The Willow Path

The
WILLOW PATH
Witchcraft, Hermetics &
the Hidden Wisdom of the Magical Arts

Kerry Wisner

Published by Troy Books
www.troybooks.co.uk

Troy Books Publishing
BM Box 8003
London WC1N 3XX

Cover design: Gemma Gary

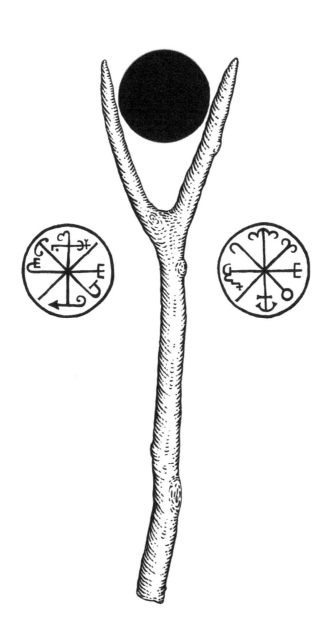

Contents

Preface   11

Chapter One: The Geassa   16
Chapter Two: The Art   25
Chapter Three: A Lady We All Know...   35
Chapter Four: The Counsels of the Art   52
Chapter Five: The Worlds   61
Chapter Six: The Worlds of the Art and the Hermetic   69
Qabalah   Chapter Seven: The Stang – The Tree   75
Rising Through the Worlds
Chapter Eight: The Magic of the Moon   84
Chapter Nine: Sun Tides   93
Chapter Ten: The Witch's Foot – Elemental Forces and the   121
Pentagram of Art
Chapter Eleven: The Miller's Stone – Numbers in the Art   131
*   Chapter Twelve: The Cloak of Danu – The*   146
Planets and Color in the Art
Chapter Thirteen: The Distaff and the Woven Thread   166
Chapter Fourteen: The Hole in the Stone   181
Chapter Fifteen: The Black Hilt Knife   184
Chapter Sixteen: Drain the Goblet Deep!   194
Chapter Seventeen: The Cauldron   203
Chapter Eighteen: The Hearth – Doorway to the Worlds   215
Chapter Nineteen: The Witch's Steed   219
Chapter Twenty: The Fe of Arianrhod   224
Chapter Twenty One: Bone, Stone, Wind and Fire   321
Chapter Twenty Two: The Apparel of the Art   238
Chapter Twenty Three: Preparing the Tools of the Trade   245
Chapter Twenty Four: Companions of the Art – 'Familiar   250
Spirits'
Chapter Twenty Five: The Four Familiars   260

Chapter Twenty Six: The Wheel of Tlachtga   264
Chapter Twenty Seven: The Roth Fail – Circle of Light   269
Chapter Twenty Eight: The Tower and the Maze   278
Chapter Twenty Nine: In Praise of the Ancient Ones   283

Conclusion: Walker on the Land   290

Bibliography   292

Photoplates
between pages 152-153

1. *The Mistress' familiar, Bes reading Crowley*

2. *Hearth set for Harvest Full Moon Ritual*

3. *Outdoor stone circle of covenstead*

4. *Circle Hearthstone with ritual tools*

5. *The author's personal Familiar 'Alraun' root, carved from an Ash tree*

6. *Outdoor harvest ritual, Besom joined with the Stang before the Cauldron*

7. *Household doorway amulets - Green Man mask, Green Man's Hand, Corn Dolly from Lughnasadh, and Oak/Rowan Cross*

8. *Indoor Hearth set for ritual*

9. *Hearth set for spirit scrying*

10. *Mirror box lined with black velvet on the outside. This is used in defensive magic by placing taglocks inside and covering this with the top which is also a mirror with the outside lined in black. The bone and black candle help to draw the baneful energy of one's enemies into the box, which is then reflected back onto them*

11. *Hearth set for spell casting with smaller Stang used for practical magic*

12. *Coven painting of the Stang as World Tree, used in rituals involving 'Traveling in Spirit'.*

13. *Author's Coven logo, 'Horns of the Moon'*

14. *Traditional Sigils of the Sun and Moon always used together to bring success. We place these on the Hearth during most spells and rituals of prosperity and success*

15. *Letter to the author from Sybil Leek*

⚜ PREFACE ⚜

When I first set out to write this book I had no intention of making this available to the public. In fact, this started as a series of notes kept in private journals. As I began organizing these, they quickly became a summation of the practices and techniques I have gained over decades of study, initiation and practical application in the Magical Arts. It was in this spirit that this work was meant to be a codification of these concepts and techniques put into a form that I (and a very small number of associates) could refer to as needed. In other words, this was to be a private grimoire.

These 'notes' soon developed into a series of books covering a wide swath of the Magical Arts; from Traditional Witchcraft through Hermetics, herbalism, divination, the use of varying tides of power, to alliances formed with other world beings including spirits, 'nature' entities as well as what can best be described as Gods. In time, at the request of others, portions of these teachings have been presented at gatherings, as well as to individuals who expressed interest in learning more. So it was that I felt that perhaps portions of these should form a series that could be presented in a public format.

This, then, is the first in a series of books, *The Geassa*, which describe the philosophy and practice of the Magical Arts as I have come to understand them. As such, these books represent the culmination of a lifetime of research and training in a variety of paths found in Western Esoteric systems. This training came through many sources.

One of the most important and which made a tremendous impact on my life was my time spent with 'Julie'. When I was in my early twenties I was fortunate to be accepted as her student. She was the matriarch of a family that practiced Traditional Witchcraft with roots reaching back to the Basque region of Europe. She was a remarkable woman who patiently worked with me until she became too ill to continue. To my knowledge I was her last student before she passed.

While Julie's teachings in Traditional Witchcraft remained an important part of my personal practices, in the decades that followed I was also initiated and trained through the various grades of a well-respected, active Hermetic Order.[1] In addition I extensively researched the practices of Ancient Egypt through academic sources and ancient texts. These three great threads of the Western Magical Arts – Traditional Witchcraft, Hermetics and Ancient Egyptian teachings - form the back drop of the techniques I present in this series.

Beyond these, it is important to know that my understanding of the Art has been greatly influenced by the teachings of Sybil Leek. She was a prolific author and speaker in the 1960's and 1970's. Recently released documents show that she had worked extensively behind the scenes with both the British and United States governments on a number of research projects related to Astrology and Psychic Phenomena.[2] In the mid to late 1970's I studied Astrology through her school. Further, it was through private correspondence with Ms. Leek that I was eventually led to Julie.

I mention this, as a deep read of the collective works of Sybil Leek reveal a tremendous amount of occult knowledge.

---

1. A Hermetic Order that follows the "Ogdoadic" current as opposed to those most frequently thought of in contemporary occultism.

2. The book, *Phenomena: The Secret History of the U.S. Government's Investigation into Extrasensory Perception & Psychokinesis* by Annie Jacobsen, documents Ms. Leek's involvement during World War II as an Astrologer who had helped to lure Rudolph Hess to surrender and her work with CIA in the early 1970's. In addition she was associated with at least one U.S. President as their personal Astrologer.

I must say that, as far as I am aware, there is no single work of hers that describes her teachings in full.[3] However, when taken as a whole, from the overall writings she left behind, as well as the many interviews she gave, these present a detailed picture of her wisdom and the tradition she had sought to carry forward. As such, I draw heavily from Ms. Leek, for I recognize her as one of the first Traditional Witches to come forward and stay true to her beliefs.

Having said this, it is important to understand that *The Geassa* series is not about Wicca. While modern Wicca has its roots in some elements of Traditional Witchcraft and Hermetics, Wicca as it has evolved over the past several decades is very different from the practices described here. Undoubtedly those familiar with Wicca will find some parallels between the two systems. However, these similarities are due in part to common older source material which is clearly documented in this work. In addition I am very familiar with Wicca.

In 1980, Julie became very ill. Before she died, she had desperately wanted to find a compatible group she could pass me to. Groups following a strictly "Traditional" form of Witchcraft were very rare. And, she informed me that the only way I could join her family was to marry into it. This was not an option I was prepared to take at the time.

So it was that she introduced me to a Wiccan group that she respected. While not Traditional in form, she felt it would be a good next step in my development. I was initiated into the coven shortly before her death. I eventually rose to be one of the leaders, remaining with them for ten years before leaving to pursue my interest in Hermetics and Ancient Egyptian studies. As such, my knowledge of early modern Wicca is extensive. I would be remise if I didn't acknowledge this training and the

---

3. Sybil Leek's book, *The Complete Art of Witchcraft* is, in my opinion, the best work of hers describing the foundation of the philosophy and tradition she taught.

many truly gifted teachers I worked with during my time with the coven.

In writing this series of books I don't want there to be any confusion regarding the intent of this work. I feel that the best way to approach this system is in the realization that this represents a blend of techniques I have learned and have been trained in. As such it is drawn from Traditional Witchcraft *and* Hermetics. With this, it is important to state that I include the very real yet often unrecognized influence Ancient Egyptian teachings have had on the Art. This influence was especially so in the centuries following the collapse of the great centers of learning found in Alexandria and elsewhere at the beginning of the current era. While I make no claims to the antiquity of specific techniques presented (simply because my teachers had received these from others before them), whenever possible I do cite all sources and present solid information on the roots of this system.

Further, these books are *not* intended for beginners or those new to the Art. Before proceeding, the reader should already have a familiarity with basic Hermetic principles, a knowledge of elemental qualities and properties, an understanding of basic Astrological and Numerological concepts, as well as experience with some magical ritual techniques. In addition it is assumed that the reader has worked with methods for attaining altered states of consciousness through natural, non-drug induced methods. These may include trance induction through self-hypnosis or meditation, as well as slipping into altered states simply through mindful 'merging' or 'becoming' in nature. Without this background much of what will be discussed in this series will be difficult to understand or apply.

This is the Art as I have come to understand and practice it. And, like all living Arts, these techniques and teachings have evolved over time, and will continue to do so as knowledge and experience grow. Each Witch and every Magician creates rituals to fit her or his own needs. Yet, it is important to understand that at its core the essential concepts and practices of the Art form a distinct pattern that has remained consistent throughout history. This underlying 'current', which I call the Geassa, represents the vital link of wisdom that lies at the heart of all Magical Arts and esoteric systems.

This series of books, *The Geassa*, represents a complete system of 'natural' magic that is based as much as possible on non-Abrahamic techniques found within Western Occultism. As such, this is a practical Art meant to put one in direct contact with intelligences and forces inherent in nature including those that exist in multiple realms. Through this system one is able to directly experience the spiritual essence of the self and one's relationship to all that is, in simple and unmistakable ways. Nothing in the Art and nothing in this system requires one to place blind faith or allegiance in any dogma, leader, messiah or prophet. Rather this system provides a means to experience different realms, forces and beings for oneself and, in the process, evolve and grow in ways that one never knew were possible.

Chapter One

✤ THE GEASSA ✤

There is power in the land; a deep and timeless essence that is alive and conscious. This is felt in the wild, remote places of nature, far removed from the confines of human structure and activity. Deep in forests, in the wind that whispers through the trees, the silver Moon shining in the night sky, in fields of grass, and the majesty of the sea. All these and more are places where the power of nature, on a deep level, can be experienced.

Our ancestors knew this. Living close to the land they were keenly aware of these energies, the cycles of the seasons, the very essence inherent in nature itself. They had an innate sense of the different inhabitants in the land, in all of nature, material and otherwise. Too, they were profoundly aware of the cycles of the heavens, the apparent movement of the Sun, Moon, planets and stars and the impact these played in the flow of energies in their world. From this grew the rich and simple traditions which evolved into a way of life that accepted these subtle forces as part of the spiritual and psychic makeup of existence.

In the west, this essence forms the core that is the underlying current and deep spiritual heritage extending back tens of thousands of years. Back to a time only remembered in myth, legend and folklore; in whispered tales told around campfires or in mumbled incantation before the hearth as the cauldron simmered over glowing coals.

This timeless essence, the underlying spiritual connection to nature itself can be thought of as the *Geassa*, the Bond, the great ancient wellspring from which all esoteric knowledge stems. It has known many forms finding expression in poem, song, art and ritual throughout history. But always the Bond remains, like a deep mountain spring. This is the essence of the Art of which this book is both an expression and extension, of.

The word Geassa, as used here, derives from the old Gaelic language meaning a magically or fated bond or duty. The word also refers to the practice of magic, requiring that certain disciplines and specific procedures be followed. Historian, Jean Markale, explains that Geassa or Geis originates from the word 'guth' and refers to "a constraining magical incantation".[4] With it there is a sense of obligation, an oath, or commitment that cannot be broken. To do so would have been considered 'taboo'. Thus, we can see in this word, hints at initiation into magical and sacred teachings. This characterizes the esoteric nature of the word itself.

However, for our purposes here, the use of this term - the Geassa - is much larger. It encompasses the entirety of ancient wisdom inherent in nature. It is the heart of the mysteries, of the land and nature itself. The image of a pure mountain spring is an apt one in that the Geassa is the very essence of the force contained in any valid esoteric system. The Geassa is our connection to all that is, on a deep, primal and profound level. Like water, it can and does, take on many different forms, appearing in a variety of images and expressions, yet at its core, the Geassa remains simple and pure. To deny the Geassa is to cut oneself off from the very living heart of all that has meaning. Still, the Geassa remains - fluid, vital, waiting to emerge in the consciousness of any who will listen.

Over generations, however, much of humanity has lost its connection to the primal forces of nature. While some of the ancient practices would come to be incorporated into local customs and folklore, the actual teachings

---

4. Markale, Jean. *The Pagan Mysteries of Halloween*. 2000.

inherent in the Geassa became fragmented, hidden, and scattered. The Bond was broken.

Still, the Geassa continued in many forms, in rural areas of Europe, Russia and the British Isles - in fact, around the globe with aboriginal peoples, in the hidden recesses of nature. Frequently, no name was applied to these practices. Rather, families, communities or even entire regions simply adhered to traditions that involved an awareness of nature, the cycles of fertility and the many different dimensions that interpenetrate our world.

For those who continued the practices in urban centers, the Bond expressed itself in Hermetics, Astrology and Alchemy. It can be found in the coded symbolism of renaissance art, drama, literature and poetry, even music. There it remained ever present, hidden in plain sight. However, for those in rural places, the survival of the Art was harder.

The dogmatic religions began to accuse those who followed the Old Ways of Witchcraft. Ultimately, the simple reality is that the varied indigenous spiritual traditions were usurped, denounced and then demonized. Before the intrusion of other religions, the 'Old Ways' - the ways of the Geassa - were simply the way people lived.

One of my first teachers was a woman who went by the name of Grandma Julie. Hers was a family tradition which, she stated, reached back to the Basque region of Europe. Julie explained that the 'Old Ways' are sometimes known as the "Willow Path" because it is the wise who know how to bend and change the course of events as subtly as one bends the fronds of the Willow. This is a term that is directly related to the Middle English word "Wiche" and later to the word "Witch". For the word "Wiche" was a reference to the use of fronds of plants that were woven or used to tie items.

Please understand that I am not proposing, as some do, that there was a single, overarching, hidden Pagan 'religion' active in Europe during the Middle Ages and beyond. The evidence seems clear that this was not the case. However, there is strong evidence that there were pockets of indigenous spiritual and magical practices scattered throughout large areas of Europe and that many of these shared remarkably similar common beliefs, world views and practices. Further, it is highly likely that communication and an interchange of ideas existed between these various branches of the tradition throughout history and into our current era. We will be examining some of this evidence further on.

In essence, we could term these practices shamanic in nature, drawing largely from the natural world with the participants consciously interacting with the forces inherent therein. As such, there was a certain parallel in practices and beliefs. Or, as we prefer to understand it, these were various expressions of the Geassa, forming a common thread and element in all.

Too, it is important to understand that over the many years that have passed, these practices have evolved as the needs of the times have changed. Some elements have been added, while others may have fallen away. Some regions may have pursued different byways within the Geassa than others, preserving elements not known to the others. Some groups may have kept more ancient techniques and teachings alive, while others incorporated methods which fit well with the original. What is important here, is the fact that the overall flow of the Geassa remains, reinventing itself as the practices evolve.

As alluded to above, once Christianity was introduced into Europe, those who followed the Old Ways were often labelled as Witches. The reality is that it is debatable that there ever was a single term or name that was used by the indigenous people to describe their beliefs. While some have noted that the root word for 'witch' stems from more ancient sources implying "wise one", in fact, many terms were used which will be discussed further on. Having said this, it is understandable that over time some of those who did practice the Old Ways would adopt the term 'Witch' as their own, simply because this

was a name used by the intruders to identify those who
didn't adhere to Christianity. In time, it stood to reason
that if one didn't accept the foreign religion, one must
be the opposite. It may be important to note though,
that Grandma Julie, as well as other respected teachers
including Sybil Leek, embraced this term, feeling no
shame in acknowledging this. However, as will be shown,
the practices of Julie and other traditional followers of
the Willow Path are very different from those frequently
thought of in our culture. The Willow Path incorporates
spiritual teachings and magical techniques that can best
be labelled as shamanic in nature, stretching across a vast
area and over many years.

As noted above, while it is uncertain that the people
actually used a specific name to identify the Old Ways,
nevertheless, there were names, terms or identities tied to
those in the community who had special abilities, knowledge
and who led the group in spiritual matters. In CE 1621
Robert Burton of England reported, "Sorcerers are too
common; cunning men, wizards and white witches as they
call them, in every village, which if they be sought unto, will
help almost all infirmities of body and mind".[5]

In her definitive work comparing shamanic practices to
historical Witchcraft, Emma Wilby explains that in England
a number of terms were used. Some of these included "wise
man or woman, cunning man or woman, witch (white or
black), wizard, sorcerer, conjurer, magician, nigromancer,
necromancer, seer, blesser, dreamer, cantel, soothsayer,
fortune-teller, girdle-measurer, enchanter, incantantrix and
so on".[6]

Beyond these, records show that in portions of Europe,
specific titles were frequently used to designate various

---

5. Burton, Robert. *Anatomy of Melancholy* 1621

6. Wilby, Emma. *Cunning Folk and Familiar Spirits, Shamanistic
Visionary Traditions in Early Modern British Witchcraft and Magic.* 2005
p.26

roles *within* the Art. These were as simple as referring to the female leaders as "the Lady" or "Mistress" linking her to the essence of the Great Goddesses of nature. For men, this was frequently "Master", though there were also specific roles such as "the Green Man", "the Man in Black", or "the Summoner". Healers were often called "strokers" because they frequently stroked the afflicted part of the body with potions and talismans.

For our purposes, we prefer to use the simple term of "the Art" or "the Arts" to designate our practice. In the Art, we find an encompassing system incorporating the different strands of the Geassa, remaining true to the ancient origins inherent to this wellspring.

From the fragmentary evidence that remains (which we will be examining further in this work), it is clear that the Geassa was expressed in the matriarchal traditions of ancient humanity. This was widespread with evidence found in most cultures of the world. In this, both male and female were seen as vital, with the divine feminine viewed as the source of all that is.

Fortunately the Art, as it has been taught to me, has re-emerged as a living system which strives to help one live in harmony with nature, while experiencing the many different energies and realities that this encompasses. As such, it is very different from most other belief systems in that it is not based on any 'revealed word', single written book or the musings of a would-be prophet, messiah or 'god incarnate'. Having said this, we do have our own teachers and leaders who have carried the tradition forward, in a variety of forms. We also have a few texts which have somehow managed to survive. However, these are seen for what they are: the teachings of our ancestors.

The Geassa, the Bond, with its rich teachings finding expression in the many forms of the Western Mystery Tradition, continues to flow as an underlying current. For our part here, our group draws from three great strands within that current:

• 'Folk wisdom' now frequently known as 'Traditional Witchcraft'. This can best be expressed as shamanic in nature. As will be seen, much of this, in our opinion, has derived from a mix of ancient practices found in earlier Pagan cultures, particularly Celtic and pre-Celtic sources, as well as 'natural' techniques drawn from the land itself.
• The Hermetic sciences stripped of any religious connotations which crept into these.
• And the rich record left in Ancient Egyptian teachings drawn from the actual texts of that once great civilization.

The root of these three distinct and yet interrelated traditions, extends back even further to a time of myth and legend, now being rediscovered and confirmed in archeological research. Each of these is important to the system delineated in this book.

Perhaps a brief description of our understanding of these three threads of knowledge is necessary at this point. The folk practices which form the body of Traditional Witchcraft as it has come down to us today will be self-evident as we proceed through this work. I will be drawing heavily from traditional sources as well as European folklore and Celtic practices, as this work moves forward. It is important to understand that Celtic and pre-Celtic society was largely matriarchal with women holding powerful roles in the culture. Bloodline descent was traced through the women. Records exist showing great warrior queens, as well as carvings of triple Mother Goddesses across Europe. In addition, pantheons of deities all were traced back to Mother Goddesses of the region where they were worshipped.[7] Clearly the role of women in the Art, as the spiritual leaders, stems from this most ancient of beliefs.

---

7. Jones, Prudence and Nigel Pennick. *A History of Pagan Europe*. 1995.
  Bord, Janet and Colin. *Earth Rites: Fertility Practices in Pre-Industrial Britain*. 1982.

The Hermetic sciences consist of the occult works of various magicians, astrologers, alchemists, philosophers and entire schools of esoteric practice which existed across Europe. These had begun as knowledge spread from Egypt, through Greek and Roman culture, eventually influencing Renaissance thinkers as Hermetic philosophy touched most regions of the west.[8] Much of current esoteric practice today can be tied directly to these important thinkers, many of whom risked their lives to keep the various disciplines alive.

That Ancient Egypt lies at the base of so much spiritual wisdom was attested to by Greek Philosophers and writers, many of whom studied in Egypt for years before developing their own schools of thought. At the beginning of the first millennia, Alexandria was the cosmopolitan center of the known world. It was here that many of the various spiritual and philosophical schools met and debated. Through them, Egyptian-based teachings eventually spread into Italy, Greece, Turkey and beyond. We are fortunate that we now live in a time when Egyptologists have been able to translate so much of the hereto undecipherable texts that had remained a mystery to medieval occultists.

The parallels between these three strands serve to enrich each other forming the balance of the Western Mysteries as a whole. The medieval 'Alchemical Splendor Solis' paintings, with their wonderful blend of these three great systems into one beautiful masterpiece, rest as an example of this rapport. Thus, any attempt to understand the core essence of the Western Mysteries requires an element of familiarity with each of these three strands. Together, they make up one of the primary methods through which the Geassa manifests to humanity.

---

8. See the work of noted Egyptologist Jan Assmann on the influence of Ancient Egypt upon Hermetics, as well as the research conducted by Dr. Alison Roberts.

There are multiple dimensions, multiple worlds, realms, realities and states of being beyond those envisioned by humanity. Many of these interpenetrate each other, cross over and influence each other and can be experienced by those trained in the Art. This volume is an introduction to our system for achieving this.

Chapter Two

✤ THE ART ✤

At its most basic and fundamental form, the Art encompasses practices and teachings that are at once simple, primeval and yet at their core, transcendental in nature. First and foremost, it needs to be understood that the Art recognizes the unique and dynamic relationship between polar, complementary opposites. This polarity - a realization of the union and interplay between complementary opposites - is a constant theme and the very foundation of much of the Art. This realization is at the very core of the Geassa.

We see this literally in everything in nature. This is best experienced through the sexes on many levels, including our understanding of, and relationship to, the divine. Further, it is the feminine which is the origin. Thus, in the form of the Art which we practice, we embrace the female in Her most elevated octave, in an adoration of the creative force. She is the center; the power *within* the land. She is creative desire, as well as the timeless essence of nature. We find Her in caverns deep, in springs and oceans, yet She is also the very essence of the star-filled night sky, the Moon that waxes and wanes, the voice of nature that speaks deep within each of us. She is the Great Mother.

He, on the other hand, is *of* the land, the wild wind rider and voice of the trees. He is the force that moves through the trees and over the fields, the warm summer Sun and the thunder that rolls in the sky. He is the horned piper calling all to join him. Both forces, Goddess and God, appear in multiple forms and expressions, one and yet many, alive and a vital part of all that is in nature.

It may be important at this point to explain that rather than relating to these powerful forces as separate deities, some Traditional Witches view these in the form of a single horned deity that incorporates both male and female features and characteristics. Given the animistic nature of Traditional Witchcraft, this is completely logical. Beyond this though, some may feel that a single hermaphrodite, otherworld being with horns, used by medieval Witches, was a natural reaction to the monotheistic dogma introduced by the Christian church. In other words, some believe that medieval Witches worshipped an archetypal entity corresponding to the Christian 'devil' and that this was in direct rebellion to the introduction of the Abrahamic tradition. In my opinion, this explanation is far too simplistic and not logical. In fact, if we dig deeper into history we can find similar examples of horned deities incorporating both sexes *before* the Abrahamic era.[9]

Perhaps the best known example of this comes in the form of the great creator God of Egypt, Atum. This deity is traditionally shown as a ram or a ram-headed man. Yet Atum was known as "the Great He-She". This was done to indicate a unity or singularity of spiritual forces. For the Egyptians, Atum was seen as having distinctly feminine and masculine forces within. These were expressed in the form of specific Goddesses and Gods,[10] yet Atum remained as the completed balance of these dynamic energies.

Please understand that I am not saying that the Ancient Egyptians influenced the eventual incorporation of such a being into traditional European Witchcraft. On the contrary,

---

9. The term 'Abrahamic' is a reference to the three religious dogmas which dominate the western world – Judaism, Christianity and Islam.

10. In particular, the Goddesses Hathor, Issuas and Nebet Hetepet were seen as independent in their own right, while being the feminine 'aspect' (for lack of a better word) of Atum. On the masculine side, the Gods Ra and the Goat headed Khnum were seen as being incorporated into Atum.

I know of no evidence to support this. However, there can be little doubt that people living close to nature and working with the forces of the land could tap into the same root essence that the Egyptians had. In this manner, they may have easily incorporated images and symbols that those forces most readily 'came through' in; including a horned hermaphrodite, otherworld being.

For our part, our group recognizes these forces in the essence of otherworld beings who are distinctly feminine and those who are distinctly masculine, in the realization that together they incorporate the full spectrum of complementary energies in nature. I have to say that this is done, not because of any personal bias on our part but rather, in our practices we have had direct experience with specific beings who have made their presence known to us and whom we work well with. The specifics of such arrangements are private, involving our internal teachings and ritual techniques.

In either case, whether a single hermaphrodite being or complementary Goddesses and Gods, each represents the esoteric principle of Polarity. Understanding and working with this is vital in all aspects of the Art. This cannot be over emphasized. In the Art, in all of nature, the greater the *creative* tension between opposites, the greater the energy they produce. Without this complementary and dynamic interplay there is no manifestation of energy. The energy released by their union is able to be used for creative purposes. Carl Jung felt that this energy, in a "psychic" form, could be directed "by transferring it to something similar in nature to the object of instinctive interest",[11] the equivalent of magic.

It needs to be understood that this dynamic polar attraction of complementary opposites is, in turn, expressed as actual living beings of a variety of natures – the Ancient Ones, the Watchers, also known as the Gods.

---

11. Progoff, Ira. *Jung's Psychology and Its Social Meaning.* 1973

The Gods are real living deities who exist in, and partake of many different realms and realities. It is for this reason that myth and legend have always been an important part of the expression of the Geassa. They convey the essence of the Gods in symbolic form revealing their character as an expression in and of nature.

At this junction, it may be important to explain that the Gods - the 'Mighty Ones' - are sentient beings of a more complex order than we. They are 'powerful spirits' of a high and ancient order of being. Yet, they are also expressions of the ultimate wholeness of consciousness - just as we are. Nature, the universe, experiences itself through the multitude of forms and forces, across a breadth of realms and realities which we can only begin to envision. Thus these beings are inherent in nature itself.

So, in the philosophy behind the practice of the Art, we see at once a sense of oneness, wholeness and singularity in all that is and yet as expressed above, an understanding of the dynamic polarity and ultimately the multiplicity that is all. This compelling and vital concept needs to be fully grasped before one can progress far on the Willow Path. For the essence of the Art is based entirely on the knowledge that all comes from, and is part of, a stream of energy - consciousness - which is indestructible but has a part of itself which can change just as matter can be changed. In essence, all is consciousness.

Because all is consciousness, all is alive and all is ever-changing in form, yet there is a continuity of consciousness throughout. As with most shamanic teachings, in the Willow Path we are taught that everything has an element of consciousness within: spirit. Humans are not superior to nature; we are one with and part of nature! Nothing ever dies, rather it changes form. Change the vibration of thought or matter and you can change its form, yet it remains as part of the whole. The difference between cold and hot is only a matter of degree. The difference is only a matter of moving along the same scale. So it is with all. With this knowledge those of the Art can bend reality, creating circumstances and results which they desire.

This leads into an understanding that there is a rhythm to everything. Energy moves along the scale between extremes and must inevitably swing back and forth. In this way balance is maintained. A steady rhythm assures harmony. However, the further the extreme that the pendulum swings, the further to the opposite it must return. It is for this reason that those of the Geassa seek balance in all that they do.

If one changes their state of consciousness one changes their state of being. This is the basis of all esoteric Arts as well as the transcendent nature of the cycles of life, itself. As such, the practice of the Art begins in the mind. Thought is an energy that is powerful and vibrant. It is for this reason that ritual is used so frequently in the practice. Not only is ritual the acting out of inner thoughts and realities in symbolic form, the use of ritual can be vital to the projection of consciousness in order to change reality in fundamental ways.

Those who practice the Art, experience the tradition through ritual devotion and magical application. Whether in small groups or in private, ritual is a vital, even essential, part of the practice. Those of the Art recognize and adore the Gods in the world around them and in nature, itself. The individual recognizes that she, too, is part of nature. As such, the Gods also reside within her. For these reasons, ritual practices of those of the Art will most often involve several key elements:

- Recognizing and thanking the Gods as the living expression of the forces within nature. With this comes communication and interaction with these beings, an expansion of one's awareness and access to the tradition's deeper teachings.
- Communication with spirits and otherworld entities inherent in nature or in the locale where the practice is performed.

- The raising of power that may be directed toward the Gods in adoration.
- Instructional, as various members are skilled in different areas of study. Within this element we can place initiation of new members. This is fairly rare and comes only after a long period of instruction by a sponsor.
- The use of magic to effect change on the material plane.
- The use of trance and altered states of consciousness in meditation and for astral travel is a common element in these meetings.[12] With this comes further spiritual communion with the Gods, an experiencing of different realms and states of being, as well as a growing awareness of the essence that is one's true self.

The times in which we practise our Art follow certain natural tides of power. These may vary from group to group depending on the tradition. For our part, we work closely with the tides surrounding the cycles of the Sun and Moon. These will be discussed further in this work.

These practices are best experienced in small, close-knit groups; the most obvious reason for this is the need for secrecy. Being experiential in nature, the Art is very private. This is not because of any elitist attitude by its members. Rather this is a remnant of the ancient mystery teachings that lay at the core of the earlier pagan and shamanic practices. Only after training and preparation is one allowed into the deeper mysteries of the tradition. As such, this is not a path for everyone. Each

---

12. This term is used loosely here, but in fact is meant to relate to any number of occult practices including 'sending forth the fetch', 'riding the mare', 'traveling in the body of light', mental projection (which has become known as 'remote viewing' in recent decades), to certain Hermetic techniques that include 'rising on the planes' and 'path working'.

person is unique with their own needs which vary from life to life. Thus, the need for secrecy remains.

Small groups are also preferred due to the fact that these can be far more efficient, magically. They are able to focus on individual goals and the needs of the members more easily. Within these too, the need for deep trust becomes imperative. Rarely, can one work magic with others whom they don't trust. During the persecutions, one's life depended on the integrity and ability to keep silent by each member of the group.

In my time with Julie, she explained that she was aware of four distinct traditions or 'modes' of practice that exist in traditional Witchcraft:[13]

- Hearth or Family groups or clans who have managed to keep the Old Ways alive within their own families. For them, the hearth is the primary altar and symbol for their form of the Bond.
- Field and Forest groups which focus on the energies of nature in remote, rural areas. They will most frequently meet in out-of-the-way outdoor sites.
- Groups which focus on the fertility and sexual aspects of the Art. As such, these groups tend to be orientated toward the worship of Goddesses in their aspect of lover, conceiver and, ultimately, creator. They will frequently use sexuality, whether overtly or symbolically, as a means for raising power as well as worshipping the Gods.
- Groups which are orientated toward masculine forces generally. As such, hunter - gatherer images and the male as protector or guardian, as well as mate, are emphasized in these groups. So, too, can male sexual virility but it needs to be understood,

---

13. It is important to understand that this was Julie's experience in Traditional Witchcraft and how she taught the Art to her students. Almost certainly there are other modes and 'traditions' not mentioned here.

though, that women in these groups frequently embody many of the qualities of strong, warrior Goddesses, balancing the masculine energy. Thus, we might see these groups calling upon such deities as the Celtic Nuada and Morgana. Too, we can see this 'mode of practice' in many of the rites from early modern Witchcraft of Britain and Europe that centered on a single horned "Man in black".

It is not uncommon for these traditions to mix or overlap. For example, sometimes a Hearth traditional practicing group may very well meet in woodlands or other wild, natural places. Field and Forest traditions may also, on occasion, meet indoors, using the hearth as their center of practice. However, generally, the traditions will follow closely along the lines Julie indicated.

A fifth type of coven which Julie taught about is that of the "Red Coven." While comparatively rare, these are groups that consist of all men with one woman as the leader of the group. In such covens, the men are devoted to her, seeing in her the essence of various Goddesses. In such groups, it would be the Mistress who would attract the energies of the men and then direct this toward the goals they desire.

As rare as red covens are, when they form they can be very powerful, providing that the Mistress has the ability to handle and direct the energy that the men in the group project. The challenge to her will be keeping a dynamic balance of her feminine energy with the tremendous influx of masculine force raised. It can become very easy for the Mistress of a red coven to become overwhelmed. When this happens, the energies raised will not be directed toward the task at hand. Instead, they tend to create tensions in the group and almost certainly, chaos. If this happens, inevitably the group will disband.

Within traditional forms of rural expressions of the Bond, there are several different roles held by members of the inner group. The following are those which we follow:

- Masters and Mistresses - These are the male and female leaders overseeing the ritual activity and general direction of the group (to my knowledge, traditional Witchcraft groups never use the terms 'High Priest' or 'High Priestess'). As a sub-group of this, there frequently can be the Cup Bearer - a man who works directly with the Mistress and fills in when the Master is not available. We prefer to use the Gaelic term 'Trulliad'. There can also be the Maiden - a woman who works directly with the Master and fills in when the Mistress is not available. We use the term 'Llawforwyn'. Generally, though not always, the Cup Bearer and the Maiden are young adults who are in training to eventually assume the role of Master and Mistress within the group when succession is desired, or they may be groomed for the roles with the thought of eventually leaving to form their own group.
- Teachers - Those skilled in a number of different techniques of the Arts and are able to pass these on to others easily.
- Initiators - The actual process of ritual initiation is a powerful rite of magical transformation. The ability to awaken the psychic and spiritual nature in another is a specialized art. While this can be a separate grouping, frequently the Master and Mistress will also hold this role.
- Leaders - Those who have a family history in the Art and have children who may be expected to carry the tradition forward.
- Elders - Those who have been practising the Art and have been part of the group for many years, having proven their knowledge, ability and experience.[14]

14. See Sybil Leek's *The Complete Art of Witchcraft* for more information on these roles.

Within Hermetic Orders, the structure of the group and roles which each member takes will vary greatly from school to school and doesn't follow the model just given. This present volume is focused on the practices of our individual group which, as already noted, uses a combination of esoteric teachings coalescing into the structure given.

Chapter Three

❖ A LADY WE ALL KNOW... ❖

One of the primary theses of this book is that the Art has its roots in the far distant past, descended from ancient pagan and shamanic practice and that these beliefs surround humanity's relationship with the forces of nature. That these beliefs involved a deep reverence for fertility and, as such, sexuality is obvious. Within this there was, and is, a strong connection with, and worship of, the feminine in the form of the many great Goddesses of the past. This lineage is best described by Sybil Leek:

> "Not only were the early primitive religions sexual in character but they were founded on a matriarchal order of society. In this, women dominated, descent being traced through them, tribal affairs managed through them, and the deities being goddesses, with the priests and prophets mainly female. Exactly how far such an order of society extended back in the past is difficult to ascertain but there are distinct traces of such matriarchal institutions, and the Old Religion of Witchcraft is a remnant which has come through to this day and age. When Christianity became established, matriarchal rites and festivals lingered on in out-of-the-way places and especially in the country areas. The Witch, despite having been driven underground, still remains as a relic of the old priestess, cunning in the wisdom of herb and medicine, jealously preserving within her own family life all the elements of the old matriarchal system, as well as the religious implications. The times and seasons have

always been observed; the knowledge of weather lore, the uses of broom, distaff, cauldron, the pitchfork and the domesticity of animals all became symbols of the Witch in later times, simply because they were originally associated in the religious symbolism of the Mother Goddess."[15]

In this one sweeping statement, Ms. Leek claims a lineage for the Art reaching back to prehistory. She at once describes a link to early Goddess worship, its eventual suppression during the rise of the Abrahamic era and that this practice continued on, evolving in hidden small groups and families to the present day. While this is a very bold statement and difficult to prove, there is evidence which supports much of Ms. Leek's assertions. Some of the most compelling evidence comes from written records within the Abrahamic tradition itself.

If we turn to the King James I version of the Bible, we find many references to worship of the "Queen of Heaven". One of the most interesting is referenced in the book of Jeremiah, chapter 7, verse 18:

"The children gather wood, and the fathers kindle the fire, and the women knead their dough, to make cakes to the queen of heaven, and to pour out drink offerings unto other gods, that they may provoke me to anger."

This statement is alleged to have been made by none other than the Abrahamic deity himself. He then goes on to describe how he will destroy the people and their lands for their worship of the Queen of Heaven and not him.

Further acknowledgment of the Goddess worship can be found again in the book of Jeremiah, chapter 44, verses 15 through to 17. In this, Jeremiah is condemning the people for making offerings to the Queen of Heaven instead of to

15. Leek, Sybil. *The Complete Art of Witchcraft.* 1971 p.170-171

the Abrahamic deity. The Bible reports that the assembly of people told Jeremiah:

> "We will do everything that we have vowed, burn incense to the queen of heaven and pour libations to her, as we did, both we and our fathers, our kings and our princes, in the cities of Judah and in the streets of Jerusalem; for then we had plenty of food and prospered, and saw no evil."

This and the previously quoted passage are telling, for they indicate that not only was Goddess worship an established part of religious life at the inception of the Abrahamic traditions, it was the primary spiritual discipline in these areas of the Middle East, given sanction from not only the common people but also the ruling class, its 'kings' and 'princes'. The book of Jeremiah tells us more. Verse 18 continues:

> "But since we left off burning incense to the queen of heaven and pouring out libations to her, we have lacked everything and have been consumed by the sword and by famine."

This passage is particularly interesting as it clearly states that once the people had abandoned Goddess worship (as the leaders of the newly-formed Abrahamic tradition had insisted) and began worshiping the Abrahamic deity, only misfortune befell them. Finally, verse 19 states:

> "And the women said, "When we burned incense to the queen of heaven and poured libations to her, was it without our husbands' approval that we made cakes for her bearing her image and poured out libations to her?"

This is perhaps the most revealing passage. For this indicates that when famine struck, the women returned to their earlier worship of the Great Queen. From this, one can easily see the parallel between this secret group of women and the beginnings of the 'Witches Coven' worshipping Goddesses centuries later.

One simple question keeps nagging as one reads these passages; why were they left in the Bible? Over the centuries, the Bible has undergone numerous edits and rewrites with entire books being removed. Yet in the King James I version, dating from CE 1611, these passages remained, where they continue in versions since. One has to wonder if there wasn't a reason.

CE 1611 would have been the height of the Witchcraft persecutions of Europe. Could it be that perhaps these Biblical accounts (along with the Abrahamic deity's punishment of the people that followed) were left so clearly in the popular Bible because the same may have been ongoing in rural Europe? Were they left in, because groups of people, i.e. covens, were still worshipping the Queen of Heaven? If so, this text then may have been meant to dissuade the common people from these older beliefs. Perhaps, these were left so prominently in the Bible to help justify the persecution of those of the Art.

It may be important to note that in CE 1597, King James I had published "Daemonologie" which outlines his fear of Witches and the need to destroy them.

In CE 1604, the English law "Acte against Conjuration Witchcrafte and dealing with evill wicked Spirits" was passed. As such, it seems to be too much of a coincidence that this was left so prominently in the Bible. With this, it does imply a certain continuity reaching over many centuries. Further written documents from Christian sources reveal more.

In CE 906, Benedictine Abbot Regino of Prum penned a two volume manuscript at the petition of the Archbishop of Treir. The request was for a collection of witnesses, both clerical and secular, to give a description of the various folk beliefs from the townships and woodlands of Germany at the time. Included in the descriptions were the practices of "certain wicked women" who rode "beasts" to secret gatherings in the service of "the Pagan Goddess, Diana." In these meetings "they obey the will of the Goddess as if She were their Mistress; on particular nights they are called to wait on Her."

During the same period, Ratherius of Verona (CE 890 - 974) lamented that many people still worshipped a Goddess. They "acknowledge Her as their sovereign, nay as their Goddess." He continues, "In their lamentable de-mentation they claim that the third part of the world is subject to Her sovereignty." In this same text, he attempts to link Diana with the Biblical Herodias - the woman who had ordered the beheading of John the Baptist. This attempt to link an ancient Goddess with a well-known Biblical villainess would appear to be a clear example of the Abrahamic tradition's demonization of older beliefs generally and of the divine essence of the female, in particular.

In fact, over and over again, we find a clear pattern of misogyny on the part of the newer Abrahamic cult toward the ancient Pagan religions due to their worship of the divine feminine. This is evident throughout Abrahamic writing.

Approximately one hundred years later, Ratherius of Verona, Burchard of Worms (CE 955 - 1025) composed a series of questions cataloging a list of folk beliefs which were, for the most part, in contradiction to Christian beliefs. Included among these were discussions on the belief that women rode with "a throng of demons transformed in the likeness of women" as they went to meetings in honour of "Holda." In Germany, Holda was a fertility Goddess who, in an early thirteenth century text, is described as the "Queen of Heaven."

These are not the only references to be found regarding Goddess worship in medieval Europe. In approximately CE 1277, the Goddess Habondia, or Dame Habundia, the Lady of Abundance, makes an appearance in the poem "Romance of the Rose" as an important part of folk life. While in CE 1313, Giovanni de Matociis reported that villagers in

Northern Italy believed that there was "a nocturnal society headed by a Queen: Diana or Herodia." Again, we find an attempt to identify the ancient Goddess with the Biblical villainess Herodias.

This is significant as several centuries later, Italian Witches would identify the daughter of Diana as Aradia in a manuscript presented to folklorist Charles Leland in the nineteenth century. Historians would later attempt to identify Aradia as an incarnation of Herodias. If so, it would seem that the church's attempt at demonizing Diana had gone full circle, for now Herodias as Aradia becomes Diana's daughter and has returned as a female messenger of the Great Goddess! It is interesting to see how after eight hundred years, Italian Witches embraced the Christian attempt to demonize their Goddess, turning Her into the very embodiment of the being who would teach them. Perhaps even more interesting, the Leland text shows that Aradia was now the being who would save them from the evils the Christians had wrought on them.[16]

Each of these examples is significant for many reasons. Firstly, they directly reference gatherings of people, predominantly women, in worship of a Goddess. These gatherings were largely considered to occur at night. In many cases, the ancient Roman Goddess of the Moon, Diana, is given clear reference. This strongly suggests that these gatherings coincided with the lunar cycle. It also suggests that Diana's cult had spread far from Italy, *or* that those

---

16. It is important to note that another possibility exists for the origins of the name Aradia. For the Greek Goddess who weaves the thread of destiny and the labyrinth is named Ariadne. Her name spread throughout Europe finding its way into a series of 'prophecies' attributed to Merlin in the twelfth century. In addition, some scholars felt that there was a connection between Ariadne and Arianrhod of Welsh traditions. The names appear to be very similar across cultures. It would not be too difficult to see that Witches in Italy may very well have had knowledge of Ariadne.

chronicling Goddess worship had inserted Diana's name into their texts, when describing Goddess worship in their areas of Europe.

While the Christian texts discussed here make mention that the writers clearly believed that these people were being deceived by demons, there is little or no worship of the Christian devil itself. Rather it is a Goddess, in each case noted, that is the primary threat to the church. This isn't to say that "the devil" doesn't also figure highly in the official records regarding those accused of Witchcraft, which he most certainly does. Rather, in the cases noted here, it is a Goddess who is the primary antagonist of the Christians and the center of worship of the Witches involved.

These references reach across Europe; from Italy to Germany, Scandinavia, France, England, Ireland and Scotland. Clearly, this was no small group of worshippers isolated to a single region of the continent. Rather, Goddess worship appears to have continued on in rural areas across Europe, traversing several countries and languages.

Perhaps more telling, though, is the time span involved. Regino of Prum documented the gathering of Diana in CE 906. Ratherius of Verona recounted the worship of the Goddess close to one hundred years later making reference to a Goddess whom texts two hundred years later would refer to as the Queen of Heaven. Finally in CE 1611 the King James I Bible uses the same title in a description of Goddess worship. This is a seven hundred year stretch of time, giving clear reference to secret assemblies of people, mostly women, in service to a Goddess! The manuscript provided to Leland would suggest that the worship of this same Goddess once again is documented in the nineteenth century, close to four hundred years after King James.

It is interesting that in CE 1608 Susan Snapper of Rye, England was a well-known healer and was considered to be a 'white' Witch. She was famous for her ability to use "plant water" (potions) to cure. When she was brought up on charges of Witchcraft she stated that she frequently communicated with spirits. She went on to explain that on at least one occasion she was "taken in a vision to meet the Queen of the Fairies."[17] The reference to the Queen of "Fairies" almost certainly represents an otherworld being; a Goddess of nature. Unfortunately, Ms. Snapper was executed for her devotion to the Great Queen.

Further historical records as well as archaeological evidence bear out an ancient tradition of Goddess worship. Until the seventeenth century shrines were kept by older women who taught "the rites of Venus" to younger women throughout Brittany. During the same period the Goddess of "Heaven and Mother of all" was known in Wales as Brenhines-y-nef. In France, CE 1625, it was reported that while ploughing, a Goddess statue was unearthed. Locals built a shrine for the image, and regular pilgrimages were made to the site even after the statue was destroyed during the revolution.[18]

Lewis Spence states that reports of groups of women gathering on islands off the coast of Brittany for the sole purpose of practicing magic and worshipping ancient Celtic deities extend back to ancient Roman days. There, they are alleged to have gathered in the many stone circles located on these islands in ceremony.[19] He goes on to indicate that accounts exist showing that, at various seasons, women would retire to certain isles off the coasts of Ireland and Scotland in learning and worship of various Goddesses, one of the most prominent being the Celtic Goddess, Bridget.[20]

In his book from 1889, T.F. Thiselton-Dyer states that in Friesland, The Netherlands "no woman is to be found

17. Fletcher, Anthony. *A County Community in Peace and War: Sussex 1600-1660*. 1975 p.162

18. Jones, Prudence and Nigel Pennick. *A History of Pagan Europe*. 1995 p.105

19. Spence, Lewis. *The Magical Arts in Celtic Britain*. 1993 p.53

20. *Ibid.*, p.24

at home on a Friday, because on that day they hold their meetings and dances on a barren heath."[21]

This worship of the Great Goddess continued on. In Romania, researchers, Jones and Pennick, report that as recently as the twentieth century, the Moon was worshipped as a Goddess, given the title of "Queen of Flowers" and "Sister of the Sun".[22] In England, as recently as the eighteen-hundreds, the Goddess, Gwen Teirbron, was appealed to as the patroness of nursing mothers. It is reported that nursing mothers would offer a distaff and flax to this Goddess in hopes of having ample milk for their infants.[23]

In the opening statement of this chapter, I quoted Sybil Leek and her claims that the Old Religion was carried forward through family tradition as a sacred heritage.[24] This is perhaps one of the hardest claims to verify and yet records remain which shed light on this. For example, for centuries a sacred well near Abergele, Denbigh, Wales, was watched over by a single family. This well, known as Ffynnon Elian, was one of many seen as a gateway through which one could commune with the Mother Goddess. In the early 1800's, John Evans, a member of the family who owned the property and watched over the well, was imprisoned twice for opening the sacred well after it had been sealed by a Christian priest. The records continue indicating that the family matriarch acted as a "priestess", overseeing rites at the well before it was closed. Finally, in CE 1829, the church succeeded in destroying the well, at least temporarily.[25]

---

21. Thiselton-Dyer, T.F. *The Folklore of Plants.* 1889

22. Jones, Prudence and Nigel Pennick. *A History of Pagan Europe.* 1995 p.190

23. *Ibid.,* p.105

24. As a family traditionalist herself, Grandma Julie insisted that the Old Religion had remained alive through certain families including her own.

25. Jones, Prudence and Nigel Pennick. *A History of Pagan Europe.* 1995 p.107

As for the rites performed at such wells, we have some historical records which give us a clue as to what these may have consisted of. In Wales during the 1860's, two men reported that on the first Sunday of May (corresponding to the Celtic fertility festival of Beltane) they caught sight of a group of women gathered at a well. There, the women had fastened their skirts up under their arms exposing their naked bodies as they joined hands and danced around the well. Next to the well sat an older woman, who proceeded to dip a vessel into the water and then sprinkle its contents on to the encircling women.[26] Clearly this was meant to be a fertility ritual, passing the life-giving properties of the Great Mother to the women on this sacred day.

Historian, Keith Thomas, is very clear on the point of how magic and Witchcraft traditions were transmitted. He explains that a Witch's "technique was learned verbally from some relative or neighbour".[27]

Further evidence suggestive of family traditions, can be found elsewhere in the British Isles. Lewis Spence reports that, in Scotland, magic was taught frequently from "father to daughter and mother to son".[28] This is important not only because of the family lineage suggested but also because this helps to show the ancient custom of the power passing between the sexes discussed elsewhere in this work.

A University of Warwick research paper on "Cunning Folk and Wizards" reported "As in many trades, parents often passed their knowledge on to their sons and daughters so they could take over their magical profession once they were gone".[29]

---

26. Bord, Janet & Colin. *Earth Rites: Fertility Practices in Pre-Industrial Britain*. 1982 p.99

27. Thomas, Keith. *Religion and the Decline of Magic, Studies in Popular Beliefs in the Sixteenth-and-Seventeenth-century England*. 1991 p.272

28. Spence, Lewis. *The Magical Arts in Celtic Britain*. 1993 p.63

29. *Cunning Folk and Wizards in Early Modern England*. Warwick, RI. ID Number: 0614383. 2010 p.19

We see a similar account of family traditions of Witches echoed in the words of a seventeenth-century Italian "Witch Hunter" Francesco Guazzo. He wrote:

> "The infection of Witchcraft is often spread through a sort of contagion to children by their fallen parents ... and it is one among many sure and certain proofs against those who are charged and accused of Witchcraft, if it be found that their parents before them were guilty of this crime. There are daily examples of this inherited taint in children ..."[30]

In CE 1775, Betty Strother of Yorkshire, England died. She had been renowned in the community as a "White Witch" selling sigils, potions and casting spells to help those in need. She had stated that she had learned the Art from her mother "Migg of Lastingham". In the course of her workings she had used, among other items, a "magic looking glass, a crystal ball, magic cubes, and a Witch's garter."[31] The account goes on to explain that she was accomplished in casting horoscopes showing at least some familiarity with Hermetic principles.

A report from CE 1628, discusses the case of a woman in Scotland who was brought up on charges of Witchcraft. When questioned, she claimed that her family possessed a book of magic given to her by her grandfather. She went on to claim that this book was far older.[32]

Many critics have suggested that if there was a long history of Goddess worship and worship of Pagan Gods which had remained in place, albeit in seclusion, there should be texts used by these secret groups. Of course, it is important to remember that much of the populace was

30. Grimassi, Raven. *The Ancient Roots of Italian Witchcraft.*

31. Harley, Marie and Joan Ingilby. *Life and Tradition in The Moorlands of North-East Yorkshire.* 1972, 1990 p.123

32. Spence, Lewis. *The Magical Arts in Celtic Britain.* 1993 p.78

illiterate. On top of this, many older traditions were largely oral, passed from teacher to student in an apprentice-style relationship. Much of the teachings of the Druids are lost to time partly because of this. Yet, the historical record does show that Pagan texts did exist. For example, Horace of Rome reported in BCE 30, that women devoted to the worship of the Moon as Diana, celebrated secret rites at night. He stated that among their possessions was the *Libros Carminum*, the "Book of Incantations".[33]

Again, the words of the seventeenth-century Witch Hunter, Francesco Guazzo, may shed some light on this. He wrote that Witches "read from a black book during their religious rites." He goes on to state: "For the Witches observe various silences, measuring, vigils, mutterings, figures and fires, as if they were some expiatory religious rite."

During the persecutions, records show that when a Witch was killed, in many cases, books belonging to them were destroyed as well. For the most part, any records of the books, themselves, have vanished. Yet, there are some exceptions. In his "Directory for Inquisitors" Dominican inquisitor, Nicholas Eymericus, lists the names of the magical works he had personally taken from the accused, read and then destroyed. In this, he listed such works as "The Treasury of Necromancy" and "The Table of Solomon". Records from the Venetian Inquisition recount an incident in which the home of a woman accused of Witchcraft was searched, uncovering a handwritten book of spells and rituals.[34] We can only guess at the number of secret texts that were destroyed during the Abrahamic frenzy.

Yet, in fact, a number of simple spell books continued to exist, later published as grimoires, 'dream books', 'fortune telling books', 'Pow-wow books' and more. Most of these, however, are an odd combination of spells and herbal knowledge, acting more as books of notes put together

---

33. Illes, Judika. *Encyclopedia of Witchcraft*. 2005 p.112
34. *Ibid.*

without much organization. This, of course, would be what one would expect from someone collecting spells over time.

The simple reality is that throughout history, the Abrahamic traditions have systematically destroyed most texts from older civilizations and other religious or magical traditions, which did not adhere to their own beliefs. We see this in the repeated burning of the Library of Alexandria, the destruction of what few books the Celts had penned, any number of grimoire in the middle ages, to the systematic destruction of the writings of Central American indigenous peoples, most notably the Mayans. Among certain factions of the Abrahamic tradition, this is ongoing today.

When taken as a whole, these strands within the historical record begin to form a pattern strongly suggesting that the Geassa continued to emerge and be practised throughout Europe, despite centuries of relentless demonization and persecution. Furthermore, this shows that Goddess worship remained a vital part of this. While there was no one singular, overarching Pagan religion as some would like to believe, it is obvious that the indigenous magical and spiritual practices of the European people did exist and continued to be adhered to. Moreover, within these, definite parallels and patterns of ritual and belief lay just beneath the surface and were common to all, despite the differences of region, language and even era. Some of these common parallels included:

- The recognition of the divine manifest in nature;
- The dynamic and complementary nature of divinity represented in both sexes;
- As well as the recognition of the divine female in a role that was quite often seen as more spiritual and frequently more powerful to that of the male because She was the source of life and transformation.

The primary thesis of our work states that the Art is an expression of the underlying force of nature; which we term the Geassa. With this, those who practise the Art tap directly into this current of wisdom. A telling pamphlet written by Edward Johnston, Esq. in Sudbery, Suffolk, England in CE 1645, laments the methods of the "Witche Fynder Generall" calling into question the tactics used to 'discover' Witches, by such individuals. Instead, the pamphlet gives methods which reveal a very different Witch than those normally thought of. Rather, it points to a recognition of the qualities of those of the Art and their ability to draw wisdom from nature.

> "If ye would know a Witche, there are ways more sutil to detect them, then the pricking of a supposed Devill's Mark, or submitting of their boddies to cruell Torture. Mere appearance telleth ye naught, for Witches doe come in divers shapes and sizes. They may aye be born gentil or humble. Accident concerneth us not: Substance is true Essence. Hear ye then how our fathers before us discover'd the Witche:
>
> Mark well their manner, for it is quiet and assumeth naught. It is in peaceful tones they speak, and oft seem abstracted. Seeming to prefer the companie of Beastes, they converse with them as equalls.
>
> They will dwelle in lonely places, there better (as they say) to know the voices of the Wind and hear the secrets of Nature. Possessing Wysdome of feldes and forrests, they doe heale and harme with their harvests.
>
> They concerne themselves not with idle fashion, nor do worldly Goodes hold worth for them.
>
> Be not so confused as to thinke that only Womankynde harbour the gifte in this matter. Of Men there bee many that holde mickle power."

This is a remarkable description of the traits of those of the Art. These characteristics could easily apply today. I find that this simple pamphlet is yet one more piece of evidence showing a continuity in the mysteries despite the centuries of persecution and then denial.

This chapter started with a powerful and sweeping claim of ancient linage reaching back to the dawn of history and extending well into our own era. If looked at objectively, there are definite clues which show that the Geassa has survived, leaving its mark in the historical record. Many today try to deny this, stating that the Art of today is a relatively contemporary 'invention' with no real basis in historical fact. This would seem to be the ultimate insult inflicted by the patriarchal religions of the current era; firstly demonize the ancient teachings, then attempt to destroy all evidence including committing the equivalent of genocide by killing any living adherents and then finally, deny that the beliefs existed altogether.

Today, even among occultists, it has almost become vogue to ardently claim that Goddess worship has no place in 'real' Witchcraft. Rather, they insist that this was solely a modern, some even use the term 'new age' invention of neo-paganism. However, clearly the evidence presented proves the opposite. In my opinion, Goddess worship has been *the* vital linking force throughout much of Pagan tradition from the dawn of recorded history.

For some, the confusion comes from those practices that were strictly acts of sorcery, as opposed to the esoteric traditions of Pagan cultures. As the Abrahamic cult continued their relentless onslaughts of persecution, techniques of sorcery were preserved often times divorced from the ancient esoteric, spiritual traditions. This is understandable given that in many cases it was the only tool the people had to push back against the harshness of life at those times and the dictatorial nature of the Abrahamic cult.

In such instances, it was common for some of these sorcerers to incorporate Christian elements into their magic. Over the years, this became more prevalent. On the one hand, this was because some felt that there was some power in using the new religious symbols of the day. Others incorporated Christian icons into their magic purposely so as to help avoid persecution. In these cases many would state that they were simply praying to the Christian deity.[35]

Yet, even here, the old Gods, often times, were evoked. For example, one spell from Lincolnshire, England, dating to the early modern era begins with an appeal to "Father, Son and Holy Ghost" but also the Saxon Gods Woden and Loki, are called upon in the same incantation.[36]

In our system of the Art, we embrace both practical magical techniques coupled with the spiritual teachings of the older shamanistic Pagan systems. And, again, evidence exists to show that these spiritual teachings were carried forward through time. In his book "Mastering Witchcraft" Paul Huson expresses this well:

> "Witchcraft remains, in its broadest sense, the shamanism of the West, the underlying, barely organized bedrock of magical practice, on which all later religions and metaphysical schools of thought rest; any substantial attempt to deal with it as a semi-"established" faith is doing it the utmost disservice and is entirely at odds with the idea behind the practices."[37]

In the end, whether the Art of today has been carried forward through family tradition and secret esoteric groups as Grandma Julie and Sybil Leek maintained, or that the Art had been completely suppressed and eventually annihilated as others would have us believe, it doesn't matter. For the Geassa continues on, regenerating itself anew. The Gods, the Ancient Ones, are alive in nature and through our Art they manifest again. Anyone with the dedication, sincerity and courage to follow this path can readily experience these forces and spiritual beings for themselves.

---

35. *Cunning Folk and Wizards in Early Modern England*. Warwick, RI. ID Number: 0614383. 2010

36. Walker. *The Witches*. 1970 p.59

37. Huson, Paul. *Mastering Witchcraft*. 1970 p.209

The reality is that the Art is constantly evolving. The fact that this embraces the worship of the forces of nature, particularly the divine feminine, carries with it a deep and lasting spiritual connection. This is the heart of our tradition. The Great Queen is our Mistress. She is our spiritual connection. Without Her, there is no true essence to the Art as we understand it.

In our opinion, the evidence is clear; the practices did survive. At times the bond was broken and yet the well spring of the Goddess, the Geassa, continues to renew itself. The Art continues on.

Chapter Four

✤ THE COUNSELS OF THE ART ✤

As with any discipline which involves the use of power within the Art a code of conduct, frequently known as the Counsels, has been adopted. The Counsels of the Wise, in fact, are not a set of 'rules' or 'commandments', rather they describe a way of living. As such, they can be applied to all aspects of one's life as well as the practice of wielding the energies in the Art. Sybil Leek referred to these as 'tenets' describing these in detail, in portions of her books. Grandma Julie, too, emphasized that those of the Willow Path worked under code. I offer a similar set here, drawn from multiple teachers including some of the insights Ms. Leek presented.

Harmony with Nature

While it is obvious that we cannot survive without nature, it is also clear that nature would certainly continue if humanity disappeared from the planet. We are part of all that is. Recognizing this in all that we do is essential as a person practicing the Art. Nature is the manifestation and expression of the life force, the divine. Sybil Leek explains that "life is an all pervading spirit expressing itself in a myriad of diversified forms."[38] All is alive, all is connected and ultimately part of the divine. Furthermore, all is consciousness. Change your state of consciousness and you change your state of being. I can't emphasize this enough. Living in harmony with nature brings us in harmony with

---

38. Leek, Sybil. *The Complete Art of Witchcraft.* 1971 p.56

our true self - our inner spiritual self that is the core essence of who we really are.

This is the exact opposite of the ego-centered individual who is a victim of conditioned thought and upbringing which so often creates a neurotic need to compete with and please others. When taken to the extreme, ego-centered individuals become victims of their own greed. It is precisely this which has alienated so much of humanity, pitting them against the very nature which lies at the core of personal existence. This creates a terrible imbalance that, on a personal level, leads to psychosis, disease, bigotry and so much more that afflicts humans today. When this imbalance occurs in society, we find the terrible conditions of global greed, business and governmental corruption and tyranny, to say nothing of the devastating destruction and pollution to the environment itself.

Trust
When commitment is made there must be the trust that one will follow through with that confidence. This includes commitments to secrecy and confidentiality. This aspect of the Art relates to the reality that one must be true to one's word. In magic, one's literal word spoken in ritual exudes a force of will meant to change reality. So this should be in all aspects of one's life. As such, integrity and honesty are paramount.

Furthermore, without trust, love cannot last long. Love is the state of joy that exists when true harmony occurs. This relates back to the first counsel of Harmony with Nature. However, one does not give trust, and thus, love, blindly or indiscriminately. To do so is to open oneself to delusion, as well as possible exploitation by others who may not be as evolved or hold the same values that one of the Art may hold. Trust and thus love, have to be earned. As such, the statement *Perfect Love and Perfect Trust* found in some circles is, ideally, a reference to those who have earned that condition.

The use of this term implies that one can rarely work magic with those whom they do not trust explicitly. The phrase, itself, almost certainly became important as the persecutions took root, as absolute trust was essential for survival. Unfortunately, many contemporary Wiccan circles have debased this simple phrase as a means of demanding blind trust and love from potential followers and initiates, without earning this. This, of course, is in direct contradiction to the essence of this counsel's original meaning.

Humility

This is the opposite *not* of pride, but of vanity. It is normal and healthy to take pride in oneself and one's accomplishments. However, to place oneself above others is at once judgmental and self-delusional. An acceptance of reincarnation quickly makes one realize that most people are, hopefully, all moving in a steady progression of evolution. Some are further advanced than others. With this understanding comes the knowledge that at one time we, too, were in all likelihood in a similar state of development as those who may currently not appear as evolved. The Art teaches first and foremost that one must take care of oneself and one's needs. You cannot help others until your own life is in order. While this may at first appear selfish it is the opposite. Rather, this is a state of understanding which can put one in a position to help others who may truly need it, precisely because one does understand and is aware of their own needs. In concert with this counsel is a simple statement that Julie used to say, "Boast not as this is one of the quickest ways to lose power."

Tolerance

It is only natural that after humility, tolerance for others must follow. There are many ways of viewing reality, many paths which must be taken. There is no "one, true and only" religion, philosophy or way of life. The way of the Art is not for everyone. As such those who practise the

Art recognize the wisdom in many paths. Still, those of the Art realize that there are many who may hold distorted understandings with views that have been created by a handful of manipulative, controlling and power-hungry individuals who do not have the best spiritual intentions of the aspirant at heart.

Those of the Art recognize wisdom when it is presented, ignorance when it occurs, stupidity when demonstrated and the manipulative underpinnings of those who would seek nothing but domination and control over others when it is being perpetrated. Perhaps it is because those of the Art have been victims of intolerance that we can best recognize people's motives and know how to tolerate differing behaviour accordingly. Ignorance, stupidity, manipulation and intolerance almost always appear in offensive and bigoted acts as well as language. In the history of Witchcraft this intolerance toward the Old Religion has manifested in physical acts of violence. I personally find Sybil Leek's description accurate and helpful:

> "For all offensiveness we also have remedies that do not require the inflicting of physical hurt; it is because of our superior knowledge of magical practices that we can afford to be very tolerant of, and even smile at, offensiveness."[39]

Learning

With the realization that there is more than one path and more than one view of reality, comes the counsel of Learning. We are all in a state of evolution and development. For those of the Geassa, learning is an on-going, never-ending process. This is seen in the Art, itself. William Grey points out that the Pagans he had encountered in Wales had obvious traditions going back into the ancient past. Still they had also, over time, incorporated aspects of ritual magic,

---

39. Leek, Sybil. *The Complete Art of Witchcraft.* 1971 p.128

recognizing the Geassa in each of these. The same holds true for the family tradition which Grandma Julie embraced. She, too, claimed a long lineage. However, when we talked about other systems including ritual magic and Qabalah she explained that the Witch uses "whatever works for her." That Hermetics, as a direct offshoot of Ancient Egyptian teachings, is found to be compatible with European Pagan traditions is important. The similarities between these strands serve to enrich each other, forming the balance of the Western Mysteries as a whole.

Leading a Balanced Life

Throughout each of these counsels the underlying theme is one of living a balanced life. This is almost a sub-root of living in harmony with nature. The difference here is to keep a balance within one's own life. In the Art, there are no dogmas and no sense of sin. One is expected to live life fully and in keeping with one's own inner nature. However, nothing should be done in excess. A balance in life is essential to healthy, happy living. So if one wants to drink, eat and make love, there is nothing in the Art which prohibits any of this. All that must be maintained is a balanced and healthy lifestyle. The Art begins with the study and understanding of the self, free from delusions. One must be true to oneself, know oneself, living in harmony with the true self and not as a victim of self-delusion and ego-centered, conditioned thinking.

Reincarnation

The individual involved in the Art also embraces the reality of reincarnation seeing each life as a grand adventure to be experienced, lived and enjoyed. Through this one learns and accepts the responsibility that comes through constant, unending growth, evolution and spiritual development, while seeing the connectedness of all that is. In essence the universe is alive and conscious experiencing itself through us - while we are a part of the living consciousness of the universe ever changing and evolving through life after life.[40]

The clear realization that life is a continual procession of growth and development, to be experienced and enjoyed in the great cycle of return is at the heart of the Geassa - all Western Esoteric Mystery Traditions. This was an accepted part of the ancient Celtic people's beliefs long before the invasion from other religions.

Responsibility (Law of Return)

With the acceptance of reincarnation comes the knowledge that there are responsibilities and consequences for the choices made in life. Every action creates an effect which, inevitably, returns to the individual. This simple truth forms the essence of ethical practice within the Art. When confronted with the need to defend oneself the first choice is a strong psychic protection, followed by reflecting the destructive influences back on its source. One authority uses this saying "bless rather than banish, banish rather than bind, bind rather than blast." Having said this it may be important to consider Sybil Leek's comments:

> "Most Witchcraft laws have a tribal quality to them. Death, because of the belief in reincarnation, is not the ultimate desolation. It is a tribal rule in Witchcraft that when there is an injustice generally to more people than one, then the satisfaction extracted by a revenge motived curse is actually a means of expurging the person who commits the crime."[41]

---

40. We use the word universe to encompass all that is. As ancient teachings affirm and quantum physics, including string theory, are beginning to discover, there are multiple universes and realities. We will discuss this further in this work. Our use of the word universe here is meant to embrace these multiple dimensions and realities.

41. Leek, Sybil. *Cast Your Own Spell.* 1970 p.118

Sybil reiterates this point in several books. In "Diary of a Witch" she explains that sometimes it may be justified to use negative magic - to blast - when it is for the greater good of the whole.[42]

Beyond these counsels noted here some traditions also include the Counsel of Growth and the Counsel of Mastery.[43] Essentially, with these counsels, those of the Art strive toward constant growth and improvement in whatever they seek to pursue. This is especially so in the development of one's spiritual self, as well as one's magical skill set. This, of course, leads to Mastery. With this one seeks to be proficient in the Art, and by extension any area of one's life which holds meaning.

Julie emphasized that as students of the Art we are expected to live by a code that is simple and yet embraces a high ethical standard. She summed this up with the following four qualities:

Responsibility - The Witch takes responsibility for her or his actions and follows through with promises made.

Understanding - The Witch seeks to understand all around her, whether this is gaining knowledge of the subject at hand, or seeking to understand other's situations and perceptions.

Truth - The Witch seeks the truth in all situations. In addition, she will speak the truth or not all.

Honesty - Integrity is the hallmark of the Witch. As noted elsewhere in this work, in the Art one's literal word is their bond. In ritual, to speak a thing is to make it real. As such, a Witch's integrity is vital to her moral code.

---

42. Leek, Sybil. *Diary of a Witch*. 1968 p.93

43. In particular the Byanu Grove in Boston, Massachusetts had referenced these in an internal grove paper presented in 1983.

Julie also stressed that one must never destroy another's sense of beauty. In stating this, she explained that while others may hold different beliefs and world views that may not be the same as ours, they nonetheless draw strength from these. For them, in this point in their evolution, the path they have chosen assists them in life. To take that away is to deprive them of the expression they need to continue to grow. This, of course, harkens back to the counsels of tolerance and humility, with an emphasis on understanding philosophical and religious differences. These Counsels mark the commitment we, as followers of the Geassa, live by.

Lastly, we need to look at the concepts of 'good' and 'evil'. For those of the Willow Path we view life as the means in which spirit seeks to attain absolute good. Sybil Leek discussed this concept at length in her writings, particularly in the second chapter of her book "The Complete Art of Witchcraft". In the Geassa, the concept of absolute good is best understood as spirit fully evolved, self-actualized, in harmony with the universe and in balance within oneself.

This evolution takes place through the process of reincarnation, in each life according to one's state of spiritual development. As such, we seek absolute good by living our lives according to the Counsels. We come to realize these tenets, instinctively, through successive incarnation and through the application of reason, intuition and passion. The spirit retains elements of the various personalities and experiences from each incarnation. This returns with us as "conscience". This, then, is the residual essence of the personalities and experiences from previous incarnations.

Conscience then becomes the standard against which we weigh our thoughts and actions and act accordingly. It is, at once, the looking glass allowing us to see who we were and the path we followed in previous lives. It is also the faculty by which we look within ourselves, seeking to bring into harmony those parts of our own life which fall under our power to change. Our thoughts are the seeds out of which our actions grow creating vibrations which blossom as effects bearing good, or ill, fruit. Thus, one must act in accordance with conscience.

Evil, on the other hand, is an unharmonious state which arises through imbalance and from the misapplication of will and passion, as an excess towards one extreme node of polarity to the determent of the opposite. Thus, for us, evil is not a natural state. Rather, we hold that good lies in the active aspect of a person - in the essential core of a person. Evil can only manifest by one consciously and willfully seeking it, seeking excesses and imbalance. Those of the Art hold that the essential part of oneself cannot be affected by any action over which one is not capable of controlling through one's will. As Sybil Leek explains:

> "We believe that no evil can happen to the essential part of man, the spirit, which is related to the original source of purity . . . unless man's own will decides to seek evil, consciously preferring it to good."[44]

Thus, evil is the end result of an imbalance consciously chosen and taken to the extreme, to the determent of one's spiritual development. As such, our understanding of the concepts of 'good' and 'evil' are tied directly to the counsels discussed earlier; leading a balanced life, harmony with one's environment, tolerance, learning, humility, reincarnation. These tenets, taken as a holistic lifestyle within the Geassa, bring one closer to absolute good.

To walk the Willow Path is to walk a path of wisdom. For as the word Geassa implies, there is a bond that is formed, with oaths of responsibility and with it, keys to power not understood by most.

---

44. Leek, Sybil. *The Complete Art of Witchcraft.* 1971 p.29

Chapter Five

❖ THE WORLDS ❖

As human beings experiencing the world through our material bodies, most people are only aware of reality as it relates to them through the five senses. For them, the world is limited and material. Anything beyond this becomes the realm of fantasy and faith. For many people now, though, this view has expanded as technology has developed instruments which can detect and use energies not normally perceived.

Radio waves, magnetic fields, radiation, the detection of "invisible" or "dark" matter are all examples of human understanding developing to a point of awareness of realities beyond those that were previously not known; yet they exist beyond our normal senses. Less than a century or two ago, many of these examples were well beyond the paradigm of people living in those times.

For those of the Bond practising the Art, the knowledge and experience of multiple realities is the foundation of the tradition. As noted earlier, ultimately all *is* consciousness manifesting in infinite forms and realities. We, as conscious beings, partake of and can experience these various worlds, if only we alter our consciousness.

With this in mind we need to begin to examine the magical universe as we of the Art have come to know *and* experience it. This is being done with the understanding that with each new discovery, each ritual and magical technique earnestly performed, this view expands and develops. As such, like science, this is a work in progress and an exciting adventure leading to discovery.

In many esoteric circles, there has long been a temptation to view this material realm, our physical world, as the 'bottom' or the 'fallen' world - the end result of the 'higher' spiritual realms which had somehow fallen out of favour of a superior force or deity. This linear view of reality with its strong religious overtones, sense of failure and 'sin' attached to it sprang largely from the grafting on, and influence of, the Abrahamic traditions with their insistent linear view of 'good versus evil'. It is unfortunate that this limited and guilt driven paradigm has entered so many occult schools of thought.[45] The older traditions with teachings closer to nature held very different views on reality.

In the Art, we recognize that there are multiple realms of being and within each there are an infinite number of worlds. Ancient teachings confirm that the material world is not the last in the realms of reality. Rather, it is but one layer in a series of dimensions, coalescing at this point but influenced and interpenetrated by the realms nearest to it.

It is probably best to begin this discussion with the information we have on what we have come to call the Annwn. The Welsh word *annwn* or *annwfyn* is traditionally translated as "otherworld," and is akin to some of the Irish worlds of the Gods such as *Tír na mBéo*, "Land of the Living". In an ancient poem from The Book of Taliesin, the speaker declares the Annwn to be underground, or more specifically "below the earth." The word itself brings with it connotations of being "very deep" as well as being an "un-world" showing its distinctly non-material nature. This is an important point, which I will be returning to shortly.

For our purposes we can think of the Annwn as a realm that is vast and multidimensional, yet holding a cohesiveness all its own. This is a realm described as having worlds or kingdoms of wonder and beauty. Legend explains that it is rich in treasure - not necessarily material wealth, but rather treasures which cultivate the soul, rejuvenate the land and

---

45. We will be discussing this further in the next chapter.

people, as well as enhance magical abilities. Legends from the Celts describe different realms within the Annwn as 'castles' or 'caer' each with their own distinct natures, inhabitants, beauties and dangers. Many legends tell of adventurers from the material world journeying into the Annwn in quest of knowledge and 'treasure.'

The Annwn, too, is the realm of faery; otherworld beings living in nature but just beyond the veil of this world. These are sentient beings as alive as any in the material world. Magicians from many traditions, ancient and modern, have regularly interacted with these realms and the beings inhabiting these.

In an effort to better understand the worlds of the magician, of the Bond, I want to suggest a *nonlinear* model. In doing so I want to make it clear that while this is based on ancient teachings it is far from perfect. This is simply an attempt to describe realities in terms that our limited three-dimensional thinking can begin to grasp. At no time should the reader assume that this is absolute or complete.

With that said, one way to view this is to think of the Annwn as a sphere; a large ball within which multiple realities, realms or 'planes' exist. The mention of planes of existence suggests layers. So we can begin to see this sphere as being similar to an egg, or an onion. At once it can be understood that this sphere contains all that is and yet it changes in nature as one goes deeper toward the core.

We begin by proceeding from the outer edge of the sphere. As we move inward, passing through the successive layers of the Annwn proper, the material world manifests as one of these layers. Here the raw, regenerative energy of the underworld of Annwn gives creative impulse to our world. The very life and power within the land comes from the hidden regions of the Annwn.

However, our world, the material world, or 'middle earth' as Celtic traditions often describe our realm, is 'thin'. It is not nearly as diverse as the Annwn underworld - the outer ring in the model of the sphere which I have suggested. Still, within our dimension there too can be found countless worlds, stars, galaxies and in a very real sense, the material realm is vast and rich. Yet, as expansive as the material dimension is, in terms of the transcendent nature of consciousness, the material realm is limited and yes, 'thin'.

Quite literally other realms penetrate this world. It is for this reason that there are places in nature, as well as seasons of the year when the 'veil between the worlds' is thin. Folklore tells us that some people have literally transferred from this world to that of faery, bodily. These legends are abundant both in the Old World and the New, and in fact, similar legends can be found in Ancient Egypt.[46] In the same way, the inhabitants of the underworld can transcend the veil and interact in this world.

Whether the stories handed down are true or not, it stands to reason that consciousness - the stuff that makes up all that is - does transcend these worlds. As such ritual becomes a primary tool for becoming aware of and interacting with these other realities. Again I want to stress that if one changes their state of consciousness, one can change their state of being, and for this discussion, their awareness of other realities.

In many respects our material dimension can be seen as a *threshold* between these other worlds. That is, our realm exists between the Annwn and the next realm which we will now consider, the Abred.

Moving further into this model of the sphere one encounters the Abred. This is a mysterious realm of myth and shifting images. Some have tried to pin the label of

---

46. The Legend of the "Cow Herder" is a possible example. In this a cow herder is tending his cows. As the day wears on a mist seems to appear. When this clears an additional cow has joined the herd. As he approaches this cow she turns into a beautiful naked woman with long flowing hair. He comes to realize that she is none other than the Goddess Hathor and that he has somehow stepped beyond the material realm to one in which this great deity could appear.

this realm as being 'evil.' Again, these are human value judgements and do not reflect objective reality. One cannot place a value of 'good' or 'evil' on a place or dimension. Rather, for this work, the Abred can be equated with the 'astral plane' of contemporary, occult thought. This is a realm where emotions energize 'thought forms' to create images that can eventually influence and, given enough power and time, manifest on the material.

Like the worlds described thus far, the Abred holds within it many realms and realities; astral kingdoms of beauty and some of terror. *Emotion powers thought* in this realm, which can create structure out of the Abred. This is not unlike our material world, where we may take the raw elements of nature and create the many objects which we count on in our daily life.

Nevertheless, there is a raw power and beauty in the astral with currents which flow throughout, like tides answering to certain times and seasons in their own natural rhythm. These currents are useful to those of the Art, as one can take advantage of these to influence magical working, which is discussed further on in this work.

As we move closer to the core of our model, the Abred slowly gives way to the Gwynfyd. Here the concepts, the images and words available in our language are inadequate to describe the reality of this dimension. It can be best expressed as approaching some of humanity's loftiest ideals of the spiritual. Like the realms before, this is a place that holds many realities and worlds within.

However, just before we enter the Gwynfyd, we need to consider that the point at which the Abred and the Gwynfyd meet is similar in many ways to that point in which the Annwn and the Abred meet. Both phases can be thought of as thresholds between two major realms. Where these mix we find sub-realms which are the product of both.

Where the Annwn and Abred meet, our material dimension exists; interpenetrated by the two realms. Where the Abred and Gwynfyd meet, a similar situation occurs. Here, the astral imagery with its ability to be moulded by thought and emotion of the Abred mingles with the energies of the Gwynfyd to form the various 'heavenly' realms, paradises and nirvana of human understanding. Yet, this isn't the Gwynfyd 'proper'. This is a world between realms which leads into the Gwynfyd.

The Gwynfyd is the realm of the Gods in their form that is most accessible to the shaman, witch or magician. While the intelligences that are the Gods permeate all that is in nature, in the Gwynfyd they take form most easily. It is here that one can have direct communication with these powerful beings.

Typically, the Gwynfyd is experienced in terms and symbols of peaceful images and rich natural settings. The Elysian Fields of the Greeks, the Field of Reeds of the Egyptians, and the Summer Land of Celtic Traditions are all examples of this realm. This can almost be thought of as a solar realm of light and beauty. Here, deep and powerful spiritual experiences can occur to those of the Geassa.

Beyond the Gwynfyd, laying deep in the core of our model rests Caer Wydyr, the Castle of Glass, the Castle of the Goddess Arianrhod, also known as the Crystal Mountain. One can only describe this realm in very abstract and symbolic terms. This is a dimension of celestial beauty with the expansiveness of the starry heavens being some of the only material images that can begin to touch upon the spiritual wonder that is the Castle of Glass. This is the center of the circle. This is the origin of All. Yet we need to keep in mind that the primary symbol of the Goddess Arianrhod is the Silver Circle; the Moon with its ever cycling movement of life throughout these dynamic realms.

Thus, while Caer Wydyr sits at the center of this model as the highest spiritual concept that we can understand, it also is found in legend as a realm hidden deep within the Annwn! This can seem to be a paradox. Yet, again, we need to keep from thinking in linear terms as we consider this.

The Annwn is the great sphere or cauldron that contains All. It is evolution, regeneration, transformation; the raw energy that is all consciousness moving in cycles through the worlds and back again, ebbing and flowing in renewed forms and life. One of the primary symbols of the Annwn said to be housed in the Castle of Glass – in Caer Wydyr – is that of the Cauldron of Inspiration. Legend explains that this is rimmed with pearls and beneath it, a fire is kept kindled by the breath of nine women.

The symbolism is clear. The cauldron is the great womb of regeneration; the divine feminine containing all. The pearls allude to the silver circle and the lunar nature fulfilled; while the raw energy of transformation is symbolized by the fire which heats this, attended to by nine women. This is yet another powerful representation of the Goddess, as nine is a number long associated with the Moon. Furthermore, it is from their breath, the breath of life, that the universe and all magical worlds flow - emerging, continually evolving and revolving.

The center of the circle is the cauldron in Caer Wydyr, the creative center at the heart of the celestial worlds. Yet the cauldron is all, the Annwn itself folding in on itself and expanding outward, ever flowing. Caer Wydyr is the central core resting at once just beyond the Gwynfyd, yet sitting at the deepest heart of the Annwn. This, then, is the Great Mystery, the Grail sought by all. Here, we see the great spiritual realms merging, bending back into themselves, rejuvenated through the Cauldron of Arianrhod. This is the Willow Path with its ability to bend and shape.

So, in this model, we see the symbolism of the three circles used in ritual. In our system of the Art, we work within three concentric circles; the outer circle as Annwn drawn with the knife, the middle circle as Abred cast with the Stang or ritual staff surmounted by two horns and the third inner circle traced with the wand.[47] At its center rests

---

47. The Stang as both a ritual tool and as a powerful symbol, representing a 'Pagan Tree of Life', is discussed further on in this work.

the cauldron - the Great Goddess - the Castle of Arianrhod, celestial and divine. Yet it is She who is the raw essence that is the Annwn itself.

For the sake of ritual practice too, the tree or Stang can be used to describe this model. Its base rests in the Annwn, the shaft rises through the middle earth and Abred, only to branch out at Gwynfyd where the masculine shaft of the Stang merges with the feminine yoni, formed by the branching horns outlining the chalice in its shape and form. Between these, just above, is the circle of Caer Wydyr - the Castle of Glass and the realm of the Great Goddess.

Combining these images, one could see in our model the circle of Annwn resting as a base, rising in a cone upward through the worlds to the peak that is the Castle of Glass. The danger in using these images is to *not* assign values of 'good' or 'evil' to any of these. Each of these worlds is equal, existing as one. Nevertheless, the image can be helpful when using practical techniques to traverse and experience these realms. It may, very well, be that it is from this innate awareness of the worlds that the 'Witches cone of power' comes.

Another way that one could look at this paradigm would be to consider this as similar to the light spectrum. Within light itself we find multiple 'bands' or frequencies. Each is separate, blending into the next. None are necessarily 'good' or 'evil'. They simply are. These too, run in a succession yet are part of a whole, merging and bending back on to itself.

Chapter Six

❖ THE WORLDS OF THE ART ❖
and the Hermetic Qabalah

It may be prudent here to explain that the Worlds of the Art as discussed thus far should in no way be confused with the Hermetic Qabalistic "Tree of Life", as the differences between the two systems are profound. In contemporary Hermetic traditions, the Qabalistic Tree of Life is a consistent tool used to describe various realms and the flow or progression of energies between these. For many, it can be a worthwhile aid, clearly describing realms and modes of being through numerical value, color association, planetary correspondence and more.

It was of a relatively recent time frame that the Hermetic Qabalah as it is understood today came into being. Beginning during the eleventh century, a series of Qabalistic Trees were written of or depicted. Yet each is drastically different. In his work "The Qabalistic Tarot", Dr. Robert Wang discusses this history with clear examples of the various "Trees" used. He depicts four different versions and discusses a fifth that was in use in the Middle Ages.

For example, one that was adapted from the CE 1617 book "Complete Works" by Robert Fludd, shows a single stalk or path leading straight up. Atop of this, one realm is depicted. At the base, another realm is shown, while along the main path eight more realms are depicted, four on each side. This is very different from the Hermetic Qabalah used by magicians today. Dr. Wang makes an interesting observation regarding the "Tree of Life":

"The most that can be said with certainty is that the Tree of Life has evolved over centuries, following ever increasing public interest and, not coincidentally, reflecting the perspectives of contemporary philosophy".[48]

On close examination, the Qabalistic Tree of Life is a linear model. This, in our opinion, poses severe limitations. Given the number of 'versions' of the Tree that have evolved over the centuries, the Hermetic Qabalah really can best be thought of as a manmade flowchart, not unlike those that would be used in any corporate setting to understand the hierarchy of departments and stations. While useful in the business world, these types of maps are difficult to apply to dimensions beyond our own.

The analogy of a corporate flowchart showing its hierarchy is, in my opinion, a very appropriate comparison. For while a corporate flowchart helps one to understand which person or department controls another, the literal structure of the buildings, layout of the offices, etc., is going to be very different. So it is, in the understanding of the Worlds.

On the other hand, the model used by us in the Art as shown in the painting later in this book, is our 'map' of the Worlds as we have come to understand them, presented in highly symbolic form. Having said this, the 'hierarchy' of powers having influence over different 'departments' or 'conditions' of life may be very different. It is my experience from initiation and work within a fully contacted Hermetic Order that the Qabalistic Tree of Life, as it is currently used, is an attempt to understand the relationship and sphere of influence that different powers have, not necessarily their literal placement.

In fact, in his work "Magick in Theory and Practice" Aleister Crowley severely criticized fellow magicians of his day for their belief that the universe was set up 'literally' on this structure.

---

48. Wang, Dr. Robert. *The Qabalistic Tarot.* 1983 p.31

Aside from the obvious linear limitations of a 'flow chart mentality' in trying to understand other worlds and dimensions, there is the real danger of falling into the paradigm of "the fall." Essentially, this is the religious view introduced by the Abrahamic tradition that the material world "fell from grace" or out of favour from a higher divine patriarchal authority figure. In this view, the worlds described in the Qabalisitc model were seen as also having been subject to this 'fall'.

In many ways, it is understandable that this view came to affect Hermetic teachings given the influence that Hebrew, Christian and Islamic thought had on Hermetic magicians of the medieval and modern eras. With this influence came the idea of "lesser worlds" and realms - the further 'down' the flow chart or Tree of Life the 'less good' the world in consideration must be.

It is unfortunate that many Hermetic magicians today see our material realm as somehow being the world most removed from the Divine, having 'fallen from grace' and in need of 'redemption.' This view is diametrically opposed to the Shamanic/Pagan view which understands Nature to be an expression and embodiment of the Divine. It is important to note that in our model, each realm is held in equal regard with no connotation of good, or evil, attached.

In researching the origins of the Hermetic Qabalah, the trail eventually leads one back to ancient Pythagorean/Greek and Egyptian teachings, with the use of numerical powers among other values, to begin to understand aspects of the Worlds. Again, this is, in my opinion, completely valid and can be exceptionally useful in working with certain otherworld forces. The danger came when this was eventually grafted on to the religious cult beliefs of the Abrahamic tradition.

This was done, in part, because there have been some brilliant occultists who were devote members of the Abrahamic tradition. As such, they felt a need to convert ancient teachings to fit their world view. The Geassa can find form in many ways, though often it can be distorted when projected through the lens of religious bias. In my opinion, *if* one can avoid any assignment of 'good' verses 'evil', 'sin', as well as 'fallen' worlds and strip away the patriarchal and religious symbolism that has found its way into this system, the Hermetic Qabalah can be of exceptional value, navigating certain realms described.

In laying the Hermetic Tree alongside our model, it seems clear that one could interpret this as helping to represent *some* of the energies described. Primarily, one could see this in play for some of the regions between the threshold which is our reality - the material world - moving through the Abred and on into portions of the Gwynfyd.

As such, this can be useful for working through certain aspects of the astral but it completely misses major areas known of in ancient Pagan traditions. The Annwn is overlooked utterly, while the celestial realm of Caer Wydyr is only vaguely glimpsed through the mysterious "Veil of Isis" or Ain Soph Aur and is never fully experienced.

As a result, for many magicians trained in contemporary schools of the Western Mystery Tradition, when the influence of the Annwn comes flooding through, most can't account for the powerful feminine and regenerative forces at either end of the spectrum. So, on the one hand, the divine feminine is almost completely ignored or else She is shut away behind a veil or "holy of holies", where none can experience Her. In this regard, She is almost always seen as hidden, non-sexual and virgin. While on the other end of the spectrum, Her raw sexual power of regeneration was made into some kind of sexual sin and perversion. Her presence in the Annwn caused this to be seen as 'Hell' by the Abrahamic tradition. From such vile interpretations, the "Whore of Babylon" and similar images were created.

Speaking honestly, the dogmatic, patriarchal mind set of the Abrahamic tradition, for the most part, loathes and fears the Great Goddess (as we saw earlier when examining the historical evidence). This is unfortunate for the Hermetic tradition. For Hermetics is, in many respects, the heir to so much of the great esoteric knowledge of Egypt. It would seem that many within Hermetic practices today, have fallen victim to the flawed and dogmatic world view of later religious doctrines. So, while the Hermetic Qabalah can be useful for exploring certain realms of the Abred, its limitations are obvious.

Conversely, ancient Pagan Western teachings revisioned here, embrace the Goddess and Her realms in powerful forms. The Pagan World Tree or Stang which we will discuss at length in the next chapter recognizes the majesty of the Gods in their manifestation in Nature and throughout all Worlds.

The Four Hermetic 'Modes' & the Shamanic World Tree
Before ending this discussion, I need to mention the role of the four Hermetic 'modes' of manifestation: conceive, create, form and express. Contemporary Hermetic magicians use the Hebrew terms for these. Each is tied directly to one of the four traditional elements (as discussed in our chapter "The Witch's Foot"). Many Qabalistically-minded magicians will ascribe each of these 'modes' to specific worlds and with this, to specific areas on the linear model described in the "Tree of Life". This, too, leads them to associate certain classes of beings with various degrees of power to these modes and to specific areas of the "Tree".

Our view of these modes is significantly different. We maintain that each of these modes manifest in *every* realm, whether Annwn, Abred, Gwenfyd or Caer Wydr, as well as the countless sub-worlds within each of these realms. We have found that these four Hermetic modes, embodied in part in the elements, correspond to the means by which energy - consciousness - exists and manifests in *every* world. And, like Hermetic teachings, we agree that beings and intelligences of various powers exist in these modes. However, we feel this is true on all worlds, all realms and is not limited to specific areas of any given map or Tree.

Conceive, create, form and express - these are modes of manifestation whether in the astral realms of Abred, the threshold of our material world, the underworld of Annwn or in the celestial realm of Caer Wydr. And, with this, beings of the mode of "conception" (Atziluth in Hermetic circles) do exist in each of the worlds of the Geassa. So it is with the other modes. No single world or realm is more sacred than the other. All are means through which the Divine, as consciousness, manifests and is aware of itself.

Having said this, the nature of the realm in which forces exist can color the way in which the intelligence comes through. So, a being of the Atziluth mode manifesting itself in Annwn, will be very different from the way in which a similar being in Caer Wydyr would. Again, we need to stop thinking in linear models and, instead, recognize the spiritual component and completeness of each realm. Each is unique in its own right, yet all is connected.

Perhaps what is most interesting is that while we have determined that consciousness transcends all of the realms, these four modes - conceive, create, form, express - also lay as a backdrop and means through which consciousness manifests *in these worlds*. This is important and explains why the traditional elements of the Art form such an important part of our practice. It will also help the apprentice to understand the importance of these when we examine them in the "Witch's Foot".

Chapter Seven

✤ THE STANG ✤
The Tree Rising through the Worlds

One of the oldest and most prominent symbols of the Geassa is the Stang, or as it is called in Gaelic, the Gwelen. Yet this has been one of the most overlooked tools of the Western Tradition. A Stang is a simple wooden staff terminating in two points which branch off from the main shaft. In essence, this is a basic pitchfork. When first seen, the two points immediately remind one of the horns of a bull, or the antlers of a stag. This is a uniquely Pagan symbol with roots that extend back through much of Europe and Great Britain.

Some of the earliest records of its association with Paganism come from accounts of Witchcraft during the Middle Ages. German woodcuts dating from as early as CE 1410 depict Witches flying to their meetings not on broomsticks but on the forked Stang.[49] Similar woodcuts continue to be found throughout Europe. One dating from CE 1489 shows Witches disguised as animals riding to a Sabbat, once again, not on brooms but on Stangs.[50] An intriguing woodcut from CE 1510 depicts a group of Witches, naked, at a meeting. In this, they appear to be evoking a tempest from a cauldron. All around them, a series of Stangs can be seen. Some of these are lying on the ground, while overhead one Witch is shown riding a

49. Cooper, John Michael. *Mendelsson, Goethe, and the Walpurgis Night: The Heathen Muse in Europe.* 2010.

50. German work *De Lamiss* by Ulrich Molitor 1489.

goat, holding a Stang with a cauldron resting between its two forks.[51]

While these sources are all from artist renditions and imaginings drawn from medieval European Witchcraft, records show that the Stang continued to figure highly in Great Britain. The custom of 'Swearing on the Horns' was a common practice extending back to at least the sixteenth century and continued well into the twentieth century.[52] This involved the taking of an oath while holding a Stang which consisted of a wooden staff surmounted by a set of antlers.

It is important to note that the Stang has survived through the centuries as a viable ceremonial tool for traditional Pagan groups.[53] In his book "Western Inner Workings", William Gray discusses the practices of a small number of traditional Welsh Pagan groups and their use of this tool in ritual. He found that these groups saw the Stang as being similar to an altar. This served as an embodiment of their beliefs with a strong correlation to the Celtic World Tree and its ties to the cyclic death and rebirth of Sacred Kings.[54]

To understand the deeper meaning contained within this seemingly simple form, we must look closely at the symbolism of the Stang itself. At its most obvious, this is a representation of the God of the Forest at a primal level. Made of wood and cut from the limb of a tree, each is individual, drawing from the land on which it grew. In some groups, the Stang figures most prominently at the Celtic festival of Samhain. In this ritual, the Stang is carried by the Master honouring the Lord of death and regeneration. While a valid use, there is so much more that this symbol relates to.

---

51. Hans Baldung Grien woodcut from 1510, Germanisches Nationalmuseum, Nurember.

52. *The London Encyclopedia.* 1983 p.379.

53. The use of the term "traditional pagan groups" refers to families and traditions that predate contemporary Wicca, however modern Wicca has incorporated some of these teachings into itself.

54. Gray, William G. *Western Inner Workings.* 1983 p.151-152.

As mentioned the Stang is strongly identified with the sacred tree of Celtic tradition.[55] Not to be confused with the Qabalistic Tree of Hermetic teachings, the Celtic stang shows a path through the Pagan spiritual worlds of Annwn,[56] Abred and Gwynfyd,[57] all leading to Caer Wydyr.[58]

As a form of the Celtic Tree of Life, the base of the Stang can be seen as resting in the world of the Annwn. As we had seen in the chapter regarding the Worlds, the Annwn is the mysterious realm of the underworld; a place of transformation, regeneration and the power inherent in the land itself.[59] The Annwn is multifaceted and holds within it the realm of Faery where the stories of Tam Lin,[60] Thomas the Rhymer and Queen Medb of the Sidhe hold sway.[61] These are not the diminutive figures of Victorian fairy tales. The realm of Faery is a separate dimension closely related to the natural energies of the land itself, yet not normally perceptible through our usual five senses. Ritual magician, R.J. Stewart, describes the inhabitants of this realm as 'Otherworld Beings' with natures and orders of beings as complex as any seen in our material world.[62]

---

55. Gray, William G. *Western Inner Workings*. 1983 p.151-152.

56. Stewart, R.J. *The Underworld Initiation* gives extensive details on the Celtic Tree as a path through the worlds.

57. The worlds of Annwn, Abred and Gwynfyd are discussed at length by Spenser, Lewis in *The Magic Arts in Celtic Britain*. 1993.

58. A discussion on the Castle of Arianrhod in relation to traditional yet living pagan practices can be found in Gray, William G. *Western Inner Workings*. 1983 p.144-147.

59. Spencer, Lewis. *The Magic Arts of Celtic Britain*. 1993 p.131.

60. *Ibid.*, p.130.

61. This is specifically discussed by Spencer, Lewis in *The Magic Arts of Celtic Britain*. 1993 p.130. Also the reader is advised to see Stewart, R.J. *The Underworld Initiation*, which discusses the esoteric meaning of these ballads in relation to the Faery tradition at length.

62. Stewart, R.J. *Living the World of Faery*. 1999.

It is in the Annwn that the solar heroes of myth, journey into the depths of the earth seeking treasure.[63] Inevitably, though, the prize is their own transformation and renewal. Echoes of this theme can be found in the Arthurian legends,[64] as well as the struggle and transformation of the Holly and Oak Kings at the winter solstice. In this continual cycle, the Sun God or hero descends into the Annwn only to rise again in the Abred with its highest point at summer solstice being on the threshold between Abred and Gwynfyd.[65] All of this can be tied symbolically to the seemingly simple staff of the Stang.

In the diagram depicted in this chapter, the lower circle corresponds to the cycle of the Sun. At the base of the painting, resting in the 'roots' of the tree lays the position of the Sun at the winter solstice. Here He is deep within the Annwn. As the circle moves upward halfway, the Sun sits at the point of the equinox and the threshold between the Annwn and Abred. This is our realm - the material world, or as ancient Pagan traditions taught 'middle earth'. Continuing on, the summer solstice marks the height of the solar cycle as it arrives at the threshold leading into Gwynfyd - the sunlit Summerland of the Gods.

It is important to note that the Goddess as the Moon, too, cycles through the worlds and on the Stang, as shown in the upper circle on the diagram. Her journey begins in the Annwn with the New Moon at the base of the staff but circles higher into the tree than the Sun does, with the Full Moon resting on the threshold between Gwynfyd and Caer Wydyr, high between the two horns. While the Sun's highest point leads into the Summerland of the Gods, the Moon goes further, resting as the Silver Cauldron in the celestial realm from which all came. This is the cauldron of inspiration, the Great Mother as the center of all. From a

---

63. Squire, Charles. *Celtic Myth and Legend*. 1975 p.273.

64. *Ibid.*, p.319.

65. Spencer, Lewis. *The Magic Arts of Celtic Britain*. 1993 p.129 & 131.

practical point of view this is important and forms a vital link to understanding the phases of the Moon and the Oracle of the Moon.

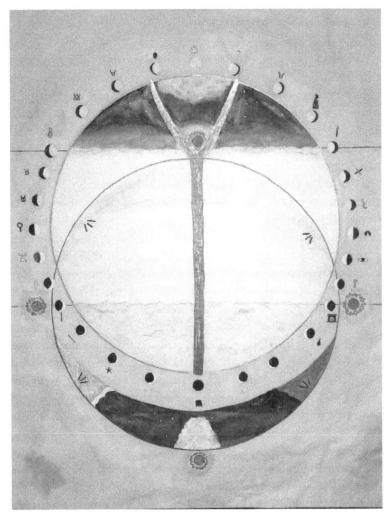

1. The Stang - Rising through the Worlds of the Geassa

Returning to our discussion of the Stang itself, the shaft rises from Annwn through the worlds to the Abred. This world was seen as being equally as intricate as the

Annwn with diverse layers but the Abred has always been understood to be a natural extension of the Annwn. In private workings, we have found that the Abred contains the lunar astral world of contemporary occult teachings. This is the realm of energy and magic where one's creative imagination will take form.

When considered further as a representation of the journey through the Celtic worlds, the shaft of the Stang can be seen as divided into two parts; the lower quarter representing the underworld of the Annwn and the remainder of the shaft as the Abred. Between these two realms lays the material world, our plane of existence (represented in the diagram as the horizontal line a third of the way up).[66]

It is important to remember that the deepest levels of the Annwn rest below the base of the Stang's shaft, or as we prefer to think of it, as the 'roots' of the tree. In the diagram, you will see a tremendous amount of symbolism placed in the bottom quarter of the painting. While subtle, these are meant to represent the cyclic energies and realms of power within the deepest recesses of the Annwn. Some of these include the red and white rivers, roses and dragons. In Egypt, these were represented in the red and white crowns of the pharaoh. Also are shown the realms of sacrifice and transformation, the lush green lands of faery, the deep celestial pool and lake of the Goddess reflecting the stellar realm of Gwynfyd. In the center of this lake lays the pylon that holds the Cauldron of transformation in which the Goddess rejuvenates the God as the Sun at midnight forging the link with the source in Caer Wydyr.

As mentioned in the chapter regarding the Worlds, the material realm (located on the diagram a third of the way up the shaft of the stang) is not as solid as our current western

---

66. It may be noteworthy to point out that several internet sites state that the material world is solely a part of the Abred with no connection to the Annwn. Others claim that the material world is the Abred. Few of these sites give references to their sources.

paradigm would like to have us believe. Resting between the Annwn and the Abred the material realm partakes of both of these other dimensions and is influenced by both. As such, these can overlap. In the Celtic understanding of reality there are places in nature in which the veil dividing the worlds is very thin. It is taught that in some places one may cross over between the realms easily.[67] Locations thought of as faery hills, ley lines, certain hallows and rock formations can all carry properties that, to the sensitive person can allow access to these other realms.[68]

At the top of the shaft the two horns of the stang branch to either side. This corresponds to the sunlit world of the Gwynfyd. This is the Celtic realm of paradise, the Summerland of Shamanic traditions throughout European culture. Here the dead rest and are rejuvenated before returning to the material realm reincarnated.[69]

It is interesting to note that despite the apparent masculine nature of the horns rising to either side, they form a lunar crescent resting on its back. This is extremely reminiscent of the cup, chalice or goblet which is the sacred symbol of the divine feminine. So here in the top third of the Stang two strong, even overt symbols come shining through. The phallic horns of the God and the womb of the Goddess are combined. Through this dynamic composition of complementary forces the realm of harmony and bliss epitomized by the world of Gwynfyd is maintained.

Where the shaft meets the yoni of the horns this union creates a fountain of energy flowing from this point. Male and female unite, and through this the dynamic energy involved becomes available to those of the Art. It is for this

67. See Robert Kirk's *The Secret Commonwealth of Elves, Fauns & Fairies*. R.J. Stewart has reissued this ancient manuscript in a new form with commentary.

68. Bord, Janet & Colin. *Earth Rites: Fertility Practices in Pre-Industrial Britain*. 1983 p.219-240.

69. Spencer, Lewis. *The Magic Arts of Celtic Britain*. 1993 p.129-130.

reason that frequently a lit candle will be placed between the horns to channel and focus that energy as needed.

Yet, there is one more stage that follows as we journey up the tree of life of the Celts. Between the tips of the horns, just above the stang the realm of Caer Wydyr, the Castle of Glass, resides. This is seen as a realm of great joy and happiness,[70] the source of wisdom which is beyond polarity. This is the stellar world that is the fountainhead of all that is.[71] The point just above and between the tips of the horns of the stang can be understood as corresponding to this sacred realm of being. It is important to note here that the highest spiritual realm of the Celts was also known as Ceugant.[72] In many traditions the Castle of Glass is equated with this same spiritual state of being. In the Welsh traditions noted by William Gray this state was also known as the Castle of Arianrhod.[73] He goes on to describe this in the practical workings of the group:

> "These particular Pagans saw their "Interior Castle" [the Castle of Arianrhod – kw] as being a sort of psychic meeting place wherein they could be conscious of their Gods and discarnate associates in a common state of inner understanding."[74]

A further reference to the Castle of Glass being equated to the Goddess can be found in Alan Richardson's discussion of Glastonbury Tor and its early associations as the "Isle of Glass." In this discussion he makes reference to the ancient belief that the Tor itself is the breast of the Earth Mother

---

70. Squire, Charles. *Celtic Myth and Legend.* 1975 p.319-320.

71. Richardson, Alan. *Priestess: The Life and Magic of Dion Fortune.* 1987 p.181-182.

72. Spencer, Lewis. *The Magic Arts of Celtic Britain.* 1993 p.129.

73. Gray, William G. Western Inner Workings. 1983 p.144-148.

74. *Ibid.,* p.145.

from which "the energies from the underworld spume into the atmosphere with a sense of a fountain".[75] This symbolism is interesting for it shows that the raw energies contained in the Annwn, the underworld, rise to manifest renewed through the divine feminine into the highest states of being.

Through all of this it quickly becomes clear that far from being only a symbol of the God and the Male Mysteries, the Stang is actually a tool which encompasses the essence of the European Shamanic spiritual path. In this form we see the great tree of life itself, rising through the spiritual worlds, embracing both God and Goddess. In following the path of the Stang, one is carried to the lofty stellar realm of the spiritual cause and creative desire represented by the Great Goddess Arianrhod. Though simple in form, this two pronged staff is the embodiment of our Pagan spiritual path and heritage.

---

75. Richardson, Alan. *Priestess: The Life and Magic of Dion Fortune.* 1987 p.182.

Chapter Eight

✦ THE MAGIC OF THE MOON ✦

As has been alluded to, not only are there specific places in nature where the worlds merge and interpenetrate each other, there are also specific times when different energies surge through, bringing access to different realms. Simply put, these are tides of power which those of the Art understand, calculate and use to their advantage. Different tides bring different energies, as well as access to different worlds.

For our purposes perhaps the single most important power tide is that regulated by the phases of the Moon. This beautiful silver orb holds such a powerful sway over magic that virtually all systems of esoteric training, that I am aware of, observe the Moon's positions. For us, this is even more important simply because it represents one of the most obvious manifestations of the Goddess in nature. As such, each phase of the Moon has specific energies and attributes.

Sybil Leek explained that the most important phase to consider is that which begins with the first day of the New Moon and extends to the first day of the Full Moon. Known as the Waxing Moon this is generally a time when one can work magic related to growth, abundance, new life, gain, fertility and prosperity. Spells and rituals done in this period should be for positive, constructive purposes. For the most part, results from these operations tend to take time to manifest as steady building and growth is required, nevertheless this is a period when advances of any kind can be made. In fact, I have seen very sudden results from certain rituals which involved the generation of intense, focused emotion. As the Hermetic Order which I am affiliated to explains, the Waxing Moon generally and the first quarter specifically are useful for works "akin to all inception and growth".

For our part, we term this 'Green Magic'. Green Magic takes time to manifest, yet its effects are long lasting and powerful. Often times, steady work with repeated ritual applications, are necessary. Still, with patience, the results can be extraordinarily profound. I've seen this time and again. Grandma Julie termed this "the drum roll". She explained that this was the repeated casting of a spell over a period of time to enhance the flow of energy toward that goal. Keep in mind that she was fully aware of the occult axiom to "let go" of the spell once cast. Rather, when the drum roll is used, a period of "resting" between the castings needed to take place. In such cases, once the spell is first cast, the Witch waits a minimum of three days (usually twenty-eight days or one lunar cycle), essentially forgetting the spell and the desired goal during that time. All attention is placed in other areas of one's life. Then the rite is repeated.[76]

When we consider the Moon we need to return to the great tree of Pagan lore, the Stang, with its base in Annwn. Placing the Moon here, this is the point when the Moon is moving from dark to new, and from the crone stage to that of the young maiden. In the Art the Moon is seen as reflective of the threefold aspect of femininity: the young woman or maiden seen in the first phases of the Waxing Moon; the woman in the full flower of her sexuality as the Mistress, the Lady, and Mother in the days prior to

---

76. Grandma Julie also used the term "drum roll" to apply to those times when Witches from various regions would coordinate their efforts, directing their combined wills toward the same objective and at the same time, but from different areas. She explained that if the goal was clearly defined the "drum roll" could be very effective.

and following the Full Moon; and the Wise Crone in the Waning Moon.[77]

Following the New Moon, during the course of the lunar month, the Moon rises higher through the worlds as She waxes. At the fourth day following the New Moon, She reaches a point of transition crossing from the underworld of potential in Annwn, passing briefly through the material 'middle world' only to begin Her emersion into the realm of Abred. This journey is represented in the painting shown earlier in this work.

The Abred is that mysterious realm of magic and astral forces. The Moon as Goddess grows in light, waxing toward full. The four days just prior to the actual Full Moon are very powerful and mark the period of the Lady, Mistress or Mother aspect of the Goddess. At this time astral and etheric energies, the 'Nephesh' of Hermetic circles, is freely accessible. This is the perfect time for positive magic in all its forms. Here, the silver orb is rising higher in the worlds crossing the threshold of the Abred to enter the realm of Gwynfyd - that high spiritual realm of actualization and fulfillment.

At the Full Moon itself, the silver orb reaches its climax of power as it crosses from the realm of Gwynfyd and rests as the silver cauldron in Caer Wydyr. This is the most powerful moment in the lunar month for magic of a positive and feminine nature. The Full Moon also marks the greatest flow of inherent energy frequently thought of as 'serpent power' or 'dragon energy' latent in nature. In essence this

---

77. Some Traditional Witches today have stated that the concept of the triple Goddess is a 'neo-pagan' invention drawn from the writings of Robert Graves' "White Goddess". However, references to triple Goddesses generally extend back into Celtic lore across Europe. As for specific references to 'maiden, mother and crone, these can be found in occult writings written well before Graves' work. In fact, Crowley discusses this in his book "Moon Child" written more than two decades before "White Goddess" was published.

is the inherent power of nature rising to the call of the Moon. This is best experienced in certain places of power; caves, natural wells, cliffs, streams, hill tops, stone circles, clearings in woodlands, beaches, etc. Granite with its high content of quartz answers to this energy becoming alive with lunar power.

Too, Sybil Leek points out that the trees themselves answer to this energy reaching from the depths of the earth rising high into the sky where the Moon comes down to meet them. The Witch uses this energy to her ability gathering this into her objects of power, or directing this toward goals at hand. In such cases Sybil had explained that "moon light is warm" referring to the affect created when the living pulse of the Moon, Earth and trees merge within the Witch during ritual.[78]

I can't say enough about the beauty and power of the Full Moon. Without a doubt the most moving spiritual experiences of my life have occurred as a direct result of this celestial event. I can safely say that the sheer essence of the divine feminine, as She is expressed and experienced on this plane, is tied closely to the humble silver orb that circles our world. Her energy, wisdom and spiritual love are easily experienced by any who will take the time to enjoy an evening meditating under Her watchful gaze.

With the Full Moon, the gateway to other realms swings open. For those of the Art, no other time is as powerful or useful for accessing these realms whether through divination, spell and incantation, or mental and astral projection. Spirit communication, as well as invocation of the Gods is very effective now. So, too, is communion with the elemental forces of nature. The Full Moon in any season is a magical time open to all with the knowledge to use it.

Because of the access to 'Nephesh' or astral energy at this time, the Full Moon is optimum for the evocation of spirits or otherworld entities. At this time, given the right formula,

---

78. See Holzer, Hans. *The Truth About Witchcraft*. Copyright 1969.

these beings can manifest in terms which even those who are not normally psychic can perceive.

Leaving Caer Wydyr, during the three days following the Full Moon, the astral energies are still strong as the Moon slowly descends back down through the Gwynfyd. The Hermetic Order in which I have been trained, states that this can be an effective time to perform magic with the understanding that the etheric Moon-Power is less than that at the Full Moon. On the fourth day following the Full Moon, it begins its transition back into Abred.

Sybil goes on to explain that the next most important phase of the Moon begins with the first day following the Full Moon until the day that the last quarter begins. Here the Moon is Waning. This is the period when the removal of unwanted influences in one's life can begin. Rituals performed in this period tend to act the quickest but are of a negative nature designed to get rid of those forces hindering the individual.

From the fourth day past Full Moon until Dark Moon this orb corresponds with the Crone aspect of the Goddess. She is the Crone as teacher, guide and wise sage, as well as the dark queen who destroys in order to transform.

Sybil makes it clear that the last quarter of the Moon is very negative. She explains that nothing of a positive nature can be done now and that if these works are tried in this period they will almost certainly rebound back on the individual bringing the opposite results. Sybil goes on to warn that those involved in dark aspects of the Arts will use this period to attack. Evil spirits are much more active now as well.

For our part we have found though that we are able to use mirror magic, the setting of the Wards, as well as other protective measures at this time to repel negative forces casting them back upon the persons who had initiated the attack in the first place. This is an excellent period to use the fire cauldron to remove negative influences from a home or area.

On the fourth day prior to the Dark Moon, the waning orb briefly crosses through the realm of the material 'middle earth' and moves into the Annwn, marking its darkest and most destructive influence.

During the Dark and New Moon, the inherent power of nature and the land, the 'serpent' or 'dragon' power, lays fallow. Again, this reiterates this time as a period for getting rid of unwanted people, influences, etc. Blasting and cursing are best done now.

Conversely, at this time, encounters with underworld spirits can be sought. This is a period of introspection, seeking understanding into the nature of those things which may tend to hold one back, as well as communication with spirits of the deceased. For such rites the use of a black mirror for scrying may be the best tool available. Essentially, for magical purposes the Dark Moon period is best approached with great care. Having said this, there are groups that meet regularly at the Dark Moon in order to tap into the powerful transition which occurs when the Crone transforms once again into the Maiden.

For us, the Full Moon is the most important and powerful period in any lunar month. The following is a list of the names and meanings used in our tradition for the Full Moons throughout the year:

- Snow Moon - Occurs when the Sun is in Scorpio, and the Moon in Taurus. This heralds the dark season and the beginning of winter. This coincides with the death of the old year at Samhain and the first snows of the season.
- Oak Moon - Occurs when the Sun is in Sagittarius, and the Moon is in Gemini. As winter is upon us the sacred tree of the Druids, the Oak, withstands the hardships of winter and the cold. The Oak, revered as one of the mightiest and longest lived of trees comes from within the small acorn. The acorn is phallic-shaped and hence an emblem of life.

- Wolf Moon - Occurs when the Sun is in Capricorn, and the Moon is in Cancer. The wolf is a fearsome creature of the night as well as a faithful companion to the God Cernunnos. As the God has returned and we are still within the dark months, the wolf is a symbol of strength.
- Storm Moon - Occurs when the Sun is in Aquarius, and the Moon is in Leo. A storm is said to rage most fiercely just before it ends. So, too, winter follows suit. This will be the last of the winter months and the fierce storms that mark this time of year.
- Chaste Moon - Occurs when the Sun is in Pisces, and the Moon is in Virgo. The Goddess returns as a virgin and so we greet her and the spring with a clear soul. Yet virgin does not imply innocence of sexuality. Rather the term 'virgin'is used here to represent the raw and pure essence of nature; the elemental energies and resources full of potential for fulfillment in the future. This marks the time of beginnings and spiritual growth. Future plans are being shaped.
- Seed Moon - Occurs when the Sun is in Aries, and the Moon is in Libra. Spring is in the air. Depending on your location this can be a time of sowing. This Full Moon is a time to re-affirm the goals set forth with the Spring Equinox which also occurs during this month.
- Hare Moon - Occurs when the Sun is in Taurus, and the Moon is in Scorpio. The hare is a sacred animal associated with springtime and fertility. The hare is sacred to the Goddess and this is her time of the year. Beginning with Beltane, which occurs during this month, all is green and growing and fertility of mind and spirit is as important as that of animal and field.
- Dyad Moon - Occurs when the Sun is in Gemini, and the Moon is in Sagittarius. Dyad is the Latin

word for pair and equates to the twin stars Castor and Pollux.

- Mead Moon - Occurs when the Sun is in Cancer, and the Moon is in Capricorn. Mead, honey wine, is the sacred drink of the Gods. Traditionally, honey was linked with the vaginal, sexual fluids of the female, while wine was seen esoterically to be symbolic of semen, sexual fluids of the male. Thus Mead is the perfect mingling of these.

- Wort Moon - Occurs when the Sun is in Leo, and the Moon is in Aquarius. Wort is the old Anglo-Saxon word term for herb or green plant. This is the time of the first harvest when these herbs and plants would be taken and dried; prepared for storage for the winter months to come.

- Barley Moon - Occurs when the Sun is in Virgo, and the Moon is in Pisces. As we are in the sign of Virgo we see the virgin (its symbol) carrying a sheaf of barley. This is also the time of the Great Harvest. Barley was one of the hardiest of the grains, and stored well for use in the Winter months.

- Harvest Moon, sometimes called Wine Moon - Occurring in late Autumn, this can fall when the Sun is in Virgo or Libra. This is the final harvest of the seasons.

- Blood Moon - Occurs when the Sun is in Libra, and the Moon is in Aries. This Moon marks the season for hunting. The crops have been stored for the winter; now the hunt begins. Blood is the essence of life and it must be spilled to feed the tribe. We offer up wine as symbolic of the hardships as well as the bounty from the past. We pour wine on the earth as thanksgiving for all that we have, as the hunters used to pour the blood of the animals in offering. This Moon also marks the season of the culling of the herds, harvesting livestock in order that meat will be plentiful in the dark months to come.

Each Full Moon tide is linked to an influx of energy that is distinct and different from the others. For those of the Art, we can use these tides weaving the threads of fate in accord with our will.

Beyond the general phases of the Moon described so far, each day of the lunar month holds meaning. Each day brings with it a different force as the Moon tracks Her way through the worlds. In this way, we of the Geassa refine the effects of the Moon in our magical practice. For our part, the actual forces contacted and used on each lunar day are very powerful. This is of such a nature that space in this current volume doesn't allow for us to present this material here.

Chapter Nine

❖ SUN TIDES ❖

L ike the Moon, the Sun answers to a cycle of its own as it, too, passes through the worlds. Ancient legends, from Egypt to the farthest corners of Europe and the British Isles speak of solar heroes, Gods, journeying through the worlds. In each, the hero is challenged along the way while experiencing ordeals which, once faced, transform them into new and stronger incarnations.

We see this in the nightly death of the Egyptian Sun God Ra, as He sinks into the underworld only to encounter the twin Goddesses at midnight. Here on an island surrounded by water, He is made new through the power of the two who reside there. This is the Sun at midnight, the center; the womb of the Goddess Nut. Here, in the depths of night, Ra is transformed as He journey's toward dawn to be born the next morning as the young and radiant Sun disk.

Celtic stories follow a similar pattern. The legend of the 'Spoils of Annwn' speaks of the solar hero, frequently Arthur and his knights, entering the underworld in search of treasure. Each faces an ordeal. Many face death. But this is death as an act of transformation and initiation. In the heart of the underworld the Castle of Glass emerges. In this lays the supreme symbol of the Goddess, the great silver lunar cauldron of inspiration, rimmed with pearls and attended to by nine maidens. This is the ultimate treasure of the Annwn. This is the cauldron of rebirth. Having visited the Castle of Glass, the solar hero returns to the world of humanity, strong, new and with the authority of the Goddess, so that he can rule justly.

The Sun's journey through the worlds brings with it different tides of power reflected in the seasons of the year. These were measured by certain important celestial events. For the Celts these were the four Great Fire Festivals of Samhain, Imbolc, Beltane and Lughnasadh. Equally spaced in the year, these correspond to the height of the season in which they occur. Historian, Jean Markale, explains that originally, while the celebration of these could extend over days or even weeks, the height of the festival was carried out on the Full Moon closest to the mid-point between the equinoxes and solstices.

This point is important, for while some doubt that the equinoxes and solstices were observed by the Celts themselves, the indigenous cultures before the Celts did observe these. This is evident in certain archeological monuments pre-dating even the Celts. The fact that the Celts used these astronomical markers to calculate the four great fire festivals suggests that the equinoxes and solstices did hold significance for them as well.

Today, in the practice of the Art which we follow, the equinoxes and solstices, as well as the fire festivals, hold strong spiritual meaning for us – however, the fire festivals are considered more powerful. The reasons for this will become clear as we examine the journey of the Sun through the year and through the worlds.

Famed astrologer, Dane Rudhyar, explained that the exact midpoint between the equinoxes and solstices are times in the year when tremendous amounts of energy are released. These are the point at which the Sun reaches the fifteen degree mark in each of the fixed signs - of Scorpio corresponding to Samhain, Aquarius corresponding to Imbolc, Taurus corresponding to Beltane and Leo corresponding to Lughnasadh.

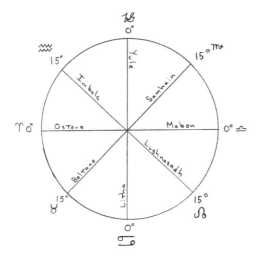

These midpoints represent a tremendous opportunity to both experience and to tap into, the energy of the season. Mr. Rudhyar went so far as to refer to these as "Avatar Gates" stressing the spiritual energies which flow through into this realm on these dates. To quote Mr. Rudhyar "an 'Avatar' in ancient terminology is in fact a *release of cosmic energy* [italics are Mr. Rudhyar's]".[79]

It is important to note that until the 'adjustment' to the calendar by Pope Gregory, essentially moving the calendar back by approximately seven days, the fire festivals of the Celts fell almost exactly on the astrological midpoint of the fixed signs noted above. The importance of this cannot be over-stated. For this is clear evidence that our ancestors who were practicing the Art and living close to the land were aware of, and in tune with, very powerful spiritual forces that are recognized and confirmed by contemporary Astrology.

Mr. Rudhyar went on to explain that the seasons marked by the Solstices and Equinoxes correspond to elemental energies which are gathered in at these events and then released at the mid-point; the fire festivals. He states that the seasons can be tied directly to the elements. The element of

---

79. Rudhyar, Dane. *The Astrology of Personality*. 1970 p.240

fire corresponds to the period of time between the Spring Equinox and the Summer Solstice. He explains that the elemental energy of fire is generated at the equinox and then released at the mid-point of Beltane. The element of water corresponds to the period of time between the Summer Solstice and the Autumn Equinox. The elemental energy of water is gathered and generated at the Summer Solstice and then released at the mid-point of Lughnasadh. The element of air corresponds to the period of time between the Autumn Equinox and the Winter Solstice, with the elemental power of air being generated at the equinox and then released at Samhain. Lastly, the element of earth corresponds to the period between the Winter Solstice and the Spring Equinox. This is then released at the mid-point of Imbolc. This is remarkably similar to the teachings of Grandma Julie who had ascribed the elements to the seasons.[80]

In the Art ritual has been the method by which we acknowledge the spiritual essence of each of these festivals. Sybil Leek expressed this well during an interview in 1969:

"Our rituals are linked with the seasons - spring, summer, autumn, and winter - and we keep so very much to the universe. What we're really doing is giving a general hymn of praise to the universe and all the things in it."

"The quarterly meetings, then, are linked with changes of the season, since the seasons are quite important to man in his own state of seeking harmony."

"Every invocation changes according to the season. The invocation in the spring has within it the means that the

---

80. Julie's correspondence are virtually the same except that she reversed Air and Water, placing Air as beginning with the Summer Solstice, and Water with the Autumn Equinox. Both systems are valid. Dane Rudhyar's implicit logic is detailed in his work *The Astrology of Personality* p. 234 - 245.

seed that is planted may grow; the invocation in August is that the harvest has been good and may we use it and divide it amongst us; and the invocation at Halloween [Samhain] is concerned that the long, dark winter may have within it the means for survival for you. It's a complete cycle of life, always acting and re-acting."[81]

While deeply tied to seasonal changes and what would obviously be celebrations in the agricultural year, there is something much deeper and richer occurring here. Each of these celebrations mark the transition and release of universal energies, as focused through the lens of the celestial event that marks the festival. The cycles of life within the agricultural calendar corresponding to these events represent the material manifestation of these overarching forces that flow from the depths of the spiritual worlds to us. As such, it is more than appropriate for us to decorate our circles with the foliage, fruits and symbols of the season. The Witches Counsel of 'harmony with nature' and 'leading a balanced life' are reflected beautifully in the simple dance that are these annual celebrations.

Samhain

In the Art, we begin our year with Samhain at the height of the fall season. Pronounced "*SAH-win*" or "*Sow-in*," this occurs midway between the autumnal equinox and the winter solstice. It is from this Celtic festival that the customs surrounding Halloween originated. Samhain, meaning summer's end, marks the transition between the old year and the new. For the Celts the year began with Samhain. Being the transition between two years this festival, in particular, was, and is, seen as being a period when the gates between worlds open. This is the time when the Sun is at the midpoint of Scorpio - the sign governing transition, death,

---

81. Interview published in *Psychic* magazine, October/November 1969, San Francisco, U.S.A.

transformation, sexuality, passion and power. All of these characterize the essence of this fire festival.

Looking to the diagram of the journey of the Sun in relation to the worlds and the Stang as tree of life, at Samhain the Sun has moved from the Abred well into the Annwn. And, like Thomas the Rhymer from the old Scottish ballad in which he joins the Queen of Elfland and journey's with her into the underworld, on our diagram the Sun is quickly approaching the red river, the river of blood. In this context, blood represents death. This is the death of the Sun as He sinks into the underworld. Yet, this isn't death as oblivion, but rather death as the process of transformation and initiation. Remember, too, that blood is life. Without blood the body can't live. So here on the threshold, the most prominent night of the year when the gates of the other world are thrown open, the Sun crosses the river of blood, dying - or rather leaving the realm of the living.

This theme is reminiscent of the Osirian mysteries of Ancient Egypt. Though these were calculated using the lunar calendar, generally they corresponded to the same time of year as the Samhain season. This is important for the Osirian mysteries were an enactment of the death of Osiris, having drowned in the river Nile, His body then cut to pieces and scattered across Egypt becoming one with the land. In these mysteries, two priestesses representing the twin Goddesses of Isis and Nephthys gathered the pieces together in the symbolic form of barley seeds. They then planted these in a coffin-shaped in the form of Osiris. This symbolized the rebirth of Osiris in the underworld where He became lord of regeneration. This simple myth helps to characterize one aspect of the meaning of this season.

At each of the festivals you'll see that the single common theme is the relationship and interaction between the two dynamic and complementary forces represented in our dimension as female and male, Goddess and God. These are energies, forces and living beings that are manifest in all of nature including ourselves.

At Samhain the Sun God, the solar hero, enters the underworld seeking the Goddess. In many legends, He is greeted by a female guide. For the Egyptians, this was His young daughter, not as a submissive youth, both rather as the vibrant embodiment of the divine feminine in Her form as the potential for new life. In faery traditions, She would be the Queen of this realm. In other cultures, this may be the powerful and seductive Goddesses of death (transformation) and sexuality (the raw power that brings all life into being), such as Morgana. Sometimes, She is veiled beneath a dark cloak, appearing as the Wise Crone who, in fact, has wrapped this aspect around Herself - hiding the potential of new life and sexual power within. In all traditions though, She is a powerful representation of the feminine creative force - at once wise, active and vital.

It would not be out of place to state that the Sun God submits to Her, dying at the gate of the underworld before being able to rule there. But She is constant. While it is the Sun God who makes the journey, She is the wheel in which He travels. Her form may change, but only in regards to how these two dynamic forces interact.

So here at the turning of the year, Samhain, in the northern hemisphere all in nature is dying away, or falling into hibernation. Many birds have begun their migration south. The leaves have turned, falling to the ground. The warm summer breezes are replaced by the harsh and wild winds, as Herne of the Hunt rides through the sky with His otherworldly company of spectres.

For many, it is a frightening time of year, when people's worst fears regarding the occult and death are forced into everyday consciousness. For us of the Art though, we find it to be an exhilarating time. We celebrate with large bonfires on high forest hills and journeys into woodlands to commune with those who have gone on, or seek council from those of worlds not normally perceived. The gates are open and we welcome the energy of the season along with the interaction of entities from other realms.

The hearth is set with horn, bone, stone and candle. Dried oak leaves are arranged on the table of Art, forming the triangle through which the spirits come. This is the time when we seek wisdom from the ancestors, the leaders of our tradition who reside in realms other than this. This is the time when the Great Queen guides us deep into the underworld. This is the time when the Great King, nature itself, embraces death and welcomes us into His world of transformation and with it initiation and ultimately rebirth.

So don't fear the season of Samhain. Yes it can be somber as we say good bye to the past and look forward to the year to come. Yet it also holds the promise of potential yet unfulfilled. This is the time to prepare. The harvest of the past year is in. The meat for the winter months has been slaughtered and prepared. The home fires in the hearth have been rekindled with the wood felled earlier, in order to weather the snowy months to come. This is the season when the land lays fallow, sleeping, waiting for the warmth of spring. So, embrace this season as you move inward, both literally into your home and spiritually turning your vision within, searching for your own potential that waits at the core of your being. Like the dying God who is greeted by the Lady as He seeks His own rebirth, you, too, can reach out to Her as you seek your own true self and spiritual potential.

Winter Solstice/Yule

As the year progresses, the Sun continues to move deeper into the Annwn. Crossing the red river, the solar hero enters the depths of the underworld, where dimensions are symbolized as hours in the Egyptian tradition, while in the Celtic system these are represented as castles, mountains and lakes. In both systems, many of these realms are seen as unique paradises, each with their own qualities and otherworld beings specific to those regions.

At the winter solstice, Yule, in the north we face the longest night of the year. We are in the darkest times of the winter. The northern snows are falling and the temperatures drop. The Sun is at its southern most point in the year. Yet Yule is a time of hope and renewal. For, following this night, the Sun begins to slowly cycle northward.

This festival is marked with the decorating of the Yule tree, while circular wreaths of holly, evergreen and mistletoe symbolizing the womb of the Goddess giving birth to the Sun, are hung. This was largely a Saxon and Scandinavian Pagan tradition that was later adopted in other areas of Europe and Britain. It beautifully captures the spirit of life and renewal during the darkest period of the year.

Outside, large bonfires are set atop hills to hasten the return of the Sun, while inside the Yule log, usually an Oak, Ash or Beech specifically selected, is prepared for the fire place. This can be decorated with ribbons, or notes attached by those in the home. On the notes, each person's hopes and goals for the coming year are written. Sometimes, cider or ale will be poured over the log. In chalk, the figure of a man, frequently with horns upon his head, is etched on the side of the log. He symbolizes the God of Nature and the Sun. He is Cernunnos or Cernowain the Horned One, Bel, Herne, Pan, Faunus, Khumn and so many others. The log is set with care in the fireplace and ceremonially set ablaze while the ancient Yule ritual is performed at the hearth.

For this ritual, like most others, the cauldron figures highly. This is because it is from the Goddess, the all comes. It is within the cauldron, the womb, that all is transformed. She is the center. She is the cause.

In looking to our model of the Stang as World Tree we see that the winter solstice rests at the base of the staff. Here the Sun God enters with the underworld lake as He seeks the isle on which Caer Wydyr rests. In Celtic legends, it is on this isle that the solar hero encounters the silver cauldron of inspiration, rimmed in pearls and tended to by the nine priestesses of the Moon.

In the Egyptian tradition, this period marks the point of midnight. The Sun God has reached the island in the lake on which the vessel of transformation resides. Here, the older

Sun God encounters the transformative power of Ausir/ Osiris, Lord of the Underworld. The two merge becoming one being and from this, the Sun shines new at midnight. The God is now able to begin His journey toward birth at dawn. Yet none of this is possible without the attention and desire of the twin Goddesses Aset/Isis and Nebet Het/Nephthys. Theirs is the embrace that transforms death into life. In the Mysteries of Osiris this act was frequently portrayed either symbolically or in ritual actuality as a sexual union. In many cultures, sexual orgasm is described as the 'little death'- for in that moment one loses them self in the ecstasy of another.

This is the power of the Goddess that transforms. For She is outside of time, yet present in all that is. It is through Her that all is transformed. He, on the other hand, represents the process of change, evolution, and the tides of power that we all answer to.

So, at the winter solstice we find hope and transformation. The darkest time of the year holds within it the potential for the greatest power from which we can draw.

There is a great mystery in this season as well. For here the Sun rests in Caer Wydyr, the Castle of Glass, the Crystal Mountain. This is the very same realm that sits at the height of the worlds beyond Gwynfyd. But here, this sacred realm was reached through the underworld of Annwn. While Caer Wydyr is the same, the means by which it is experienced is different. When approached through the paradise realm of Gwynfyd the Castle of Glass is experienced as a realm of joy where ecstatic union with the highest spiritual forces which we can relate to flood our consciousness. However, when the journey is made through the Annwn, we are tested through ordeal, as the keepers of the gates question our progress. This is the quest for the grail, the Great Goddess.[82]

Passing each trial of the Annwn eventually brings one to the interior of the Castle where the cauldron rests. Here,

---

82. Originally a Celtic legend of knights seeking the cauldron before it was hijacked by the Abrahamic tradition.

while this is the same cauldron that rests in Caer Wydyr above Gwynfyd, with the same intense spiritual force flowing from it, the cauldron becomes the vehicle through which our own transformation occurs. Like the Sun God emerging from the waters of the underworld lake to be embraced by the Goddess, those of the Art who seek this path through the Annwn, experience their own death and rebirth. For this is the path of initiation.

This theme is repeated in the construction of ancient neolithic tomb site of Newgrange, Ireland. For here, even when the entrance is sealed, once a year at winter solstice the first rays of the Sun shine through an opening in the womb shaped mound piercing to the very center of the chamber within. Sun and Earth unite, God and Goddess embrace, and all that was old is transformed into that which is new.

So at the winter solstice sing the praises of the Goddess who embraces the God, bringing His death and His rebirth. For this is the moment of transformation. As He gives Himself over to Her in the ecstasy of their embrace, She transforms Him into the child who journeys toward new potential and rebirth.

In the Egyptian tradition there is an added dimension to this season. The winter festival of the Navigation of the Goddess occurs at this time. In the Egyptian calendar there were two such festivals - one occurring near the winter solstice, the other near the summer solstice.[83] The winter navigation involved the symbolic

---

83. The Egyptians ran two calendars concurrently. One was stellar based beginning with the rising of the star Sirius at dawn. The other was lunar-based. The lunar was the calendar by which the majority of religious festivals were calculated. Being lunar, these could vary from year to year. However, the lunar calendar was tied directly to the more regulated stellar calendar. As such, the festivals rarely fell far from the seasons in which they were intended to be celebrated. For more information see Parker, Richard. 'Egyptian Astronomy, Astrology and Calendarical Reckoning', *Dictionary of Scientific Biography*, vol. XV, Suppl. I New York: Charles Scribner's Sons, 1978, p.706-727.

representation of the God of wisdom, Thoth, being sent south to convince the Goddess Hathor, as the Eye of the Sun, to return. For all joy was linked to Her and only the return of the feminine aspect of life and light would bring abundance to the land.

Imbolc

As the Sun continues its cycle moving through the year, it approaches the mid-point between the winter solstice and the spring equinox. Imbolc, known in the Christian calendar as Candlemas, is one of the four great fire festivals of the Celts. Pronounced "*i-MOLG*" or "*i-MOLC*" this is the mid-point occurring as the Sun crosses over fifteen degrees of Aquarius. And, like Samhain, we celebrate both this date and the Full Moon that occurs nearest to this event, for both hold considerable power.

In the north, the days are beginning to grow longer. While we are still in the depths of winter, periods of warmth and the promise of spring begin to show. There is a sense of anticipation, as all of nature waits for the burst of energy that will thrust life into bloom.

Traditionally, this is time when new love is celebrated. For the Celts, trial marriages were frequently begun now. In these cases, a couple would walk toward one another, kiss, and be considered married for a period of a year and a day. If, at the end of that year they decided to end the arrangement they would return to the place, turn back to back and walk away.

This festival is a celebration of light. Dedicated to the Celtic Goddess Bride or Bridget, the emphasis is on the growing sexual tension that forms in new love. Here we find the cauldron as a central element of the ritual. But instead of being filled with liquid, in its place we build a small fire. Whether through the use of a candle or, for added affect, we use alcohol for a more robust flame, the goal is the same.

"God of Glory,
God of Fire,
Burn, burn, burn
With lusty desire!"

This was the chant used by a coven I was with for many years, in their Imbolc ritual. As basic in imagery as this is, the ultimate outcome is clear. Winter is fading and in its place, the passion and power of life embodied in the youthful dance of courtship, comes forward. This is the awakening of power within the land - the power that will help bring new life to the earth. This is the awakening of power within ourselves, giving us the energy to reach our goals in the months to come. This is the time when the twin red and white dragons of earth energy rise from their slumber.

Grandma Julie was quick to point out that the Art celebrates fertility. Sexuality is a natural expression of the dynamic interplay of complementary energies found in all that is. And, as Sybil Leek explained when discussing the subject "Far from pretending that it did not exist, early men elevated the whole concept to one of refinement and beauty; he incorporated sex into his religions". She continued

> "When, therefore, the sexual urge is felt, realize that this is part of the marvelous mechanism that is you, accept it, and do not try to suppress it. In our religion, it is not considered a virtuous attribute to lead a celibate life. . . we advocate a healthy attitude toward sex, and that a balance be achieved between mind and body . . . it is essential to see certain desires as natural, not as anathema".[84]

In our image of the Stang rising through the worlds, the Sun approaches the white river. This is the opposite of the red river that was crossed at Samhain. Together, these are

---

84. Leek, Sybil. *The Complete Art of Witchcraft.* 1971 p.114.

the red and white dragons of Celtic lore. Both are powerful complementary forces hidden deep within. These are the red and white crowns of ancient Egyptian teachings, the twin serpents that guide and guard the Gods. These are the red and white roses of medieval and renaissance Alchemy; Sun and Moon, male and female. Resting on either side of the Annwn, they are the raw power of the universe. By crossing the white river at this time, Imbolc is the festival which evokes these forces enabling them to merge and create.

With Imbolc, this union of opposites has not yet occurred. Rather, the desire awakes. The powerful urge of passion within youth is stirring. The Goddess Bridget, Bride, seeks Her mate and the young Lord responds. Yet it is She who decides. As Dion Fortune states, "She is the awakener, calling that which is latent into potency."

Like the other festivals, this is a time when bonfires may be lit atop hilltops signaling the return of light. If weather permits we will visit the sacred glen, the grove, the crystal well hidden in forest. For us though, more likely than not, the weather in New England is too harsh at Imbolc. In which case, our rite is held indoors with a large fire in the hearth, the cauldron set in the center of the circle as flames from both, herald the passion of the Gods and the return of the Sun.

Other traditions associated with Imbolc included placing food and drink out, and making a bed available. For it was believed that on Imbolc the Goddess Bride would visit the home, blessing the house and inhabitants. It was believed that She would stay the night. Frequently a Fe (a wand of white wood, usually birch) would be set by the bed. The symbolism is obvious with the Fe being an overtly phallic object. Offerings of milk would frequently be given. In Ireland, *Bridget Crosses* would be made and left at sacred wells.

It is interesting to note that the winter hag of the Cailleach was thought to go out on Imbolc to decide if she needed more winter wood. Folklore states that if winter is to last another six weeks she will make the weather on Imbolc fair as she doesn't like to gather wood during poor weather.

Spring Equinox/Ostera

As the year progresses, the Sun crosses the equator. In the northern hemisphere, this marks the spring equinox. The equinox, whether spring or fall, signals the two times in the year that day and night are of equal length, no matter where one is on the planet. While little evidence exists specifically showing the same enthusiastic ritualistic and celebratory practices as the other festivals in the ancient world, it is clear that these were observed if for no other reason than to act as markers in the year by which the great fire festivals were calculated.

Having said this, a number of Pagan spring folk traditions associated with this time of year were later adopted by the invading Christian church. Many of these involved the symbolism connected with the rabbit or hare which is an ancient Pagan totem for the energies of earth, fertility and abundance. The egg also figures highly in the traditional celebrations of this season. Both of these were brought into the Christian traditions surrounding their celebration of Easter, the name of which was drawn from the Goddess Eostre. She is a Germanic Goddess of Spring whose name relates to the dawn and whose totem animal is the hare.

This is significant as the church calculates the timing of Easter as the first Sunday following the Full Moon after the spring equinox. It would seem that the connection with the spring equinox could not be clearer.

In the Art, as we practice it today, the spring equinox represents a time of balance and with it, the first rush of light and energy which comes through at spring. On the mandala of our Stang as it rises through the worlds, we find the Sun at the equinox is crossing the threshold between the Annwn and the Abred. As such, it has burst into our world, the realm that rests between these two great strata. This is a time when the land awakens with new potential. With the

107

Sun sitting on the threshold, its power is particularly strong, manifesting in our world as the thrust of life.

The equinoxes, both spring and fall, mark a great turning in the psychic and astral tides. This means that occult works begun in the months preceding this, may need to be reset following this festival. In particular, we have found that protections - the setting of boundaries and watchers around the home or around one's magical working space - will need to be changed out and set anew. If not, the old protections will tend to fade, losing power and effectiveness. Over years of practice, we have found it best to take the time to perform the rituals that set the boundaries at these times of the turning tide.

Throughout the cycle of the festivals of power, we have seen that the single reoccurring theme is the interplay and relationship of the dynamic, yet complementary, forces of nature which are best expressed through the sexes. The spring equinox is no exception. Here, as the day and night are of equal length, the passive and active forces are in balance moving in a rhythmic dance. Each is powerful and each holds within itself the essence of the other. That the tides would turn on this day is obvious when one considers the ancient law of reversed polarity - that which is potent in one realm, is latent in the next. Thus, there is an ebb and flow occurring between worlds allowing for each to affect the next in a natural progression. It is for this reason that those things created on the astral, given enough force, eventually manifest on the material.

This principle also implies that the roles of potent and latent, active and passive, can change - reversing their effect on each other. This holds true at the equinoxes. It is for this reason that many of the old customs surrounding celebrations at the spring festival include men and women cross-dressing as the opposite sex. This was seen in the British Pace-Egg plays celebrated at Easter. The symbolism is clear. At the turning of the tide the roles of male and female, as the natural embodiment of the dynamic polarity for us humans, are reversed allowing each to experience that essence of 'the other' in a dance of fertility.

However, once the equinox has passed the energies realign. What was active before this, is now passive. What was lying dormant before the equinox has been awakened and is now potent; while that which was potent sinks into a period of being fallow.

At the spring equinox, the dragon energy of the land rises up in all that is alive and growing. Those of the Art actively seek this energy, experiencing this in the trees as they reach toward Moon and Star. We experience this in the heartbeat of the Earth as the water rushes over the ground in brook and river, pooling in wells, springs, glens and lakes. This power is found everywhere in nature and we of the Geassa collect this in our tools, in stone and bone, root and Stang. Through blade and cup, wand and shield, the four elemental energies rise at this time as the pulse of life surges in the spring. This is a wonderful time of year filled with promise and hope. In ritual, both the cauldron and the wheel are prominent symbols, both seen as embodying rebirth and renewal. Sybil Leek explains:

> "At the spring equinox, we use the symbol of the wheel, which is placed by the altar - and the cauldron, the great iron pot which is beloved by gypsies, is placed in the circle. Both it and the wheel symbolize reincarnation."[85]

Beltane
The wheel turns and the Sun continues its journey through the worlds. Soon He approaches the midpoint between the spring equinox and the summer solstice. Fifteen degrees of Taurus marks the gate of power that corresponds to the fire festival of Beltane. For us, the Full Moon nearest this point is very powerful. On this night, the *sprowl*, a Cornish term referring to the vital force of nature, is alive and free

85. Leek, Sybil. *The Complete Art of Witchcraft*. 1971 p.185.

flowing. This is a night of magic and mystery. Too, the actual date when the Sun reaches the fifteen degree mark of Taurus is equally important. For both events, those of the Art will use ritual to celebrate this tide of power while directing it toward the goals at hand.

Beltane really is the quintessential point of power in the year marking both transition and fertility. This is the crowning of the May Queen, the Goddess of life and spring. Sexuality, sensuality and all that is pleasurable are celebrated now. In the Celtic tradition, Beltane marks the beginning of the summer half of the year, as opposed to Samhain and the winter half.

Records exist from the sixteenth, seventeenth and eighteenth centuries which give remarkably similar accounts of the festivities surrounding this Sabbat. Occurring over a number of days, English reports show that the festival often began with women and men of all ages running off to the woods, groves and sacred hills where they would spend the night "in pleasant pastimes". In the morning, they would return with greenery, "birch and branches" to decorate their homes and public buildings.

Then, with a set of oxen strewn in garlands, the people would bring a large, decorated maypole to the center of town and set this up. With music playing, people would begin dancing around the pole as the local festivities grew in enthusiasm. As night fall came, fires were lit and many couples once again returned to the forests to enjoy the pleasure of each other's company. These and many other customs were recorded as happening all across Europe from ancient times. Many of these still continue to this day, in some rural communities.

Another wonderful and ancient custom associated with Beltane is the collecting of morning dew. It is believed that morning dew collected on Beltane has the power to preserve one's looks and youth. As such, it was common for people to wash themselves with dew on Beltane.

In the Germanic Celtic tradition, this was celebrated as Walpurgis Night. Originally, Walpurga was the name of a

Goddess appearing as a beautiful woman dressed in white, wearing a crown, carrying a spindle and a mirror that reveals the future. As with Bridget in Ireland, Walpurga was later canonized by the Christians as St. Walpurga, clearly in an attempt to transfer the worship of the ancient lunar Goddess of spring to the invading religion.

Also called *Hexennachat*, 'Witches Night', mediaeval accounts claim that this was *the* major festival. The records state that Witches would gather from across Germany, building bonfires in the mountains dedicated to the Goddess Freya. Particularly, the Brocksberg Massif, the highest of the Harz Mountains, was reputed to be the central region for this gathering. In time, the Christians became so fearful that, as a custom, they would go out at night and shoot their guns into the air in hopes of killing flying Witches.

This simple custom illustrates the tension that ran between the Old Ways and those of the invading religion. Eventually, Walpurgis Night was seen in Germany as sinister in nature, with the fear that the Witches were assembled in order to cast their curses down on the villages below.

At Imbolc, the great festival of mid-winter, we saw the dynamic tension of attraction played out between the sexes. However, here at the next great fire festival that tension is realized and released in the actual mating of the two. Goddess and God, as two opposite poles of the same force merge in a dynamic union. The Bel fire is lit high atop the hills in forests and stone circles as the hieros gamos, the sacred marriage, is enacted. Whether symbolically or in actuality the purpose has always been the same; the union and merging of complementary opposites in a dynamic act that builds and releases energy. Whether the outcome ultimately results in actual offspring or not, doesn't necessarily matter. Rather, this festival is about the raising of power through the union and the sheer enjoyment that comes with it. How this force manifests depends largely on the participants.

Beyond the overt fertility aspects of the festival, Beltane is every bit as powerful a point of transition as Samhain.

In our experience, it isn't uncommon to undergo tension and a sense of anticipation, even among the general populace who are totally unaware of the festival. Those of the Geassa embrace the season in all its joy and ecstatic celebration of the life force, as we use this energy directing those toward our goals.

As the counterpart to Samhain, we find that this season, also, is a time when communication with otherworld beings is very strong. As far back as the ninth century, written records give accounts in Celtic myth in which solar heroes seek the spring Goddess, such as Pwyll's vision of the Goddess Rhiannon; or as in the story of Lludd and Llevelys with the portents foretold in the fight of dragons. For our part, we find this to be a time when the gates open wide. Yet, instead of the ancestors or spirits of the deceased, at Beltane we find the emphasis is on those beings just beyond the veil that surround us in all of nature seeking to come through.

Because of this, it is at this time, specifically, the Full Moon of Beltane that we, in our system of the Art, will often collect and prepare the Alraun; the 'spirit' root. Alraun is a German synonym for "Witch", with pre-Christian roots referring to Germanic women who were the priestesses, wise ones, shamans and healers of the community. Roman historians encountering the Germanic people referred to the "aurinia" as endowed with magic and as "loose haired, bare-legged Witches".[86]

Cut from an Ash tree root, the Alraun is carved into the form of a human in the opposite sex of the magician. Through ritual, this becomes the physical 'body' for a nature spirit drawn from the land itself. Thus, the Alraun then becomes a powerful companion to the Witch in all her works.

On our map of the Stang rising through the worlds, the festival of Beltane falls at the mid-point of Abred, halfway

---

86. Illes. Judika. *Encyclopedia of Witchcraft*. 2014 p.323.

between our world and the threshold of Gwynfyd. This is the center of the astral realm, that reality in which energy is molded and transformed through thought and emotion. Desire and passion take shape, clothing itself in the power and essence of the astral. There, once formed, it begins to manifest in our realm. Thus, Beltane is a festival of magic, the season when the forces of fertility and desire can be directed with ease toward the goal of choosing. For the most part, this is an excellent time for acts designed to bring prosperity, success, joy and abundance.

As with Samhain, the lighting of the fires has always been important, whether it be a great bonfire or the rekindling of the hearth. At Beltane, this was accompanied by livestock being driven between two fires to remove any evil and protect them in the months to come. Too, a common practice still done to this day is the jumping over the fire by those celebrating. The purpose is essentially the same; cleansing and protection to say nothing of the sheer joy of it.

The simple fact is that Beltane is a festival of joy, pleasure and the enthusiastic exuberance of life in all its forms. So, of course, the primary representation of this natural force is sensuality and sexuality as the passion of the season. The Great Goddess of spring is crowned as the Green Man of the forest rushes to Her. Together, they are the force of life, nature and the universe.

Summer Solstice/Litha

This, in turn, brings us to the midsummer festival, the summer solstice. What a wonderful season this is. The Sun is at its northern most point. For those of us in the northern hemisphere this is the peak of summer. This is the longest day of the year. Traditionally, this was seen as a particularly magical time. Once again, great fires are lit in circles deep in forests and on hilltops. Frequently, the eight-spoked wheel is present in rituals. Often times, these are set on fire and in some traditions rolled down hills symbolizing the Sun. Sybil describes the symbols and ritual act used in her coven:

"The midsummer festival again uses the cauldron, this time filled with water and adorned with flowers. This festival is very much associated with phallic symbolism such as the plunging of wands into water, with an incantation to Cerridwen, the Celtic goddess associated with the cauldron."[87]

In glen and woodland, it is said that the nature spirits, the faery folk, are particularly active. In many ancient cultures, these beings were actively sought at midnight on midsummer. This is the height of the growing season and with it, the passion of spring is giving way to the fruitfulness of life made manifest. For us, we begin our celebration with a search through the woods and glens for male ferns growing in a cluster of five fronds, forming the shape of the Green Man's hand. Once found, we prepare the great Belfire at the center of our circle. Over this, we smoke the fern as it begins to dry. This is then hung inside the home near the door to both protect the household and to attract prosperity and good fortune. For some magicians, the spores from the ferns gathered on this night form a special powder used to render one 'unseen'. In essence, this enables those of the Art to go unnoticed.

On the summer solstice, the Sun has journeyed through the Abred where it now comes to rest on the threshold between the Gwynfyd and Abred. This is the home of the sunlit paradises of legend. Tir-ni-nog, the Field of Reeds, the Summerland, and the Elysian Fields all can be found here.

Looking to the world tree of the Stang, the Sun at the summer solstice rests in the cleft blazing forth where shaft and yoni meet. This is the gate of life, joy and ecstasy. From here, all that is in the Abred, within our world and deep into the Annwn, has its beginning. It is to this gate that we return to, life after life, as we learn and grow. The great wheel turns. The tides of power call us through

87. Leek, Sybil. *The Complete Art of Witchcraft*. 1971 p.186.

the worlds, spiraling, evolving. Yet, at its heart, the Silver Cauldron is seen. As if a vision beyond the realm of the threshold, the Grail of Arthurian legend comes into sight. The Great Queen in Her brilliant aspect of Full Moon shines on the threshold of Gwynfyd. This is the realm of the Gods. This is the gate of wisdom. So it is that the Full Moon nearest the summer solstice, Mead Moon, holds enormous power. Remember that Mead has traditionally been seen as symbolic of the union of female and male, their essence combined, in this royal drink. So, too, we find the full ripening of the Sun and Moon at this time. So, if accessible, Mead figures highly in our rituals.

Lughnasadh

As summer progresses, the Sun moves toward the fifteen degree mark of Leo. In the Art this corresponds to the ancient fire festival of the first harvest, Lughnasadh. Named after the Celtic solar God Lugh, this festival is literally the "Commemoration of Lugh" and as such, this is a festival of the Sun. The life force of the God warms the body of the Earth so that She can give life. And life, She gives! The harvest is upon us. This is a celebration – 'The harvest home'. The first harvest of the season comes to us now. The first grains are cut. The barley and wheat are ground. Elderberries and grapes are gathered for the wine of the season. The heat of summer is upon us.

Lugh, "the Shining One", is seen as fair in appearance, powerful and in His prime. He is the champion of the Celts - Master of the Arts and glorious Sun God. He was worshipped across Celtic culture both in the Britih Isles and Europe. Now, as the summer continues, fairs are held celebrating the sacrifice the God has made. For this festival, the John Barley Corn is made. This simple custom is a cake made from the first grains harvested. One of the Priestesses I had trained with, made this from oats, honey and other ingredients, though she kept the exact recipe secret, claiming that it was passed along only through the women of the tradition. She would mould this cake into the shape of a nude man with an erect phallus, which was then baked and later used in the Lughnasadh ritual. He represented the sacrifice of the God dying for the land, so that all could live.

While Celtic in ritual and spirit, this is exceptionally reminiscent of ancient Egyptian practices. In the Mysteries of Osiris, barley was used as the primary ingredient in a ceremonial cake, shaped as the God lying prone with an erect phallus. Several examples from tombs survive to this day, representing both the sacrifice Osiris made and the procreative force of nature - Death and rebirth. This is the harvest: the grain must die so that we can live. The land must be renewed so that She can be fertile again.

Did the Egyptians influence the Celts? Did the Celts influence the Egyptians? Or was there an older tradition; a long forgotten spiritual heritage at the root of both? The Geassa continues to flow. She changes forms, shape and location. And yet She remains; the pure and ancient mountain spring that nourishes through the ages.

Traditions surrounding John Barley Corn also include the brewing of whiskeys and ales. Again, the grain that comes from the earth is sacrificed, its essence distilled to spirit, becoming a drink that alters and changes consciousness.

Yet while the Sun is beginning to slowly wane as it turns south, this isn't a sad or somber festival. Rather, this is a festival filled with promise; the promise of a bountiful harvest and the gifts the Gods have brought to us all. Our ritual reflects this, as Sybil Leek reports:

> "August Eve is a festival of thanksgiving for the growth of the crops and the riches of the earth; again dances figure highly in this, with special incantations to the Mother Goddess, for this is her great moment of manifesting her fruitfulness".[88]

---

88. Leek, Sybil. *The Complete Art of Witchcraft*. 1971 p.186.

A very old custom that endures to this day is the cutting of the 'calacht' or 'last sheaf' of the first harvest of grain, whether wheat or barley. As part of the ritual, the Master stands facing the Sun. A handful of stalks are cut, preferably with a sickle. This grain with stalk is held aloft and swung three times around the head in a "sunwise" direction. Then all chant the Sun God's name in praise and thanks for the harvest He gave. This is then fashioned into a 'corn dolly' or 'Kern baby'. This is formed in the resemblance of a woman, frequently even dressed in women's clothes. In older traditions, this was placed on a pole and held high as the group would dance around her. Then she was set at the table, given a place of honor at the Lughnasadh feast. After all was done, the corn dolly was placed above, or near, the door of the home as a talisman drawing prosperity and good fortune.

This, too, is a festival of grape and wine. The sacred spirit of the Horned One as woodland Lord, the cloven-hoofed piper who leads the dance calls to us now. The intoxicating drink of the God flows freely as we answer the call of the Master. All of nature is alive now. Ecstasy, music and dance characterize the festival of Lughnasadh. The peak release of energy of the summer season pours forth. The fire of Leo releases the water of Cancer and all of nature rejoices in celebration and harvest.

For us, in the form of the Geassa which we practice, we celebrate both at the Full Moon nearest the midpoint, as well as on the actual day of the Sun's approach to fifteen degrees of Leo. Coincidently, for our location on the globe, this also corresponds to the rising of the star Sirius at dawn with the Sun. This celestial event was perhaps the most significant marker in the Ancient Egyptian calendar. This was their New Year festival, Wep-Renpet. The annual union of the Sun disk with the Stellar Goddess was commemorated with massive temple rites, all designed to draw in the power of this moment into the living images of the Gods themselves.

Most notably, though, this marked the union of Goddess and God as Her power of regeneration and life enriched Him while His seed made Her fertile. In Egypt, Sirius was identified with several Goddesses: Sopdet/Sothis, Aset/Isis, and Hwt-Hrw/Hathor, to name a few. While individual in their own right, the Egyptians recognized that they were also one, interchanging their names frequently in texts. The following text beautifully expresses the joy and spiritual essence of the festival:

"Hwt-Hrw is the Golden One,
The star that rises at the beginning of the year!
She of radiant perfection!
Hwt-Hrw flies as a female falcon before the Ennead,
She unites with Ra in the barge,
She is the one who arouses perfection.
She who was with Ra causing creation to happen!
Hwt-Hrw the Great;
The Mistress of the sky;
Sovereign of all the Neteru;
Hwt-Hrw is brilliant in Her sanctuary on the Wep-Renpet!
She unites with the rays of the Sun!
She pleases Ra who is joyous in his city!"

This text is drawn from ancient inscriptions carved in the Egyptian temple of Dendera, a sacred center dedicated to the Goddess Hathor. The festival of Wep-Renpet is one of the most beautiful and spiritually moving rituals in the Ancient Egyptian calendar. With its close proximity to Lughnasadh, we incorporate major elements of Wep-Renpet into our celebrations, finding these completely compatible with the Celtic elements of the festival.

Looking to the Stang, we find the Sun at Lughnasadh sinking back down into the Abred. It is midway through the astral. Having journeyed to the threshold of the Gwynfyd, the Sun God begins His return through the worlds. In this, He takes with Him the transformative experience of touching the realm of the Goddess. With this treasure He now returns, bringing His message of hope, beauty, love and truth with Him.

On a more practical level, this is a time of year when evocation of entities, spirits and various astral beings is easily accomplished. In fact, magic generally is much more powerful now.

Autumn Equinox/Mabon

At the autumn equinox, the Sun crosses the ecliptic. Once again day and night are of equal length. The Sun is slowly sinking deeper, its light fading as the colder months of the year draw near. This is the festival of the year's remaining harvest season. Sybil explains:

> "The autumnal equinox sees the altar full of the symbols of the season of harvest: pine cones, ears of grain . . . . The incantation is one of thankfulness, and very much concerned with reincarnation again, for in saying good-bye to the dwindling force of the sun, there is an acceptance of rebirth through acknowledgment that other seeds will be grown, other lives will occur, and the sun or Father God is simply going into a rest period".[89]

On the Stang, the Sun now rests on the threshold between the Abred and the Annwn. This is our world, the material plane. Yet, as we have seen earlier, ours is a realm interpenetrated by these other two great dimensions. As such, they are easily accessed in nature. So, with the Sun at the autumn equinox the sense is of balance, equality and the brink between realities. At this time, the great currents of the worlds change once again - just as they did at the spring equinox. Those of the Art are aware that any protections and occult works set during the summer months will now

---

89. Leek, Sybil. *The Complete Art of Witchcraft*. 1971 p.186.

need to be reinforced. For with the turning of the great tide, older protections can become weakened.

As with the other festival rites this celebration is marked by feasting and large bonfires. In ritual, the corn dolly from the previous year will be ceremonially burned in the fire, while the new corn dolly hung at the door is toasted to, in honor of the harvest that has come this year.

Chapter Ten

✤ THE WITCH'S FOOT ✤
Elemental forces & the Pentagram of Art

It is with some trepidation that we include a chapter on the pentagram, simply because so much has been written on the subject by others. Yet given the importance this symbol plays in the western expressions of the Geassa we would be remise not to include this. Further, we find that the techniques and teachings we have been given go beyond much that is currently represented in contemporary writings.

The pentagram is a very ancient symbol with roots reaching back to Egypt in the form of the Seba; the five pointed star representing all things sacred and celestial. We find its representation in later mediaeval magical texts including "The Key of Solomon" and "The Discoverie of Witchcraft" by Reginald Scott, among others.

The pentagram really is the quintessential symbol incorporating the five traditional elements of magic, blended in dynamic harmony. Almost all authorities agree that the arrangement of the elements and their correspondence to the points of the pentagram is as indicated above.

In our tradition, the invocation of a particular element always is done, first by beginning with the topmost point and proceeding deosil (clockwise) through the form. This action draws in spirit first, to the rite in question. Then, we retrace the pentagram by beginning with the point at which the element is designated and drawing deosil from this, tracing the pentagram until this is complete.[90] Thus, a ritual intended to draw on the element of water would incorporate the tracing of the pentagram beginning at the far righthand point and following this over to the earth point, up to spirit, down to fire, over to air and then finishing at the water. To banish the influence of a particular element, the same is done, except that the pentagram is traced from the appropriate elemental point, counterclockwise.

Each of the elements corresponds to very specific energies that are expressed in nature as qualities, colors, forces, and shapes; modes of transformation and direction. Grandma Julie used to explain that a lit candle is a perfect expression of the elements. I can still see the glimmer in her bright blue eyes as she told me to think of the candle itself as being solid and thus of earth, the flame of course is fire, the melted wax pooling on the top of the candle is liquid relating to water, and the soot rising up from the flame is air. The light of the flame itself corresponds to the element of spirit.

As for the directions, it is important to note that some forms of the Art see the elements as relating to the directions, with fire corresponding to east, earth to south, water to the west and air to the north. This is particularly true of the traditions

---

90. Many will note that this method is very different from contemporary Wiccan systems which derived their system of tracing the Pentagram largely from Golden Dawn sources. In fact, the method we use as noted here comes from the Hermetic Ogdoadic tradition.

coming out of Cornwall, England. For our part, we use the correspondence more familiar to Hermetic ritual magic:

- North relates to Earth. That which is solid, material, stable, grounded, manifesting on the physical plane. The color we use for this is a rich verdant green. The hare, the bull and the horned stag all relate to the element of Earth. Each animal, though, represents a slightly different energy. The hare is the spirit of fertility and abundance. The mighty bull speaks to strength, fortitude and the raw power of lustful procreation. The horned stag, too, relates to sexuality; however, he also is the spirit of the forest sacrificing himself, so that others may live. The Celtic realm of Falias and the *Stone of Fal* or Stone of Destiny relates to the north.

- East relates to Air. The intellect, logic, the abstract and conceptual all fall under this influence. For us, the color yellow has an affinity with air and the east. The falcon and eagle, raven and crow all embody a portion of the air element. The falcon has long been seen as the keen eye of wisdom, power and protection, masterfully soaring through the sky. For us, the eagle represents the expansive power of air. The raven, crow and jackdaw embody the cunning wisdom and intellect of air. They are the messengers of the other worlds. The Celtic realm of Findias and the mighty Sword of Nuada - *Cliamh Solais* - the Sword of Light, hold sway in the east.

- South corresponds to fire and with it drive, power, heat and force. This is the energy which vitalizes and quickens. Its color is red. The lion, or wild cat, are the guardians of this energy. They are royal and powerful totems, to be approached with care and awe. The Celtic realm of Gorias is identified with the south as is - *Slea Bua* - the Spear of Victory of the Sun God Lugh.

- West carries with it the element of water. This is the home of emotion, feeling, and sensitivity - that which is receptive and fluid. The color we use is deep blue. The animals related to this direction are the sea serpent or water dragon, as well as the toad and frog. The sea serpent, of course, is the raw, unbridled power of water itself, personified. The frog represents life and fertility emerging from water. The toad holds a special place in European traditional Witchcraft. Its venom has long been used as an aid in rituals inducing altered states. Thus the toad is connected to the western realms of death and regeneration, and the ability to move between worlds. As an additional creature symbolizing water and the west, ceremonial magicians will use the eagle here, as this emblem is symbolic of the spiritual aspect of the zodiac sign Scorpio, the fixed force of water in Astrology. While valid in its own right, we prefer to use the eagle as a symbol of air in the east, as noted earlier. In the west, the beautiful realm of Murias and *Coire Dagda* - Dagda's Cauldron of Plenty - Consort of the Great Mother Danu, resides in the mysteries.
- In the center of the circle, as well as the upper most point of the pentagram, rests spirit. This is the inner spark, the point of rejuvenation, the portal from which all comes and will return. Its color is a dark stellar indigo, lapis or purple. Its tool is the cauldron of Caer Wydyr - the Castle of Glass; the Tower of Arianrhod. With their breath, nine maidens fan the flames of the fire beneath this cauldron that is rimmed with pearls. This is the creative center of all. As the lunar Goddess Arianrhod is frequently depicted as an Owl, this bird corresponds to the center.

The Guardians
In this examination of the pentagram and the elements, we need to address the subject of the "guardians" or "watchers".

Essentially, these are otherworld beings who reside in and personify the raw power and essence of the element called upon. While the images, symbols and words used to evoke them are mutable and interchangeable, there should be no mistake as to the sentient reality of these beings as living entities in their own realms. Further, as the embodiment of the elements, these beings can and do influence our realm. In evoking these beings, certain symbols and images are envisioned, while specific incantations are recited. These enchantments, essentially, are the esoteric language of the mind that helps us as beings housed in the material realm, to communicate with and give form to, forces that otherwise we would not be able to relate. This is not unlike meeting a stranger for the first time and having to find a common language with which to communicate with that person. As such, the apprentice should think of the following descriptions as magical formula through which these energies can manifest in the place of working.

East

In the east, we envision a tall, lean muscular man dressed in Celtic garb. His cloak billows in the wind. This is brilliant yellow and gold, with flashes of violet that appear and vanish in the folds of the cloak. A gold torc decorates his throat. In his right hand, he raises a sword, *Cliamh Solais,* above his head. The blade of the sword gleams in the morning light as the first rays of the Sun catch its edge. In the clear sky, a falcon circles high above. You can hear the cry of the bird of prey and feel the wind against your skin as you utter the evocation. On his shoulder, a raven sits as if speaking wisdom into his ear.

South

Facing south, the hot, radiant, noonday Sun shines high overhead. In front of us, a vast field of tall golden grasses and grain raises to meet the sky. Bees can be seen buzzing from the various white and yellow flowers that are interspersed in the field. From the horizon, a huge figure of a man strides forward as if to meet us. Like the first, he, too, is strong, lean and muscular. His clothing, too, is that of a Celtic warrior. However, his garb is a royal red with Celtic swirls of orange and green. At his feet, a great, female wild cat with golden fur accompanies him. In his right hand, the guardian holds a tall, gleaming spear. The shaft is a brilliant golden orange, while the tip is red. This is *Slea Bua*, the Lance of Lugh. You can hear the roar of the great cat and feel the warmth of the Sun on your face as you chant to evocation of the south.

West

In the west, we find ourselves standing on a rocky sea coast staring out at the majesty of the sea. While the sky is clear and blue, the ocean is turbulent and powerful. A mix of aquamarine waves capped with white foam, crash against the shore. We can feel the spray of the sea mist and taste the salt on our tongue. Across the water, coming toward us, a beautiful woman with long, flowing, copper hair can be seen. Like the others, she is dressed as a warrior. Her garment is blue merging in highlights of orange Celtic knotwork along the trim. Around her throat, a silver necklace can be seen, from which hangs a clear, polished, round crystal. In her hands, she holds a silver bowl or goblet. As you peer into her deep blue-green eyes, you can almost see the contents of the bowl - a gold liquid, honey mead reflects from the surface. This is the *Coire Dagda*, and the Cauldron of Inspiration. The guardian stands in magnificent power and strength as about her feet encircling her and just breaking the water's surface, the great orm of the sea, the living giant sea serpent of myth and legend, can be seen. Its power is one with hers and she is its Mistress. As we chant the evocation she raises the silver bowl and the power of water now protects and aids us.

North

Turning to face north the scene before us changes to one of lush green meadows filled with wild flowers. A forest can be seen in the background and just beyond that tall, majestic mountains rise up high into the sky. In the meadow, a large black bull grazes lazily in the warmth of the Sun. At the same time, just on the forest's edge a magnificent stag, his antlers held high bounds into view. In the center of it all the figure of a woman steps forward, stopping in front of us. She is dressed in lush green and indigo, with hints of gold trim, patterned as Celtic swirls. Her long blond hair spills over her shoulders. About her waist a gold belt can be seen, its buckle terminating in the image of hare. While feminine in dress, as with the others, there is no mistaking that she is a protector and warrior. Her right foot rests gently and yet purposely, on a large flat stone. This is the *Stone of Fal,* destiny. On her left arm a gold shield gleams in the Sun. The center of this gives way to a brilliant silver background on which can be seen the etched image of the cross-legged Cernunnos - his antlers high, his face jovial. About his feet, a cornucopia filled with vegetables and fruit can be seen. Near this, a pouch of coins and precious stones is inscribed on the shield. In the guardian's right hand, a razor sharp bronze sickle is plainly seen. The evocation rings from our voice as the strength of the Earth protects our circle.

The Five Qualities of the Art
The family tradition of Grandma Julie expressed that the inner qualities of those in the Art are exemplified in the five points of the pentagram:

- The first is *sex*. Water. Make no mistake about it, the Old Ways, the path of the Art, is fertility-based in all that the term embraces. Those of the Geassa, see sex as an essential and vital aspect of life. As such, it is to be celebrated and enjoyed. This is the expression of the creative force in its most basic and natural form. In this principle we see the attraction between male and female, the recognition of life, and the vehicle of regeneration. The deeper aspects of the Art hinge on this interplay of the sexes, the natural exchange of energies between dynamic polar opposites. For sex is the essence of nature itself and a point of contact between worlds. This is the union of polar, complementary opposites; two aspects of the same force merging. This first point of the pentagram also represents one's entire feeling for life itself, and can be extended to acceptance, an open mind and healthy exchange of ideas.

- The next quality of one of the Art is *self*. Earth. As stated earlier one must have a healthy respect for oneself, a respect for one's own needs. One must put one's own life in order before they can be effective and help others. As Sybil Leek explained, the first step into the Art is a selfish one; a recognition that one must understand oneself before one can progress.

- The third quality is *pride*. Air. As seen earlier, pride is not the same as arrogance or vanity. In fact, it is the opposite. One can be proud of one's accomplishments and still be humble. The quality of pride is the recognition of your own worth and ability. It is the simple statement of "I am."

- The fourth quality is *passion*. Fire. Passion is a vital part of the practice. Those of the Art must have a real passion for life and the endeavors she, or he, embraces. Passion gives meaning to life. Passion is the power and drive that makes all else happen.

- The fifth quality is *power*. Spirit. As Julie explained, power really is the sum of the four previous points of the pentagram when they work in harmony and balance with each other. To lose any one of the previous points, or conversely, to have any one of these in excess of the others, would cause one to lose one's power.

The Elements and the Hands

In the Art, the hands hold special significance. Thus, subtle but effective gestures can be invaluable. Gestures with the left hand are used in the Art for rites of removal, banishing and cursing. The left hand is also used to gather substances and energies that one may use for toward this same goal. The right hand is used in magic for positive invocation and spell casting intent on increase, growth, healing, regeneration and that which attracts or projects positive influences. Gemma Gary explains that one may use the left hand to banish an illness, and then use the right one to heal the afflicted area.[91] In the Art the five elements also correspond to the fingers themselves:

- The thumb relates to the element of earth. Thus it will be used in ritual gestures designed to affect the material world, the body, stability.
- The index finger is aligned with the element of air. Works designed to enhance communication, the will and intellect, speed and awareness will be aided by gestures involving this finger.
- The ring finger controls emotion and is ruled by water. Rites of meditation, tapping into deep feelings or memories will involve the use of this appendage. This, too, would figure highly in spells of love and romance. It is no coincidence that wedding and engagement rings are worn on this finger.
- The little finger is the finger of fire. Strength, drive, sexual passion, vitality all align with this finger.
- The middle finger is the finger associated with spirit. As such, ritual gestures designed to invoke or evoke otherworld beings, often employ this finger.

Beyond the elements, the pentagram also relates to the human body while aligning this with celestial influences. In her book *"Numerology: The Magic of Numbers"*, Sybil Leek

---

91. Gary, Gemma. *Traditional Witchcraft: A Cornish Book of Ways*. 2008.

details this correspondence. In this, she equates to the upper point of the pentagram with the head and the planet Venus. The right arm and thus the right point of the pentagram align with the energies of Mars. The right leg of the person and the bottom right point on the pentagram correspond with Jupiter. The left leg of a person relates to the bottom left point of the pentagram and is a manifestation of Saturn. While lastly, the left hand and left point of the pentagram are ruled by Mercury.

Chapter Eleven

✧ THE MILLER'S STONE ✧
Numbers in the Art

A ll energy vibrates. All that is, is energy, moving at different rates of vibration. Yet, all that is, is consciousness. Change your state of consciousness to change your state of being. Change the rate of vibration of a thing to change its state of being. Energy and consciousness are the same thing. The rate of vibration is the mode by which consciousness and energy form patterns and realities. Vibration can be measured in numbers, in colors, in musical tones, in the influence of celestial events. And, like all else, these are interconnected and have a direct influence on each other. It is through this simple understanding that the ancient occult principle of correspondence comes into being. In essence, all is connected, aligning to specific forces or lines of power. For those of the Art, being able to understand and trace these strands is vital to the success of our work.

For the purposes of this tome, I want to begin with a discussion of the relationship between numbers, as a representation of the 'rate of vibration', and the seven traditional planetary influences used in classic magical texts. While many numerological systems exist, in the occult work practiced by this tradition there are two very distinct numerological systems which we have found to hold equal value and potency. In both systems, the energies which the planets embody are expressed through these two different number sets. On the surface it would appear that neither is related, however, careful research has shown a common link reaching back at least 2500 years, possibly longer.

One of these systems is directly tied to the Hermetic teaching on the Qabalah and what has come to be known as the Tree of Life. In essence, this states that numbers represent the flow of energies from one level or state of being as represented by a planetary influence, to the next, in a succession of evolution. In this way, each number and planet represents a different reality within the Abred. These begin with Saturn at the highest level, corresponding to the number three. This is followed by Jupiter and the number four, Mars and the number five, the Sun and the number six, Venus and the number seven, Mercury and the number eight, and finishing with the Moon and the number nine. In Hermetics, the numbers one and two do not correspond to any of the traditional seven celestial bodies within our solar system that can be viewed with the naked eye.[92]

It is important to this discussion to understand that this planetary order relates directly to the period of apparent revolution around the Earth that each planet makes.[93] Thus, the Moon is the fastest, followed by Mercury, Venus, the Sun, Mars, Jupiter and finally Saturn. This ordering of the planets is often referred to as the Ptolemaic system after its codification by the famous Astrologer, Claudius Ptolemaeus, who lived between CE 100 – 178. This is, precisely, the pattern noted above.

In the Hermetic Qabbalistic system, the energies of the realm or 'sphere' above it spill over into the next, becoming a new sphere or energy. The best way to think of this is as if one were looking at a great fountain. Water pours from the top filling a cup or small pool. As the water flows the

---

92. Many contemporary magicians do claim that the planet Uranus corresponds to the number two, Neptune to the number one and Pluto to zero.

93. This is the perceived revolution of the planets as we observe them from Earth, as opposed to the actual orbits of these planets around the Sun in our solar system.

pool fills to capacity and over flows spilling into the pool just below it. This analogy is important as it will help one to understand the structure of many mediaeval magical and alchemical texts, as they symbolically represent the flow of power through the worlds.[94]

The other numerological system widely used in occult circles is one which has come to be referred to as the Pythagorean system. Drawn directly from pre-Abrahamic sources, this has its roots in the teachings of the Greek philosopher, Pythagoras. Like the Hermetic Qabalistic system, the Pythagorean came to be used extensively in practical magic and divination among many European schools of occult practice. In this system, the number one corresponds to the Sun, two to the Moon, three to Mars, four to Mercury, five to Jupiter, six to Venus, and seven to Saturn.

As stated above, both systems work well, yet they appear to have completely different meanings and uses. To understand how this can be, one must stop thinking in a linear pattern and instead look to circular models to find a compatible solution which shows the value of both. To do this, imagine drawing a straight line on a piece of paper. At one end is the symbol of Saturn, on the other the symbol of Jupiter. From Jupiter, a line is drawn at an angle, at the end of which, the symbol of Mars is placed. Then one continues to draw the remainder of lines until a heptagram or seven-pointed star is completed. The flow from point to point following the lines is exactly the same numerological pattern found in the Hermetic system:

---

94. Splendor Solis is an excellent example of this showing fountains overflowing into rivers and streams only to be centered in additional pools or vessels in the various alchemical paintings. Also some renditions of the Tarot show a river running through the major arcana from card to card, representing a similar theme.

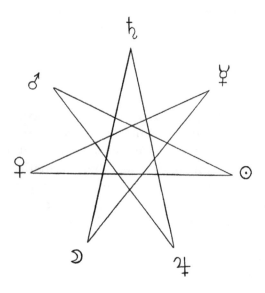

Looking at the diagram, rather than running down each line of the star, instead move around the circle from the Sun as the first point to the Moon as the second, Mars as the third, Mercury as the fourth, Jupiter as the fifth, Venus as the sixth and Saturn as the seventh point. If one were to draw this pattern it would be a spiraling, circular motion.

The use of the Hermetic numbers with their direct lines forming the seven-pointed star, show the different and unique realms which each corresponds to, flowing into the next. In practice, we have found that the Hermetic system is useful for understanding and experiencing the essence of each of these realms in *their own states* as unique dimensions. As such, the Hermetic numbering system is perfect for astral work in which one wishes to experience the essence of these realms. The Hermetic system best defines the means to enter into contact with many of the most prominent forces contained within the Abred. Many Hermetic schools use elaborate rituals involving number, color, tone, gesture and scent to align the consciousness of the magus with the realm being sought.

The Pythagorean system on the other hand with its spiral moving from Sun to Moon and on through the planets shows how these planetary energies *manifest, finding expression*. Thus their influence is practical in nature, while the Hermetic is representative of the realm itself.

We find this reflected in Celtic and Germanic traditions. The week days are named after northern European Gods that correspond to the planets and which align with the spiral pattern seen in this example. Thus, Sunday is the first day of the week, Monday (the day of the Moon) is the second, Tuesday (named for the God Tiw and Mars) is the third, Wednesday (Woden or Odin's day, equating to Mercury) is the fourth day, Thursday (named after Thor and Jupiter) is the fifth day, Friday (literally the Goddess Freya's day, equating to Venus) and lastly Saturday as the seventh day of the week.

However, this is further exemplified in Celtic myth. In the legend of the Spoils of Annwn, the heroes of the account journey to the realm of the Annwn in which the Great Cauldron of transformation awaits. As we had discussed earlier, this is described as being rimmed with pearls (a lunar symbol) and attended by nine maidens, not two. This is significant as, regardless of the antiquity of this legend, the Hermetic number of the Moon is prominent here. Despite the legend being Celtic in origin, the fact that the heroes were journeying to the realm of the lunar cauldron indicates that this is a spiritual or other worldly venture. Thus, the number nine signifying the realm itself is evident. If, on the other hand, the legend was meant to express the lunar influence as manifesting in the material world, then the number two would have been paramount.

These factors need to be considered when working ritual. When preparing for ritual, those of the Art need to understand exactly what result is intended from the work. Is the ritual of a nature in which one is seeking to experience the astral world symbolized by the planetary energy? If so, the Hermetic numbering system is the correct system to use. If, on the other hand, one is seeking to manifest the planetary energy on a material or practical magical level, the Pythagorean system is the numbering process that will yield the greatest results.

The interesting thing about this is the fact that both systems dovetail so well together, when viewed on the glyph of the circular seven-rayed star. Clearly, these are part of a larger and, in our opinion, older system.

In fact, this is true. Research has shown that much of what passes as Qabalah today, stems from Pythagorean teaching. These, in turn, were strongly influenced by teachings from Ancient Egypt. This is clearly represented in Pharonic Egyptian texts regarding their esoteric meaning of numbers.[95]

It wasn't until the thirteenth century CE that Jewish mysticism was tied to the numerical system of Pythagoras in Spain and France. This, in turn, developed into the Qabalah that is used by so many ceremonial magicians, seeing its blossom in the eighteenth century. From then on, it has continued to dominate much of contemporary Western Mystery Tradition to the present.

It is important to note that we are not saying that the Hebrew Qabalah originates from this source. Rather, there was a merging of Pythagorean teachings with Jewish mysticism in the middle ages and from this, one of the off shoots was the system of Qabalah used by many ceremonial magicians since.[96]

The Pagan origins of this numerological system are significant. Pythagoras identified specific meanings to the numbers, which are reflected in the Hermetic Qabalah. As noted above, these are also reflected in older Ancient Egyptian teachings. More importantly, though, the planetary numbering system found in the Pythagorean system relates to days of the week *and* the planetary hours of the day.

---

95. See Akhet Htw-Hrw's course of study; Bezzu lesson one.

96. For a discussion on this See Wang, Robert. *Qabalistic Tarot*. 1983.

The Egyptians appear to be the first to have divided the day into 12 hours, with the night having the same, for a total of twenty four. It was the Egyptians, too, who had two concurrent calendars, one stellar-based and one, lunar. It was the lunar calendar by which they calculated religious and magical festivals. Each lunar month was 28 days in length - the complete cycle of the Moon. Each quarter was seven days, making one lunar week. Egyptologist, Richard Parker, has presented extensive research supporting the origins of the Egyptian calendar.

That there were seven visible celestial bodies that traveled against the back drop of the stars soon became obvious to the ancients. It was but a simple step to equate a planet to a day. When applied to the days of the week, the first hour of the day is ruled by the planet of that day. Thus Sunday is ruled by the Sun. This is the first day of the week. Following the Hermetic pattern the next hour of the day on Sunday is Venus, followed by Mercury, and so on. When calculated out over a twenty four hour period the Moon falls as the celestial body governing the first hour of the next day, Monday. This is the second day of the week. Thus it continues through the week.

The interdependence of these two systems now becomes obvious. The order of the days follows Pythagorean teachings with the Sun as one, Moon as two, Mars as three, and so on. Yet the planetary hours follow the pattern of the Hermetic Qabalah; Saturn, Jupiter, Mars, Sun, Venus, Mercury, and Moon. This is simply too close to being coincidence. The two numerical systems must be related.

The Planetary Hours

Sunrise Hours	Sun	Mo	Tue	Wed	Thur	Friday	Sat
1st	Sun	Moon	Mars	Mercury	Jupiter	Venus	Saturn
2nd	Veus	Saturn	Sun	Moon	Mars	Mercury	Jupiter
3rd	Mercury	Jupiter	Venus	Saturn	Sun	Moon	Mars
4th	Moon	Mars	Mercury	Jupiter	Venus	Saturn	Sun
5th	Saturn	Sun	Moon	Mars	Mercury	Jupiter	Venus
6th	Jupiter	Venus	Saturn	Sun	Moon	Mars	Mercury
7th	Mars	Mercury	Jupiter	Venus	Saturn	Sun	Moon
8th	Sun	Moon	Mars	Mercury	Jupiter	Venus	Saturn
9th	Venus	Saturn	Sun	Moon	Mars	Mercury	Jupiter
10th	Mercury	Jupiter	Venus	Saturn	Sun	Moon	Mars
11th	Moon	Mars	Mercury	Jupiter	Venus	Saturn	Sun
12th	Saturn	Sun	Moon	Mars	Mercury	Jupiter	Venus

Sunset Hours	Sun	Mo	Tue	Wed	Thur	Friday	Sat
1st	Jupiter	Venus	Saturn	Sun	Moon	Mars	Mercury
2nd	Mars	Mercury	Jupiter	Venus	Saturn	Sun	Moon
3rd	Sun	Moon	Mars	Mercury	Jupiter	Venus	Saturn
4th	Venus	Saturn	Sun	Moon	Mars	Mercury	Jupiter
5th	Mercury	Jupiter	Venus	Saturn	Sun	Moon	Mars
6th	Moon	Mars	Mercury	Jupiter	Venus	Saturn	Sun
7th	Saturn	Sun	Moon	Mars	Mercury	Jupiter	Venus
8th	Jupiter	Venus	Saturn	Sun	Moon	Mars	Mercury
9th	Mars	Mercury	Jupiter	Venus	Saturn	Sun	Moon
10th	Sun	Moon	Mars	Mercury	Jupiter	Venus	Saturn
11th	Venus	Saturn	Sun	Moon	Mars	Mercury	Jupiter
12th	Mercury	Jupiter	Venus	Saturn	Sun	Moon	Mars

This is clear evidence that both numerological systems stem from the same source, the ancient teachings of Pythagoras and before him the influence of Ancient Egypt.[97] Yet, what is most puzzling is the fact that these numerical systems had formed such an intricate part of the myths and spiritual traditions of the people of ancient Europe. Either there was some form of cross-cultural exchange in esoteric teachings, or there had to have been an even older common root laying behind both; a long forgotten tradition that was the foundation of both the Egyptian teachings and those of ancient Europe. In either case, the Geassa remains, re-emerging in each age.

For our tradition, we equate the following significance to the numbers. Much of this is drawn directly from the research of Egyptology, yet the similarities to the Western Mysteries Tradition will become apparent to anyone who has studied this.

One - This number represents uniqueness, importance, individuality, as well as unity. Because of this, the number one holds the potential power of all the other numbers, the potential for all else that is, *before* being created. As Egyptologist, Richard Wilkinson, explains, "one contains the many, and one may thus represent the unity of many as much as it represents individuality".[98] Yet, this same number can also represent the fusion of complementary opposites. This can be seen in a number of creator Gods such as the Egyptian Atum and Nit, both of whom have male and female elements which brought about creation.

---

97. For further reading into the ancient origins of the numbering systems and the Qabalah an excellent source to consider is Kieren Barry's book *The Greek Qabalah: Alphabetic Mysticism and Numerology in the Ancient World*. 1999.

98. Wilkinson, Richard. Symbol & Magic in Egyptian Art. 1994 p.128.

Sybil Leek explained that in the Art "we see one as the life force itself, the first unit of power, the beginning of all things".[99]

Two - Duality and unity, complementary opposites (or two halves of a whole), microcosm and macrocosm, the dualistic yet complementary (interwoven) realms of the material and spiritual dimensions form the basic meaning of this number. The number two represents opposites that are intimately interlocked in harmony. The Ancient Egyptian words used to represent this number are *Wenen* meaning to 'exist', be 'perfect', or 'complete'; and the word *Kheper* meaning 'develop' and to 'become'.[100] Thus, we see two as the essence of creation that is dynamic and recurring.

Sybil explains that from the number two comes "unity and correlation, and is associated with reproduction".[101]

Three - This represents plurality. It also portrays a 'closed-harmonic' system that is interactive among its parts - the unity of an integrated group or whole.[102] We see this in a number of groupings of Gods and Goddesses: Osiris, Isis and Horus; Ptah, Sekhmet and Nefertum; as well as Hwt-Hrw, Horus and Ihy. In European myth, this is seen in the three phases of the Goddess as Maiden, Mother and Crone; or in such obvious figures as the three raven Goddesses of the Morrigu. Egyptologist, Manfred Lurker, calls the number three an "all embracing number".[103] This too is a

---

99. Leek, Sybil. *Numerology: The Magic of Numbers*. 1969 p.28.

100. Wilkinson, Richard. *Symbol & Magic in Egyptian Art*. 1994 p.129. Lurker, Manfred. *An Illustrated Dictionary of The Gods and Symbols of Ancient Egypt*. 1980 p.88.

101. Leek, Sybil. *Numerology: The Magic of Numbers*. 1969 p.28.

102. Wilkinson, Richard. Symbol & Magic in Egyptian Art. 1994. p131-133

103. Lurker, Manfred. An Illustrated Dictionary of The Gods and Symbols of Ancient Egypt. 1980 p.88.

very powerful number in magic as the triangle is used to focus energy allowing it to coalesce in ritual. This is the Triangle of Art.

Ms. Leek states "from three we get activity in all its many forms, varying from the pure action of the physical to the cohesive action of mind and spirit".[104]

Four - This is one of the most important numbers in Ancient Egyptian magic and ceremony. This number represents completeness, totality, and universality. This number further represents the concepts of time and space, the temporal world in perfection.[105]

The four cardinal points came to hold immense meaning in magical and religious practices, the world over. This includes the Egyptians, Celts, Native Americans, and so many others. With this, the four elements naturally are tied to the directions and with them the seasons, the treasures of the Tuatha De Danann and the energies each of these represent.

Looking to the Pythagorean association of the number four with the planet Mercury, Sybil Leek explains that this number is also associated with the mind, intellect and reason. It represents the ability to create order out of chaos, defining boundaries with logic and seeing patterns.

Five - For the Egyptians this number was best understood as a combination in meaning of the numbers two and three. Thus in the number five we see the process of becoming or developing into plurality and the flow of energy within a closed system. From the essence of creation as seen in the number two, creation becomes manifest in three. Thus, five is a number of power and energy. Of course this number, too, relates to the pentagram or Witches' Foot. Thus, five

104. Leek, Sybil. *Numerology: The Magic of Numbers.* 1969 p.28.
105. Wilkinson, Richard. *Symbol & Magic in Egyptian Art.* 1994 p.133-135.

is a natural progression aligning the four elements with quintessence or spirit - the harmonic on which so much of the Art is built.

Six - As with the previous number, six is best understood as a combination of three doubled, which means that the flow of harmonic energy within the closed system as represented by three is made stronger in the number six. This number is the essence of harmony, balance and union. Thus, as Sybil explains, this number brings love and comfort. This can be physical, spiritual or somewhere in between. In essence, six acts as a force of unity, blending and linking other forces, hence its association with the planet Venus in the Pythagorean system and the Sun in the Hermetic Qabalah.

Seven - This is one of the most potent numbers in magic. This number has the combined effects and meanings, of three and four. Thus such concepts as plurality, completeness and universality are conveyed. Of course, this relates to the seven traditional planets of the ancients, as well as the seven stars found in the Pleiades and Ursa Major. For the Egyptians, the number seven was strongly connected to Osiris. In the ancient temple of Abdu (Abydos) - dedicated to Osiris - a series of seven ritual chambers, each of comparatively equal size, are lined up next to each other. Each of these is dedicated to a different Egyptian God or Goddess. From left to right, these consist of: Seti I (as the personification of the divine incarnate); Ptah; Ra; Amun; Osiris; Isis; and Horus. In the back of each of these shrines, a 'false door' can be found. The so-called 'false door' was used in temples and tombs as a magical portal through which Gods, spirits and the Ka or astral form of living initiates could travel to different realms. In the shrines present at Abdu, it is clear that the different 'false doors' in each of these shrines represent pathways to the spiritual realms, which each chamber corresponds to. It should also be noted that several of the Gods have seven different aspects or Ba's. This includes Hwt-Hrw, Ma'at and Ra.[106] In the mysteries of Hwt-Hrw, the seven different aspects or cows that represent Hwt-Hrw, are the sustaining powers of the universe. This number was frequently seen as a number representing perfection.[107]

Sybil Leek describes the number seven as "the number of fate" representing a form of completion, finality and perfection. It is from this that the

"seventh child or the seventh child of a seventh child is endowed with the ability to see into the future . . . due to the fact that it comes into this life bringing with it conscious memories of past incarnations and is able to profit by the total sum of past experiences".[108]

Eight - The number eight is extremely important in the Art. For the Ancient Egyptians, this number is identical in meaning to the number four but doubled or intensified. Thus, it represents completeness and totality.[109] In the teachings of the priesthood of Thoth, the number eight figures very highly.

In the discussion surrounding the number seven, I took a look at this number in relation to the sacred architecture found in the temple of Abdu (Abydos). Perhaps the most remarkable aspect of this temple in relation to the number eight, is that in the back of the shrine of Osiris (which is one of the seven shrines to the Gods), rather than there being a 'false door' there is an actual passage to a secret, eighth chamber in the temple. Accessible only to high initiates and royalty (as representations of the Gods) this section was devoted to the mysteries of Osiris. Osiris is the God of renewal and regeneration. Thus, this hidden eighth

106. Wilkinson, Richard. *Symbol & Magic in Egyptian Art.* 1994 p.136.

107. Lurker, Manfred. *An Illustrated Dictionary of The Gods and Symbols of Ancient Egypt.* 1980 p.88.

108. Leek, Sybil. *Numerology: The Magic of Numbers.* 1969 p.31.

109. Wilkinson, Richard. *Symbol & Magic in Egyptian Art.* 1994 p.137.

chamber can be seen as a center for the transformation of the initiate through ritual. What is even more remarkable is that this hidden, eighth Osirian ritual center consists of eight smaller rooms, each of which is dedicated to a different phase in the rites of Osiris.[110]

As can be seen from this examination, the number eight was seen in the Egyptian system as a number of spiritual regeneration, transformation and perfection. Its use can be seen as a means toward transcendence and renewal. This same theme would be carried over and reflected in the much later Christian Gnostic texts that stem from Egypt, as well as Hermetic teachings with certain origins in the Hellenistic period.

Beyond Egypt, though, the number eight holds immense significance in other magical traditions. In Celtic Europe, this is seen in the balance of the four great fire festivals and the four festivals seen at the equinoxes and solstices. In Asia, the importance of the eight-sided Bagwa can't be over-stated. As a symbol of universal balance, power and harmony, the Bagwa has been in use for thousands of years.

Sybil explains that eight is a number of dynamic power, force and inspiration. But she warns that this power can be difficult to handle for those who may not be prepared or spiritually evolved.

Nine - For the Egyptians, this number represented a large, great or infinite amount of whatever was being discussed; 'All that is possible.' As such, nine is the total number of a subject. In this context, we can see a new understanding of the Egyptian Gods being grouped into the Enneads or groups of nine. They represented the total spiritual force that is the manifest world.[111] This, too, harkens to the nine women tending the fires of the Cauldron in the heart of Caer Wydyr in Celtic traditions.

---

110. Roberts, Alison. *My Mother, My Heart: Death and Rebirth in Ancient Egypt.* 2000.

111. Wilkinson, Richard. *Symbol & Magic in Egyptian Art.* 1994 p.137.

Furthermore, this ties directly into Sybil's observations when she states "nine symbolizes all that is of the highest and most noble of things, being particularly associated with the great spiritual adventures that exceed the needs of the material world".[112]

In essence, everything can be broken down to a numerical value. That number then gives a clue to the overall energy pattern inherent within. As this is a work of practical magic, the use of numerological values can be very powerful in the timing and construction of rituals, talismans, tools and in many methods of divination. While some esoteric schools follow various means of breaking letters down into numbers using Hebrew or Greek numerological systems, we ascribe to the idea that simple is best. As such, we prefer the basic method of laying out the alphabet with the following values:

1	2	3	4	5	6	7	8	9
A	B	C	D	E	F	G	H	I
J	K	L	M	N	O	P	Q	R
S	T	U	V	W	X	Y	Z	

For us experimenting with other systems, this simple method seems to get to the essence of a matter. One can breakdown a name, place, group, etc. by converting the letters into numbers and then simply reducing this down to a single digit. In this way, names, words and numbers can be incorporated in magical acts to draw on the core essence desired. For those interested in learning more on practical numerology, we recommend Sybil Leek's *Numerology: The Magic of Numbers* and David Greenacre's *Numerology and You*.[113]

---

112. Leek, Sybil. *Numerology: The Magic of Numbers*. 1969 p.32.

113. It is important to note that Mr. Greenacre ascribes the planets and numbers differently than either of these two traditional systems. It would appear that his correspondence is drawn from his own personal observations. Nevertheless, his book is an excellent introduction practical numerology. As for the planetary attributes ascribed to numbers we follow the systems outlined in this chapter.

Chapter Twelve

✤ THE CLOAK OF DANU ✤
The Planets & Color In The Art

From the significance of number, we can move into the natural power of color. Color essentially is the manifestation of the band width of the light spectrum vibrating at a level that we, as humans can see. It is interesting that not all creatures can see the entire spectrum of color. In our form as human, we only see a limited field of color. Those colors include the seven primary bands of light and the colors that result when these are blended together. In the Art, like numbers, color is used as a vehicle to access certain energies. These correspond to the forces represented by the seven planetary bodies of traditional magic. In Hermetic circles, much research has been done in regards to the use of color and how these draw upon and interact with astral forces. By and large, these relate to the seven spheres, however, differing between the four levels of Qabbalistic practice: conception, creation, formation and expression. Melita Denning and Osbourne Phillips' work *The Magical Philosophy* will prove valuable to the reader should you wish to pursue an in-depth study of these attributes.

As a general rule of thumb, drawing largely from the Briatic color scheme, Hermetic circles attribute the colors with the planets, more or less, in the following order:

Saturn: Black, Grey and in some Hermetic Orders, Indigo
Jupiter: Blue
Mars: Red
Sun: Yellow or Gold

Venus: Green
Mercury: Orange
Moon: White and Silver, as well as Lavender or Violet.

However, Sybil Leek gives a somewhat different color scheme in the following correspondence as related to the Pythagorean numerological system.

Orange: The Sun, Leo and the number 1
Green: The Moon, Cancer and the number 2
Red: Mars, Aries and the number 3
A richer dark red: Mars, Scorpio and the number 3
Clear blue: Mercury, Gemini and the number 4
Bright clear blue of the sky: Mercury, Virgo and the number 4
Indigo: Jupiter, Sagittarius, and the number 5
Yellow: Venus, Taurus and the number 6.
Light blue: Venus, Libra and the number 6
Gray ranging from light dove gray to almost black: Saturn, Capricorn, and the number 7
Electric blue: Uranus, Aquarius and the number 8
Violet: Jupiter and Neptune jointly, Pisces, and the number 9.

Sybil makes it very clear that black is only used as a "neutralizing factor" - gathering and preventing energies from working. Black nullifies other forces, negating them. Sybil goes on to explain that this is why black is used in negative magic as it negates the other powers around it.

In researching occult manuscripts, it is clear that Sybil's color correspondence matches very closely to that of contemporary Astrological enquiry.[114] This would make sense, given the fact that Sybil was a consummate Astrologer; a talent that her family had practiced and passed to her. It makes sense, as well, that as members of an

---

114. See Bills, Rex. *The Rulership Book*. 1971, 1976.

old family involved in the Art, they would have used this system for color assignment. For us, we use the following correspondence in our use of color and the Art. Like our understanding of the value of numbers, the following is drawn primarily from Ancient Egyptian sources. However, too, we include correspondence which we have observed from the magical practice of Europe and elsewhere. Again, these are all valid expressions of the Geassa.

In the Art, color helps to show the hidden or esoteric quality of an object.[115] As such, color needs to be considered very carefully when making or selecting ritual items, such as tools, amulets and emblems.

Yet, it is important to know that colors frequently hold dual meanings and which meaning is intended, depends largely on the context in which the color is being used. Sometimes, the color's dual meanings can both be evident in an item. In many cases, opposite colors are used on the same object, or in the same setting to show their completeness or wholeness.

Black - Known to the Egyptians as *Kem*, its *positive* attributes include its connection with resurrection, fertility, the cycle of death and rebirth. Osiris is often portrayed as having either black or green skin (sometimes interchanged) – thus, showing his connection with the rebirth cycle. The fertile Nile mud left by the inundation each year was black in color, showing a further symbolic connection with regeneration. Often times in Egypt, healing statues were carved from black stone as this color was considered very potent in healing the body. Black represents the land and, with it, the potential of life that can grow from this.

In Ancient Egypt, black's *negative* connotations included death as destruction. At times, a black hole was used to represent the elimination of an enemy. While on a *neutral* level, black represented the underworld and the night. Clearly,

---

115. Lurker, Manfred. *An Illustrated Dictionary of The Gods and Symbols of Ancient Egypt.* 1980 p.40.

the dualistic nature of black is evident through the ideas of life, death and rebirth, all strongly associated with this color.

In the practical magic of the Art, all of these qualities can be used when considering black. Black itself isn't a color. Rather, it is the absence of color. For practical purposes this means that black absorbs the light spectrum of the colors. So we use black in ritual to draw in and absorb, or negate, the influence of others. Thus, the outside of a mirror box, or a dual set of mirrors placed face to face, will be covered in black to draw the negative influence of those who wish to harm us into the mirror, where we then reflect this back on the person who sent it.

Black candles can be used in a similar way. They, too, can be used to draw in negative energy which we then convert to power, for other purposes. Because of its association with both death and regeneration, black candles can be a tool for evoking the shades of the deceased and, as alluded to above, used in negative magic, to blast. Yet, black is a symbol of the latent power within. As such, one will see references to the Master as the 'Man in Black'- a title describing his place as leader and his association with the earthy underworld Gods, such as Osiris and others.

Finally, it needs to be mentioned that black is associated with the Crow, the Raven and the three Morrigu - Great Goddesses of power in the Tuatha de Danann. As will be seen, the crow is the messenger of the Annwn. She is wise and cunning. 'Black' need not be negative. Rather it is of the netherworld; the realm of necromancy and spirit communication; the link to the ancestors and to the Old Ways. We welcome the Great Queen in Her cloak of black for it is only through the Dark of the Moon and Her wisdom that the Maiden can be renewed. In candle magic, generally, black candles should either be burned for one hour or completely out.

Blue - Known as *Irtiu* or *Kesbedj* to the Egyptians, this color represents life and rebirth with strong associations with the heavens and the primeval waters. As such, the color blue came to symbolize fertility, offerings and prosperity. The Bennu or Phoenix, as well as the Baboon and Ibis (both images of Thoth) were often depicted in bright blue tones. In looking to the dualistic nature of this color, blue at once can represent the clear sky, air, logic and intellect; yet, conversely, it can represent the water, the ocean's depths, emotion and feeling. Again, the context in which the magician is working will decide the meaning of the intended.

In our depiction of the Stang as the World Tree, we purposely use blue to represent both the sky and air giving way to the heavens above *and* the waters of the underworld. Each is a reflection of the other, holding the hidden essence of the Goddess and, in each, the potential for creation to emerge as the God united with the Goddess is ever present.

In practice, blue is an excellent color for bringing clarity to a situation, as well as opening lines of communication. Throughout, though, there is a sense of calm and peace. Blue candles should burn for a minimum of three hours.

Dark Blue - This is the color associated with the night sky and was considered to be very spiritual to the Egyptians. As such, this color also had strong associations with the underworld and the afterlife. The color of the hair of the Egyptian Gods and Goddesses was often this color, although, this could be interchanged with black. In ritual practice, dark blue is used to create a link with realms beyond the material. It can be used to gain knowledge and perceive events beyond one, aiding in psychic perception. Dark blue candles should burn a minimum of two hours.

Light Blue - This color is associated with the sky during the daytime and is sacred to Hwt-Hrw (Hathor). Symbolically, this tint of blue is functionally the same as green is in the Egyptian tradition. Quite frequently, ritual Ankhs were given a light blue glaze to partake in this color's attributes of fertility, life and rejuvenation. Light blue, too, relates directly to the element of Air and the intellect. This, of course, is very similar to Sybil's attributes associating light blue to Venus and Libra (Venus = fertility and rejuvenation, Libra is the Cardinal sign of Air). Burning time for light blue is three hours.

Green - In Egypt, this was known as *Wadj* and characterized life, resurrection, healing and good health. The afterlife was often referred to as the "Fields of Malachite" because of this stone's green hue. In fact, green was very strongly connected to the underworld, confirming this region's regenerative powers. In addition to black, Osiris' skin was frequently shown as being colored green. Many scenes of the underworld show a variety of deities as having skin this color. The *Wedjat-Eye* or "Eye of Heru/Horus" amulets were usually this color to denote well-being and health. This color is also strongly associated with Hwt-Hrw, as such it denotes anything that is good and joyful.

This is a color of abundance, prosperity, fertility and love. It represents all that grows. Money, stability, happiness, joy, all fall under the energy depicted as the color green. 'Green Magic' is a powerful form of the Art. While green magic takes time to manifest its effects are powerful and long lasting. In our form of the Art, we use green magic, extensively. As Sybil points out, it is a color associated with the Moon, because of the connection with growth and the Goddess. Green candles should burn a minimum of four hours.

Red - Known as *Desher* in Ancient Egyptian the color red has enormous and conflicting meaning. From a *positive* perspective it represented life and regeneration, strength and victory. Red was often used for "Eye of Ra" amulets because of its protective qualities (destroying opposition), and thus had a connection with the Sun, and the Goddesses Sekhmet and Hwt-Hrw. Red was used to signify the skin tone of men in Egyptian art with no negative connotations involved. The protective amulet known as the "Blood of

Isis," "Knot of Isis," or the "Tyet/Tet", which is a clear representation of the vulva, were almost always red in color.

From a *negative* prospective in Ancient Egypt, red frequently was used to symbolize dangerous forces that are out of, and beyond, control. This color can signify anger, destruction, chaos, wrath, and death. Red ink was often used to write hieroglyphs that signified evil, generally and destructive creatures, specially. As such, red is a color strongly associated with Sutekh (Greek name: Set). He is often represented as having red hair and eyes.

In practice, red is a powerful color to work with bringing in raw energy. This energy can be sexual and primal. Thus, it can manifest as passion, desire, seduction and love. It is blood that gives us life. Yet passion that is not tempered with structure and reason can lead to negative results. As such, the Witch must be careful when using red. Its affects are quick to manifest but often don't last long.

Like green magic, there is a branch of the Art that is 'red magic'. This relates directly to the power in the land and the energy of life and spring, passion and desire. Red covens are linked to this energy directing this from the men of the group to the Mistress. It can be very powerful but needs to be approached with care. Red candles should burn a minimum of one hour.

Red and Green together - In many Celtic expressions of the Art, the colors red and green are often used together much in the way that red and white are used in Alchemical and Egyptian systems. In this sense, red represents the fire and passion of the Sun, the male and the Horned God of nature. At the same time, green represents earth and water, love, harmony, fertility, the Moon and the Great Queen of all. Hence, the combined use of these colors in the Yule wreath, among other traditional pagan emblems. In our system, it is common for us to place a green candle to the left of the hearthstone and a red candle to the right symbolizing these great spiritual forces in union.

The Mistress's familiar, Bes reading Crowley

Hearth set for harvest full moon ritual

Outdoor stone circle of covenstead

Circle hearthstone with ritual tools

The author's personal familiar 'alraun' root, carved from an Ash tree

Outdoor harvest ritual, besom joined with the Stang before the cauldron

Household doorway amulets – Green Man mask, Green Man's Hand, Corn Dolly from Lughnasadh, and Oak/Rowan Cross

Indoor hearth set for ritual

Hearth set for spirit scrying

Mirror box lined with black velvet on the outside. This is used in defensive magic by placing taglocks inside and covering this with the top which is also a mirror with the outside lined in black. The bone and black candle help to draw the baneful energy of one's enemies into the box, which is then reflected back onto them

Hearth set for spell casting with smaller Stang used for practical magic

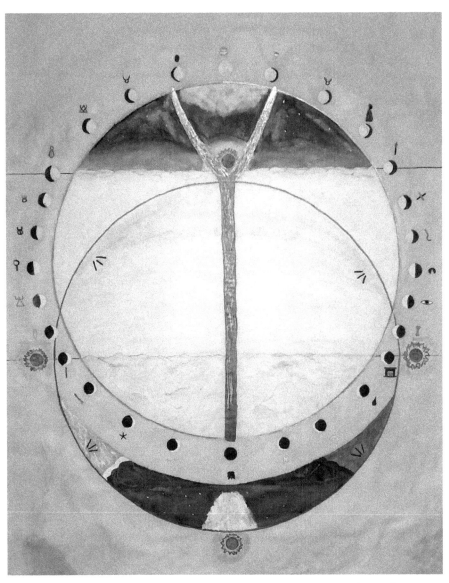

Coven painting of the Stang as World Tree, used in rituals involving 'Traveling in Spirit'.

Author's Coven logo, 'Horns of the Moon'

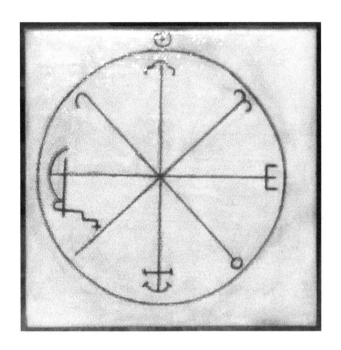

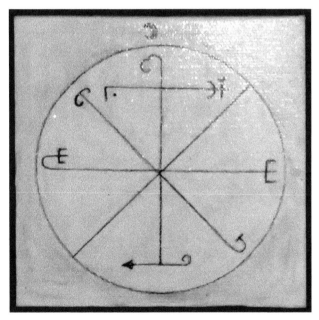

Traditional Sigils of the Sun and Moon always used together to bring success. We place these on the Hearth during most spells and rituals of prosperity and success

Diploma Award

MAC

Martin Astrology Consultants
Member A.F.A.

by SUE MARTIN Astrologer

Sybil Leek Studies

THIS CERTIFIES THAT KERRY WISNER

Has successfully completed Beginner's, Intermediate and Advanced Courses of study to the satisfaction
of the undersigned and is awarded this Diploma in recognition of achieving this goal.

Signed:

Signed:

Instructor. SUE MARTIN

Dated: May 5, 1977

Post Office Box 158

Melbourne Beach   Florida 32951

Dear Mr Wisner

          I would suggest you get in touch with Isaac Bonwits
Mother Grove Association, Box 9398 , Berkeley California 94709
I concentrate on my own coven in England and I think it is more
befitting for you to be in contact with an American. I am sure
Isaac will be able to put you in touch with someone in your
own area.

          All good wishes and good lukc in your search

                    Blessed be

                         Sybil Leek

Letter to the author from Sybil Leek

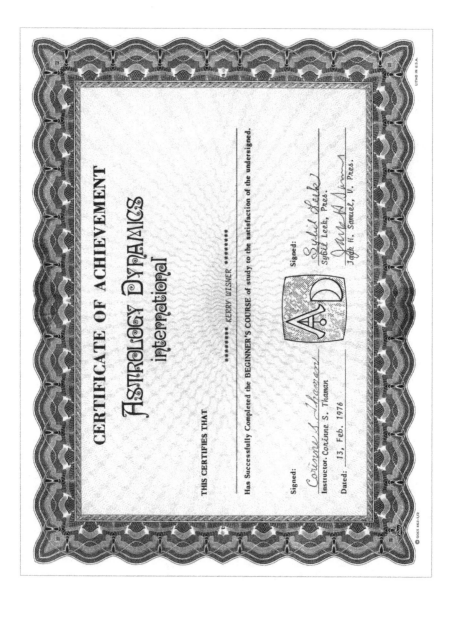

CERTIFICATE OF ACHIEVEMENT

Astrology Dynamics
international

THIS CERTIFIES THAT

******** KERRY WISNER ********

Has Successfully Completed the BEGINNER'S COURSE of study to the satisfaction of the undersigned.

Signed:

Corinne S. Thaman
Instructor. Corinne S. Thaman

Dated: 13, Feb. 1976

Signed:

Sybil Leek
Sybil Leek, Pres.

Jack H. Samuel
Jack H. Samuel, V. Pres.

White - In Ancient Egypt, white was called both *Hedj* and *Shesep*. White always denoted cleanliness and sacredness. For the Egyptians, white was associated with the Moon and the Sun, as well as the precious metals of silver, gold and electrum. The sacred lotus, the White Cow (a symbol of a variety of Goddesses across the world) and the White Baboon (an image of Thoth) all can be found to derive meaning from the characteristics represented as white. According to Egyptologist, Manfred Lurker, white signified joy.[1]

Where black is the absence of color, white is all light combined. So it represents the potential in all that is. White can be used as a substitute for any of the colors except black. Sybil explained that in her system, tall white tapers should be burned during the waxing Moon "with the silver and white flowers" present as an invocation to the Goddess.[2]

Red & White together - In the Art, when depicted together, the colors of red and white take on a deeper meaning. Red and White together express wholeness and perfection as well as a dynamic power that is best expressed through the union of complementary opposites.[3] The red and white crown of the Pharaoh best exemplifies this. The red crown of Lower (northern) Egypt was considered a talismanic object embodying the power of the protective Cobra Goddess, Wadjet; while the white crown of Upper (southern) Egypt embodied the power of the vulture Goddess, Nekhbet. Together, this powerful symbol was seen as providing the Pharaoh with these Goddesses' divine power.

In the years that followed, red and white became key symbols of Alchemy, an Art which can be directly linked

---

1. Lurker, Manfred. *An Illustrated Dictionary of The Gods and Symbols of Ancient Egypt.* 1980 p.129.

2. Leek, Sybil. *Cast Your Own Spell.* 1970 p.153.

3. Lurker, Manfred. *An Illustrated Dictionary of The Gods and Symbols of Ancient Egypt.* 1980 p.44.

to Egypt. In Alchemy, the red and white roses became symbols of the Sun and Moon, respectively. These were the embodiment of the divine masculine and divine feminine intertwined as growing roses in a garden. In Celtic myth, we see a similar image in the twin dragon - one red, the other white. The dragon or 'worm' in Celtic lore was, and is, a symbol of the power in the land, the Geassa. And, of course, this explains why the early Abrahamic traditions depicted their 'devil' as a dragon that had to be slain. It was a metaphor for their attempt to destroy the Old Religion.

Taken together, red and white represent the dynamic union of complementary opposites in harmony. This union is power. This union is all that is. Hence, in the Ogdoadic tradition of the Hermetic Arts, the interlaced squares of the Tessera, the primary symbol used in the Ogdoadic Mysteries, represent this.[4]

Yellow/Gold - This is perhaps the most depicted and thus important color in Ancient Egyptian art. As a color, yellow/gold was known as *Ketj*. However, as a precious metal, it was called *nebu*. This color represented the Sun, the stars, the heavens, as well as immortality and spirituality. It is for this reason that the Egyptian Gods are usually depicted with yellow or gold skin. This color is particularly sacred to Goddess Hwt-Hrw who was frequently referred to as the "Golden One", or simply as "Gold". Women were usually depicted with this color skin.

In the Art, generally, gold represents many different things. It can relate to material wealth and success. Yet, it can be used to represent spirituality. In the Hermetic order in which I was trained, we were taught techniques to project gold light from the center of the body filling the aura. This provides protection, yet draws attention and success on both material and spiritual levels.

---

4. It is important to note that in traditional Witchcraft the interlaced squares are depicted as red and green, or sometimes as red and blue.

On the other hand, the color yellow has been found to open the power center located at the solar plexus, allowing psychic information to enter the person. Therefore, it relates to communication and awareness. Yet, this opening can create confusion and fear as the 'programs' of others flood one's system - hence, the term 'yellow belly' to denote a coward. In such incidents, one becomes so overwhelmed that fear takes over. Still, the use of yellow can bring joy and an opening to others. I have purposely charged yellow objects with a specific intention and given this to the person I wished to influence, working on the idea that the color would stimulate their center and open them to my influence. One of my teachers had magically charged a small vial of water colored yellow with food dye, opened this and placed it strategically in a room where a gathering was assembling to make a decision about her. The result went in her favor with the members electing to let our coven into their company. Note that both gold and yellow candles should burn no less than three hours.

Orange - This color corresponds to passion, desire as well as to acts which require quick action. While not as powerful as red, orange energy is easier to control and manipulate. Spells cast using this color, tend to come to fruition quickly but may not last as long as one would like. As it is a color transitioning from red to yellow it can have uses in regards to lust and power (red) as well as communication and energy (yellow). Again, the intent of the Witch is the deciding factor. Orange candles should burn a minimum of two hours.

Purple/Violet - What a powerful and wonderful color this is. Purple corresponds to power and control, expansion and grace. It can be highly spiritual but it isn't always easy to control. Too much use of purple can result in tension and problems, not unlike its counterpart, red. Yet, its use evokes the energies of Jupiter on the one hand, bringing philosophical and spiritual energies, abundance and

155

prosperity (if used properly). It also relates to the Moon and Her energies, drawing occult and magical influences to the user. Again, intention is everything here. Change your state of consciousness; change your state of being. Purple candles should burn a minimum of one hour.

Once again, there is a real difference between traditional Hermetic teachings and that of magical practices designed to influence the material realm. Both are valid. Both work. And, as we have seen, both are derived from the same root teaching.

It would seem clear that if one is seeking to experience the astral essence of a particular realm within the Abred, the use of the Hermetic color and number is going to be the most effective. However, if one is seeking to manifest and use the power of that realm for practical purposes on the material plane, the colors given by Sybil, along with the Pythagorean number system will have the strongest and most lasting effect.

In this work, we have frequently referred to the 'influence' of the planets. The reality is that the Sun, Moon and planets, as physical 'bodies', do possess certain energies, such as gravity, radiation, electromagnetic properties and more. However, in the Art, when we refer to planetary influences, what we are referring to are the energies, forces and tides of power which correspond to and are best understood through the celestial body. In other words, the planets themselves are not the actual realm being tapped into by the magician. Rather, they embody and represent the raw qualities on a material level of a corresponding energy existent in other dimensions and realities. Just as numbers correspond to a specific vibratory rate of energy, or colors embrace the visual image of a specific force, the celestial bodies, too, draw on, represent and to a certain extent, express these deeper, richer forces.

Having said this, it is important to understand that the planet, or celestial body involved, does act as a vehicle, condensing and projecting the forces of realms beyond our material dimension in very real ways. All is consciousness, all is connected. This is the basis of Astrology. This is the basis of the occult laws of vibration and of correspondence. In this way, one can charge a talisman by exposing it to the light of the planet it is dedicated to. In this way, one can energize water, essential oils and magical tools in rites, designed to correspond to the movement of different stellar forces. In this way, too, one can commune with otherworld beings, Gods and spirits that are associated with the planet. This latter point is significant. These otherworld beings are not believed to physically live on the material planets they are associated with. Rather, these beings are intelligences that correspond to, and work through the energies represented by these celestial bodies; just as each of us manifest characteristics related to specific planets more than others.[5]

The following pages are meant to be a quick and basic overview of the essential correspondence of items which embody the forces we have been discussing. This is meant to act as a foundation on which the reader will build. This is in no way to be considered complete and inclusive.

Sun

Basic magical properties include: Self-integration, individuality, fame, ego, extroversion. This influence is used to create friendships, obtain health, acquire money and wealth, create peace, bring happiness, obtain patronage, begin new enterprises, bring success, all positive works to obtain, create or acquire.

- Day of week: Sunday
- Hermetic number for the dimension ruled: Six

---

5. To understand how and what planetary forces an individual manifests in their life it is best determined through the construction and interpretation of the Natal Horoscope. This can be a highly revealing and valuable document.

- Pythagorean number finding expression on the material plane: One
- Hermetic / Briatic color for the dimension ruled: Yellow and Gold
- Color in the material sphere of influence: Orange and Gold
- Element: Fire
- Metal: Gold
- Stone: Diamond, Gold Topaz, Yellow Sapphire
- Incenses & Herbs: Cinnamon, Bay Laurel, Frankincense, Chamomile, Marigold, Heliotrope, Yarrow, Goldenseal, Sunflower, Dandelion, Cinquefoil, Flax seed, Balm of Gilead
- Tree: Laurel, Walnut

Moon

Basic magical properties include: Visions, astral travel, spirit communication, rhythm, personality, safe travel, discovery of hidden knowledge, dreams, magic, divination, love, emotions, intuition, subconscious, all rituals devoted to the invocation and worship of the Divine Female in all Her many forms.

- Day of Week: Monday
- Hermetic number for the dimension ruled: Nine
- Pythagorean number finding expression on the material plane: Two
- Hermetic / Briatic color for the dimension ruled: Violet
- Color in the material sphere of influence: White, Silver and Green
- Element: Water
- Metal: Silver
- Stone: Moonstone, Pearl
- Incenses & Herbs: Lotus, Sandalwood, Jasmine, Almond, Camphor, Willow, Cucumber, Lemon, Poppy, Aloes, Onion
- Tree: Willow, Birch

Mars

Basic magical properties include: Activity, dynamic energy, power, courage, victory, physical body, heat, aggression, cause discord, disrupt friendship, military success, cause war, raw sexuality, anger.

- Day of Week: Tuesday
- Hermetic number for the dimension ruled: Five
- Pythagorean number finding expression on the material plane: Three
- Hermetic / Briatic color for the dimension ruled: Red
- Color in the material sphere of influence: Red
- Element: Fire
- Metal: Iron
- Stone: Bloodstone, Carnelian
- Incenses & Herbs: Dragon's Blood Resin, Tobacco, Blackthorn, Rue, Nettle, Pepper, Wolfsbane, Patchouli, Hellebore, Sulfur, Garlic, Bloodroot
- Tree: Blackthorn

Mercury

Basic magical properties include: Communication, reason, speed, duality, youth, selling oneself, business success, success in study and learning, influence over others, good time for personal success, intellect, the sciences.

- Day of Week: Wednesday
- Hermetic number for the dimension ruled: Eight
- Pythagorean number finding expression on the material plane: Four
- Hermetic / Briatic color for the dimension ruled: Yellow
- Color in the material sphere of influence: Blue
- Element: Air
- Metal: Quicksilver, Aluminum
- Stone: Opal
- Incenses & Herbs: Fennel, Anise, Ash, Vervain, Wormwood, Valerian, Dittany of Crete, Red

Sandalwood, Sassafras, a combination of Cinnamon and Gum Mastic make an excellent Mercury incense.
- Tree: Ash

Jupiter
Basic magical properties include: Expansion, idealism, ambition, career success, obtain friendship, obtain health, good luck, acquire honors; obtain wealth, strength, will, inspiration, material possessions, good fortune, optimism.
- Day of Week: Thursday
- Hermetic number for the dimension ruled: Four
- Pythagorean number finding expression on the material plane: Five
- Hermetic / Briatic color for the dimension ruled: Blue
- Color in the material sphere of influence: Indigo or Violet depending on the Sign one wishes to draw upon.
- Element: Fire
- Metal: Tin
- Stone: Turquoise, Amethyst
- Incenses & Herbs: Mandrake, St. John's Wort, High John the Conqueror root, Cedar, Ginseng, Solomon's Seal, Frankincense, Hyssop, Juniper Berries, Pine, Nutmeg, Juniper
- Tree: Oak

Venus
Basic magical properties include: Union, love, lust & desire, sexual intercourse, sexuality, sensuality, eroticism, social activities, parties, acquire beauty, friendship, to obtain love & marriage, pleasure & luxury, harmony & balance, esthetics, the arts, positive for all pleasurable emotional endeavours;
- Day of Week: Friday
- Hermetic number for the dimension ruled: Seven
- Pythagorean number finding expression on the material plane: Six

- Hermetic / Briatic color for the dimension ruled: Green, Aqua Marine
- Color in the material sphere of influence: Yellow or blue depending on the sign one wishes to draw upon or influence. Though pink, red and green can be used for certain works of love and sex.
- Element: Water
- Metal: Copper
- Stone: Emerald
- Incenses & Herbs: Rose, Myrtle, Honeysuckle, Ambergris, Orris, Rosemary, Apple, Egyptian Paradise Seed, Musk Oil, Gum Benzoin, Cherry tree Resin
- Tree: Rowan

Saturn

Basic magical properties include: Formation through restriction, protection, astral travel, spirit communication, time to study, things connected with the home, the land, real estate, esoteric knowledge, as well as curses, oppression, restriction in all forms, death, inhibitions, discipline, deprivation.

- Day of Week: Saturday
- Hermetic number for the dimension ruled: Three (Eleven for spiritual endeavors);
- Pythagorean number finding expression on the material plane: Seven
- Hermetic / Briatic color for the dimension ruled: Black, Gray and Indigo
- Color in the material sphere of influence: all shades of grey up to and including black, though black is used only to negate other forces.
- Element: Earth (Water for spiritual endeavors)
- Metal: Lead
- Stone: Onyx, Obsidian
- Incenses & Herbs: Myrrh, Hemlock, Asafoetida, Jimson Weed, Deadly Nightshade, Mullein, Patchouli
- Tree: Cypress

Putting it all together

So far in this work, we have covered a multitude of factors that those of the Art consider, when preparing for ritual. Taking advantages of tides of power can be some of the most powerful tools available to the Witch. Yet, coordinating these can be challenging. We have looked at the phases of the Moon, the tides of the Sun and elemental attributes of the seasons, as well as planetary days and hours. In addition to these, there may be times when one considers the "Mansion of the Moon", the significance of the days of the Moon, the twenty-four minute elemental cycles of the day or even the Ancient Egyptian hours of the day and night. One can even go so far as to wait for certain planets to align, to be rising, or straight over head. I remember the head of the Hermetic Order stating in frustration "it can drive you crazy" trying to get all of the factors to align.

For our part, we follow a basic formula prioritizing the factors based on the task at hand. Firstly, carefully consider the objective of the ritual. Keep this simple and direct. Make certain you understand the goal and the motive behind this. In her book "Cast Your Own Spell", Sybil Leek gives some excellent advice:

> "The main art is to formulate very clearly in your own mind exactly what you want and do not dress up your request with reasons why. Neither should you try to rationalize or make suggestions as to how the achievement should come along."

She goes on to state:

> "Every thought you think, every word you utter during the making of a spell is important . . . or should be. It is also a vibration and is not an isolated breath capable of disappearing. It has a beginning and it has a target. Therefore think well about the presentation of your

spell before you begin to perform. This is a one-take affair, blow it and you may have to wait another twenty-eight days before it is safe to do it again".[6]

By making sure you understand the goal and your motive, keeping this simple and down to the basic root desire. This will help you categorize the tides which will serve you best. For example, you may have a goal of increased prosperity. Is it just a matter of opening to the tides to allow this to manifest in whatever ways it can most easily come into your life? Or are you seeking something more specific? If along the same theme you actually are looking to receive a promotion by influencing your boss, the tides involved would be very different from those of general prosperity. What obstacles may be holding you back from achieving your goal? Does it make sense to remove these from your path before doing a ritual of prosperity?

In each of these scenarios the tides involved would be very different and yet the overall results are meant to be the same. So always consider your goal by first breaking this down into its simplest components. Remember magic, like water, follows the lines of least resistance. So, a clear understanding of the steps needed to succeed, are essential.

Also, you will want to make sure that the goal sought is within your realm of availability. If you are seeking a promotion to an executive level position but lack the expertise and training to handle the job, no amount of ritual will secure the position. Ritual may get you noticed by the people making the decision but without the necessary skill set, it is doubtful that much more would occur.

Rather, it is wise to look at the overarching goal and then break this down into steps that are achievable. Look to the first step that is within your realm of availability, do the work to get to this goal and then proceed to the next with each step carrying you closer to the ultimate prize.

---

6. Leek, Sybil. *Cast Your Own Spell.* 1970 p.77.

Beyond these preliminary stages, the first factor to consider in magical timing is *always* the phase of the Moon. This will take precedent over all other factors and should not be deviated from. Waxing, full, waning and dark are the main components that must first be considered. With this taken into account many rituals will prove to be highly effective.

The second factor to look into, is the Sun Tide. What season are you in, at the time that you wish to perform the rite? As shown earlier, the elemental energy of the season can be very potent when performing ritual. Generally, though, this energy is considered when goals meant to be long lasting and enduring are desired. Quick goals, such as having someone contact you, or influencing the people involved in an immediate decision need not be tied to considerations of season. On the other hand, larger goals such as continued spiritual development, finding a compatible life partner, or placing one in a significant career that will affect your entire life would be rituals you would want to consider in regards to the solar tides and seasons.

Generally speaking, the period between the Spring Equinox and the Summer Solstice which is governed by the element of fire is excellent for works involving new beginnings, goals that require an initial burst of energy. In the Art, this season is excellent for the evocation to visible form of otherworld beings aligned with the traditional seven planets.

The water tide beginning at the Summer Solstice marks the height of the solar year. This season brings with it a sense of nurturing and development. Works at this time can be geared toward long term goals both material and spiritual. This tide is even more effective for the evocation of otherworld beings to visible form, than the previous.

The season of air commencing with the Autumnal Equinox is excellent for rituals designed to bring results and culmination to an event, while the season of earth beginning at the Winter Solstice relates to rites of meditation and introspection.

Again the longer seasonal tides should be evaluated based on your need. In many cases shorter term basic goals can be safely performed in any season. However, you will want to be aware of the energy involved and structure your rite accordingly. Having picked the appropriate lunar phase within a season compatible to the task, the next step is to look at the planetary days and hours.

Ideally, this same formula would apply to all rites performed. In practice, this isn't always easy to do, nor is it always necessary. However, the more tides that you can get to align the more powerful your rite will be. In the final analysis though, your will, your intention and ability, are the ultimate factors that will decide the success or failure of your rituals.

Chapter Thirteen

✤ THE DISTAFF ✤
and the Woven Thread

The Art is, and always has been, an initiatory discipline. No matter the culture or era, entrance to the deeper mysteries of the Art has always been accompanied by a period of training, intense inner scrutiny and analysis, all under the direct supervision of a mentor or guide. Depending on the system, this then culminates in a ritual involving ordeal and transition characterized by a rite of passage that is equated with death itself; to be followed by rebirth - initiation. Whether this was in ancient Pagan temples, a secret chamber in a lodge or, as in more rural and Shamanic expressions of the Geassa, set before the clan hearthstone, the pattern remains the same.

In some traditions, a series of initiations are required; each representing increasingly intense stages of progression into the mysteries. In these, the first is usually seen as an introduction to the basic meaning of the symbols of the Order with oaths of secrecy and dedication being administered. It isn't until later initiation rites, conferring different 'degrees', that the deeper mysteries are opened to the candidate.

In the Willow Path, students are only chosen from those who specifically ask for training. This is never coerced. The Willow Path must be freely chosen. No one will seek to 'convert' outsiders in hopes of increasing membership. Only after careful consideration of a potential student's mental, emotional and spiritual maturity, and all in the group agree, a basic dedication rite is performed announcing the candidate's intention to train. With this, they formally acknowledge that those teachings which are exclusive to the system will not be revealed. Following the dedication, an intense period of training under the tutelage of one or more members of the group (usually a member of the opposite sex) takes place. It is only after this training is more of less completed that initiation is considered. Initiation then is the culmination, resulting in the full blossoming of the candidate's spiritual self, to the deeper mysteries of the system. As such, the time devoted to training varies from student to student. Traditionally, this was a minimum of a year and a day, though often it can be much longer.

Many never reach the point in which initiation occurs. Others are content to remain as members dedicated to the practice but not seeking the transformation which initiation ultimately brings. And there are many others who find that the path isn't for them.

Yet, for those who do take that final step, worlds open to them that others can only imagine. One is never the same again and with this comes a spiritual adventure that brings wisdom and information that simply can't be understood with the rational mind, alone. Unlike some other traditions, The Willow Path, as our group has come to practice it, doesn't employ a series of 'degrees'. Initiation into this system occurs only once. And, like other shamanic disciplines, this rite connects the individual to the sacred forces and beings who guide our tradition, helping to carry the deeper teachings forward through those who have been properly prepared.

The Distaff

To understand the reasons why initiation is such a vital part of the deeper mysteries of the Art, we must first look at the structure of esoteric schools, groups and covens (family tradition or otherwise). In essence, initiatory spiritual disciplines the world over were, and are, organized

167

structures which teach esoteric theory and practice to their members. These organizations make use of rituals which are intended to bring the initiate into direct contact with forces and beings beyond those normally perceived with the physical senses.

As a result, these groups consist not only of human members, but also of orders of beings in other worlds, other dimensions or states of existence. These beings are portrayed according to the philosophical and cultural atmosphere of the societies in which the spiritual discipline was developed. And, in fact, these beings will frequently represent themselves within the confines and expectations of a discipline. In other words, these other world beings will relate to humans through the symbols and images that the group involved can best understand and grasp. As such, they can and do appear in a variety of forms.

In Egyptian religion, we see this in the numerous shapes that a single God or Goddess can take. For example, the Goddess Hathor can appear as a cow, falcon, beautiful woman, wild cat, lioness, snake and more. These are different 'forms' that help to express Her nature. These and other forms represent the different ways that She relates to humans through patterns that we can understand.

We see this in Celtic myth as well. For example, both the Goddesses, Arianrhod and Cerridwen, are depicted as changing form repeatedly into a variety of animals. So, too, do several of the Celtic Gods. In many stories, the Gods will have any number of animal features in a given description.

It is important to explain that, in the Art, these patterns of expression for the Gods are not 'symbols' in the sense of an object, token or sign representing something that is not genuinely or actually, present. Rather, for us these different forms, including ritual objects, carvings, glyphs, statues, etc., are all seen as being the *embodiment* of the deity represented. In this sense, the use of ritual items including amulets, staffs and masks all bring the spiritual intelligence of the being into temporal expression. These

168

are not mere symbols but rather the living images of the entity involved.

Paradoxically, though, it needs to be explained that these material patterns of expression do not show the 'actual' appearance of the God or Goddess. Rather, they are the means by which a deity chooses to express itself. Dr. Erik Hornung explains this further:

> "We should not, therefore, assume that the Egyptians imagined Hathor as a woman with a cow's head. It is more plausible to see the cow as one possible manifestation of Hathor, and the cow's head and cow's horns as attributes that allude to a manifestation of the goddess or a part of her nature. In Hathor there is the maternal tenderness of the cow, but, among many other characteristics, also the wildness of the lioness and the unpredictability of the snake. Any iconography can be no more than an attempt to indicate something of her complex nature . . . pictures of gods should not be understood as illustrations or descriptions of appearances, but rather as allusions to essential parts of the nature and function of deities."[7]

Further, these patterns of manifestation do not show the *complete* essence of the spiritual force being manifest. They are the means used by beings to convey knowledge and to make their presence known. Again, Dr. Hornung sheds light on this:

> "But none of these animals, plants and objects that are related to the manifestation of deities gives any information about the true form of a deity. According to the texts the true form is "hidden" and "mysterious" . . . None of these images shows the true form of a god, and none can encompass the full richness of his

---

7. Hornung, Erik. Conceptions of God in Ancient Egypt: The One and the Many. 1971, 1996 p.113-114.

nature – hence, the variable iconography of Egyptian gods, which is seldom reduced to a fixed, canonical form. Every image is an imperfect means of making a god visible, characterizing his nature, and distinguishing him from other deities."[8]

Therefore, within a genuine initiatory discipline, it can be seen that these matrices, these 'symbols', function as tangible links to spiritual entities. The essence of the training in the Art itself then acts as a bridge between worlds, with modes of consciousness being the vehicles used to traverse this bridge. Thus, we find the deeper teachings of an esoteric organization are experienced, not taught. They cannot be communicated to others by words alone. It is for this reason that we find varying levels of training within the Art *leading* to initiation.

Still, teachings within a spiritual discipline often form a natural division. Initially, a neophyte in any initiatory organization is introduced to the philosophy through information that can be taught to, and thus, understood by, the reasoning mind. Frequently, modern esoteric orders refer to this stage of training as the 'lesser' training, 'lesser mysteries' or 'outer court' teaching. This 'lesser' level of training is comprised of learning many of the techniques, rites and sacred texts of the organization. These need to be learned by the rational self before one can advance because they serve to form the basis for the development of the individual within the discipline.

However, it is the correct use of this teaching, the correct use of these 'lesser' disciplines that lead to the ability to eventually experience the 'greater' or 'inner' teachings of the system. In a valid initiatory spiritual discipline it is the correct use of the organization's teachings that brings the student to the point where it is possible for their teachers

---

8. Hornung, Erik. *Conceptions of God in Ancient Egypt: The One and the Many.* 1971, 1996 p .124-125.

to evoke an epiphany; a state of sudden spiritual realization. This enables the student to understand the language of the deeper essence contained within the spiritual discipline. It is this understanding, this epiphany, that awakens the ability within the student to directly experience the hidden worlds not normally perceived; in other words, the Geassa.

Having considered this, perhaps we need to ask, where do initiatory spiritual systems come from, and, how valid can esoteric disciplines from ancient cultures be to the aspirant today? These two points are some of the most vocal and repeated criticisms directed toward members of the Art, today. For many contemporary thinkers, the idea of initiation seems archaic, primitive and elitist; reserved only for clubs and college fraternities.

To find the answer to this, we need to look to the Geassa, itself. A genuine spiritual system uses the rite of initiation as a means of transformation of the aspirant's consciousness. As pointed out earlier in the book, change one's state of consciousness to change one's state of being. Yet this is not a temporary change. The process of initiation, when preformed properly, facilitates this change on a deep and permanent level.

Further, a spiritual discipline involving initiation is not something that can be created at the whim of a group of people. Rather, it is the result of years, even generations of steady oral and in many cases, written custom, tradition and practice of the Art. In addition, the repeated use of symbols and the practice of ritual are an essential element. An esoteric discipline, thus, on one level, can be seen as the distilled spiritual wisdom of the culture from which it sprang. Dr. Robert Wang explains:

> "A system, whether cult, religion or meditative program, is an access pattern into the inner worlds, one agreed upon and strengthened by generations of use. It is a path into the unknown, paved with culturally-determined, though universally applicable, symbols. And within any given

school, the symbols may be manipulated and variously applied."[9]

However, the essential beginnings of such a discipline are fairly humble. Initially, when people gather to perform certain actions, think along certain lines and in the process, experience an emotional and spiritual influence associated with the gathering, there is built up, in association with the organization, what may be termed a group matrix. This composite pattern of energy contains the emotional and mental forces directed by the members during these meetings. Over time, this matrix takes on a life of its own, growing stronger with each gathering. If given enough time and energy from the members, this matrix eventually has a much greater power than the sum of the members' minds themselves.

This phenomenon is particularly true of religious organizations and magical Orders. For in these groups, there is the conscious intent on the part of the members to forge links with beings of a more complex order and frequently of different realms. The resulting influx of energy from these other worlds adds to the group pattern, considerably.

While the formation of a single group devoted to esoteric study and ritual practice will, over time, form a group-consciousness - this does *not* in itself constitute a spiritual discipline. Again, a valid initiatory system can only happen over many, many years with the steady passing of rituals and teachings from teacher to student. All the while, the overlooking essence of the group grows stronger, becoming independent and alive. At the same time, beings on other dimensions eventually form links or contacts with the system itself. Then and only then, does the gathering become something akin to an esoteric discipline. For it is through these links to otherworld beings over extended periods of time that esoteric knowledge leading to personal transformation begins to take place.

---

9. Wang, Robert. The Qabalistic Tarot. 1983 p.xvii.

It is important to note that should the group cease to meet, the overseeing matrix of the system tends to become passive and quiescent. Then, the otherworld contacts withdraw. However, should a group once more be formed that uses the same basic rituals, symbols and teachings as the first, then the original group matrix of energy reawakens. The new group, whether wittingly or unwittingly, makes contact with this intelligence. When this happens, this essence begins to work through the members of this new gathering. In this way the discipline is renewed.

But, it is not only the original matrix created by the initial organization that comes back to life. The otherworld beings who were part of the original system also take notice. Given the opportunity, these beings will begin to come through to the new group just as they had for the original. In this way, when one seeks to understand and partake of an ancient spiritual discipline, it may happen that the techniques and the teachings of the same will tend to regenerate intuitively within one's psyche.

Naturally, any impressions that are received need to be checked against the known facts, regarding the tradition. Please understand that it takes self-control, patience and a willingness to do the hard research to check one's personal insights, hunches or predilections against the facts. However, this is absolutely essential. The spiritually naive individual typically over-values their own ideas much to the detriment of their own true growth.

Having said this, I can cite numerous occasions when very clear images regarding the practice of certain aspects of the Art, have occurred. Later, through careful research, these intuitions proved to be highly accurate. It is important to understand, though, that any information received intuitively is, by definition, subjective. That is, until it can be verified through research, it needs to be perceived as potentially partisan or influenced by one's own personal views. While I am convinced that personal spiritual experience is valid, it is all too easy to allow individual and group bias to cloud such experiences.

When this happens, the actual tradition can become corrupted and the group's practices may move away from the true form of the original discipline. It is for this reason that I view personal gnosis as a guide to further research. When, during ritual or meditation, such an experience occurs, it needs to be noted and then researched for objective evidence to support the revelation.

On the other hand, when these arise but the evidence to support them isn't available, one can proceed with caution, using the material on an 'experimental' basis to check its effectiveness and relevance to the overall system. It is in this way that traditions grow and develop.

It is important to note that forging of links to otherworld beings does not in and of itself, create a valid spiritual discipline. I can think of several organizations, today, that have forged links with spirits and entities (some of the entities are of a very questionable nature) which are, in my opinion, not valid esoteric schools. While a portal to other worlds has been opened, the overarching beings involved frequently have their own agendas and purpose, with little concern for the human participants involved, other than to form a means for the entity, or entities to express themselves in the temporal realm.

Those of the Art use initiatory disciplines as a means of opening gateways to other worlds, transforming the consciousness of initiates, forging links with spiritual beings *and* become expressions of the Geassa, itself. In the Art, the natural evolution of the group is to eventually become open to the influence of the Geassa, itself.

This last step, merging with the Geassa, is at once a seemingly simple process of awakening oneself to the forces of nature and being able to listen to and recognizing these forces in all one does. Unfortunately, the more humanity moves away from nature through urbanization, the harder it is for sincerely-minded occultists to make this last critical step. In failing to do so, a group can still manage to open communication and reach teachings and information from otherworld beings but this will be limited to the scope and agenda of those beings. However, if the final step of merging with the Geassa is successfully made and maintained, the discipline now has access to the full spectrum that lies at the root of all that is. This is the heart of the mysteries, the silver cauldron laying deep in Caer Wydyr.

In considering the validity of esoteric disciplines, it needs to be pointed out that any real initiatory practice has both a system for teaching members and a means of interaction among the same. Genuine esoteric systems possess both a pattern and pool of information, wisdom and conduct that all members share in. In this way, any spiritual discipline can be viable providing its teachings carry the initiate through to a point of personal transformation and spiritual awareness.

The value of any occult system lays in its symbolic language, which forms the dynamic center of the discipline. When the symbols and myths, as the living embodiment of the spiritual forces associated within the system, are understood and developed through ritual exercise and meditation, the initiate begins to open to other worlds and dimensions. It is then that they can begin to experience and act as a mediator for those spiritual beings who are linked to the discipline. As Dr. Jan Assmann states, "Ritual repetition - the long term memory of a culture - serves to safeguard the links with another world." He continues, "Ritual regulations are precisely observed to ensure that the connections with that other world remain unbroken."[10]

So, we see that an actual initiatory spiritual discipline will contain a consistent and sacred set of symbols that not only act as a language for the deep mind to communicate and form links with other world beings but also form a means of expression embodying those same other world beings. The discipline will have expressed in ritual, legend

---

10. Assmann, Jan. *The Search for God in Ancient Egypt.* 2001 p.72.

175

or sacred text, and quite likely song, dance and drama, a set of matrices describing important aspects of the philosophy in highly symbolic and evocative terms. A real initiatory, spiritual discipline will have the modes in place through which human participants can draw in and revitalize the essence of the teachings.

Thus much of the training of the initiate consists of learning to identify, interpret and channel the higher forces represented by the symbolic language of the system. One of the hallmarks of a real esoteric school or discipline is that it provides the means for inducing spiritual energies to flow within participants along the circuits outlined by the symbolic language of the organization. And lastly, a valid esoteric discipline will have opened itself to the natural world recognizing, welcoming and embracing the divinity that is manifest, expressed and experienced in all that is the Geassa.

The Woven Thread

"For the serious-minded person who has made up her mind that Witchcraft and the Dianic cult may be the way to help her mind, body and spirit to tread a better path through this incarnation, there is a long, hard period of study necessary. Much of the studying she will do in the form of contemplation and meditation, helped as much as possible by the guru chosen to guide her. All early lessons will deal with the need to guard oneself faithfully against delusions, both self-induced and through association with others . . . No one should persuade you to seek wisdom through the areas of Witchcraft; the decision must always be yours . . . During the time before your initiation, merciless analysis of yourself will go on by your teacher, but mostly through your own assessment of the flaws in your own nature."[11]

---

11. Leek, Sybil. *The Complete Art of Witchcraft.* 1971 p.104-105.

So begins the process each must go through when seeking initiation into the mysteries, for initiation is the thread which binds those of the Art.

To begin to understand initiation itself, it is important to realize that trials and ordeals form the opening back drop to all valid initiation rites, no matter the spiritual system. To quote Migene Gonzalez-Wippler, "every initiation entails a cycle of life and death in a spiritual and mythical sense." She continues, "The initiate's old personality dies during the ritual of initiation and he is born again spiritually after the ordeal".[12] As such valid initiation ceremonies, no matter the culture or spiritual discipline, always involve certain key elements. Dr. Beth Hedva has done a wonderful job of describing five of these fundamental steps:

- Separation - Entry into the sacred through rejection of, or forced isolation from, the status quo of the community.
- Purification - Initiatory ordeals and ritual tests and trails to shock the initiate into a sacred expanded state of consciousness.
- Symbolic death - The conscious and ritual release of personal inhibitions or status quo prohibitions to the sacred expanded state.
- New knowledge - Receiving a spiritual teaching which gives meaning to the initiatory ordeals.
- Rebirth - Integration of the spiritual teaching as it relates to the fulfillment of one's new role and reentry into the community.[13]

In the Art there is also an additional stage not mentioned by Dr. Hedva. Between the stages of 'new knowledge', and

---

12. Gonzalez-Whippler, Migene. *The Complete Book of Spells, Ceremonies and Magic.* 1978 p.49.

13. Hedva, Beth. *Betrayal, Trust, and Forgiveness; A Guide to Emotional Healing and Self-Renewal.* 1992, 2001.

'rebirth', there is a point of transference and merging of energy between the initiator and the individual being initiated. In this setting, the initiator ceases to be an individual. Rather they become a conduit for spiritual intelligence and energy that is brought through in the ritual for the sole purpose of facilitating the transformation of the individual being initiated. This, too, links the new initiate to the tradition itself and those who have gone before. As such, in my experience, initiation brought about through a trained teacher is far more potent than any would-be "self" initiation. In the ceremony itself, this is done through specific ritual actions. In some cases, this involves the placing of hands on specific areas of the body and willing the spiritual energy to pass through the initiate. In other cases, this involves the 'breathing' of energy into specific centers of power in the initiate. This latter gesture is the source of the medieval stories of 'kissing the devil's backside'.

This transformation brought on by the ceremony of initiation frequently brings a period of challenge; usually occurring in the weeks and months following initiation. These almost always involve new and difficult events and hold a distinct purpose for the development of the new initiate. Ceremonial magician Gareth Knight explains:

> "These may be regarded as tests, but in reality are more likely to be a reorientation of the direction of life from what it had previously been assumed to be."

He continues:

> "An initiation is a step towards a clearer realization of reality, which will thus bring about a certain amount of reassessment, often apparently triggered by external events."[14]

---

14. Fortune, Dion & Gareth Knight. *Principles of Hermetic Philosophy.* 1999 p.86-87.

After initiation, one is never the same. The world looks different and the individual seems different to oneself and to others. This ceremony marks a major transition in the evolution of the individual and this transition touches every aspect of one's life. The influx of spiritual energy drawn in through this ceremony is for the sole purpose of awakening the candidate to the true essence of existence. This same energy quite literally transforms the individual, forever. Frequently, the ego has a difficult time adjusting to this awakening. As a result, old impressions and old misconceptions about the self and reality will be challenged and systematically stripped away in order that the individual can grow into the spiritual being that a valid initiation is meant to bring about.

This 'stripping away' is not something that one's initiators or teachers purposely induce. Rather, the process of initiation itself, set up through the energies brought in by the ceremony, create a chain of events which force the individual to reexamine their character, their lifestyle, and the very view they hold of them self. This "reorientation" as Gareth Knight stated can be extremely intense. The period following initiation can be very difficult for some because of the challenges that the spiritual forces throw at them. In reality, these challenges are brought on precisely because one's previous held opinions, beliefs and conditioning simply were not in alignment with spiritual actuality. However, once the individual reconciles these conflicts and comes to an understanding of the sublime meaning that transcends the individual ego, then they progress deeper into the esoteric system in which they were initiated.

Death of the old self, isolation and ordeal that brings about a spiritual transformation, leading in turn to rebirth in renewed forms; this is initiation and it is far more than metaphor or myth. When performed correctly, the energies that are called upon in a true initiation are profound and life-altering. Initiation is a vital part of the Art, opening the doors of the Geassa to those who can make the ascent.

In my early life when I was seeking training and initiation into the mysteries, the following quote from Sybil Leek gave me strength and hope which indeed did blossom into the goal sought:

> "If reason bids you to pursue Witchcraft, even though the way may not seem clear at the time, then you can rest assured that you will be able to pursue it. Someone will come into your life like a guide, taking your hand and leading you along the paths, step by step, until you can be passed on to someone else who will guide you still farther. If you have a deep certainty within you, free from delusions, free from thinking in terms of personal power and willingly to go on into new realms of thought, philosophy, and religion, then your pursuit of spiritual understanding will be easier and you will be accepted wholeheartedly into the strange, mysterious realms of Witchcraft.
>
> Meditate on your awareness, analyze your emotions, your waywardness, your vices and virtues, and then if the idea still pleases you, the spark of the Divine Being within you will lead you to the gates of understanding - where someone will guide you, and see what achievements you have reached in the past and where you are likely to go in the future. First know yourself before you struggle to know others, for the first step into Witchcraft is a selfish one and concerns *you* and no one else. Think well of yourself, but think truly and sincerely. So mote it be ."[15]

15. Leek, Sybil. *The Complete Art of Witchcraft* 1971 p.160.

Chapter Fourteen

✧ THE HOLE IN THE STONE ✧

In the practice of the Art, it is important that the Shaman, Witch or magician understands that tools used in ritual are not symbols 'representing' forces that one wishes to employ. On the contrary, the tools of the Art are the *physical manifestation* of those occult forces. As such, the tools that the Witch uses are extensions of these forces, just as one's hand is an extension of one's physical ability to manipulate the world around oneself. The hand doesn't 'represent' one's will; the hand is the manifestation and means by which one expresses the will. So it is that the tools of the Art express and, thus, are manifestations of the forces. This understanding is critical to the practice of the Art.[16]

As we continue in this study of the Art we will be discussing a number objects used in our formulation of the Geassa. Each has a long history which we will explore through historical record, ancient texts, myth, folklore and practical magical application. These are not 'archetypal images' or mere symbolic representations. They each are the embodiment and expression of the forces which they are part of.

---

16. While we understand that the tools used are manifestations and expressions of the forces involved in this work we do refer to the symbolism contained within the tools themselves. It is important that the student understand that this is not a contradiction of our statement regarding expression and manifestation. Rather the use of terms such as 'symbolic' or 'representative' come more from the limitations of the English language. Again, it is vital that those of the Art understand that each of these items are, in fact, part of the forces involved as opposed to being merely a construct 'representing' those forces. These items are, in essence, the force they evoke.

To understand this, it is best to think in terms of the four worlds or 'modes' found in Hermetics. As noted earlier, these are: conceive, create, form and express. A simple example that ritual magician, Gareth Knight, had used in his writings was to begin with the concept of 'purity'. From here, one could create any number of ideas of how purity could be present. For example, purity could be brought to bear on the creative impulse to clean. This, in turn, would lead to the need to find a form or vehicle through which cleanliness occurs. This would be the step of 'forming'. Finally, this could lead to any number of material objects used in the cleaning process, for example, a broom.

In this example, one can see that the simple broom, ultimately, is an expression of 'purity'. Again, it is vital that the student understand that the broom does not 'represent' purity; rather, it is the manifestation and, thus, an embodiment of purity. They are one in the same.

This is exactly how those of the Art understand the tools, sigils, plants and herbs - in fact all of the physical items used in ritual. They are the actual forces of nature, of the Worlds, manifest in our dimension. This explains why the preparation and handling of the tools are done with such care. They are sacred and powerful; from the simplest amulet to the finest handcrafted wand or statue.

Within this scope of expression, the actual form a tool takes will vary from tradition to tradition, Order to Order, family to family. Those inclined to Hermetic ceremonial practice will have elaborately designed tools rich in imagery and detail. However, in the more rural expressions of the Geassa, the tools tend to be very simple, frequently though not always, unadorned. They could pass as household objects; a simple kitchen or hunting knife, a broom standing in the corner, an old iron cauldron hung near the fireplace, and a plain pewter goblet on the mantle. This was done out of necessity. On their own, each looked like any household item found in anyone's home. In order for the Geassa to survive, those who practiced had to hide their tools in plain sight.

In our system, we have employed both versions. Yet, for us, practice has found that simpler is better. As such, the practical tools we use most frequently are those which tend to be elementary in form. Some of the most powerful of these come directly from nature in to form of wands, stangs, roots, rocks and bone. This, by no means, is a requirement. There is real value in the careful preparation of highly elaborate ritualistic tools. In my time with the Hermetic Order, each item from the ritual robes, the sigils and pentacles, to the sword of power all were carefully crafted and consecrated in accord to the tides of power.

Again though, for the form of the Art which we have found most practical and powerful, our experience leads us toward the basic methods of the rural traditions.[17] In the chapters ahead, we will teach these fundamental principles as manifest in the tools of the Art. We leave it to the sincere student to determine which works better for them.

---

17. There is little doubt that some of this leaning toward rural expressions of the Art stem from previous incarnations, as well as, the influence of Grandma Julie and Sybil Leek early in this life.

Chapter Fifteen

✥ THE BLACK HILT KNIFE ✥

Ritual swords and knives have a long and venerable history in the Art. Some of the earliest references to the blade as a magical tool can be found in the Celtic legends surrounding the Tuatha de Danann. These myths reach back to the oral traditions of the Celtic people. The version that has come down to us through history describes the Tuatha de Danann, or Tribes of the Goddess Danu,[18] as a mythical race of beings who came to Ireland from four different realms: Findias, Gorias, Murias, and Falias.[19] Viewed as Gods, they brought with them four sacred tools; *the Cauldron of Plenty, the Stone of Destiny, the Spear of Victory* and *the Sword of Light*. These were the forerunners of the four major tools of the Western Mysteries: the ritual sword or knife, the chalice, the wand or staff and the pentacle. Nuada, king of the Tuatha, brought *Cliamh Solis, the Sword of Light*, from the realm of Findias.[20] Nuada was seen as a Sun God and the only one who could use the sword. As will be seen, the sword represents the power of the land awakened through the Goddess. Only the king, as Her agent and guardian can wield this. Legend explains that the *Sword of Light* was "invincible . . . from whose stroke no one ever escaped or recovered."[21]

18. Squire, Charles. *Celtic Myth and Legend.* 1975 p.48.

19. *Ibid.,* p.71

20. Fitzpatrick, Jim. *The Book of Conquests.* 1978.

21. Squire, Charles. *Celtic Myth and Legend.* 1975 p.51 & 71.

One of the most telling aspects of this legend reveals the magical nature of the sword. When the Tuatha arrived in Ireland they battled with the Fir Bolg, a race already inhabiting the isle. During the battle of Moytura, the chief Druid of the Fir Bolg, evoked an ancient demon to defeat the Tuatha. Despite their best sorcery, the Tribes of Danu were unable to counter the power of the demon. It was then that Nuada went into a battle frenzy invoking the power of the ancestors and the Sun itself. In this state, he faced the demon alone with his sword, Cliamh Solis. The legend explains that the sword began to glow with power as Nuada drove this into the head of the demon sending it back to the realm from which it had come.[22] This was a major turning point in the battle as the Fir Bolg's magic was broken and the Tuatha were eventually victorious.

All of this gives clues into the nature and properties of the magical sword, as well as the black-handled knife which figures so frequently in traditional Celtic magical lore. Cliamh Solis, with its title of *Sword of Light* and its ability to drive evil back, can easily be seen as the prototypical image and form for the black-handled knife, later given the title of 'Athalme' or as Sybil called it the 'Athalme'. [23] [24]Clearly, Cliamh Solis was the embodiment of the drive, will and power of the Sun God. These motifs repeat themselves in later accounts concerning the Athame and sword.

As a magical instrument, the sword makes its appearance again as the famous *Excalibur* of Arthurian legend. The symbolism contained in this epic tale is too vast a subject for this simple examination here. However, two aspects

22. Fitzpatrick, Jim. *The Book of Conquests*. 1978.

23. There is much controversy over the origins and name of this as a tool of Witchcraft today. This is discussed in detail later in this chapter.

24. Leek, Sybil. *Diary of a Witch*. 1968.
Leek, Sybil. *The Complete Art of Witchcraft*. 1971.

of the legend need to be mentioned, as they shed light on this important tool. In the account, *Excalibur* first appears stuck in a stone that only the rightful king can remove. This harkens back to Celtic and pre-Celtic traditions which identified the king as one with the land. In the ancient Pagan traditions of the British Isles and Europe, the king was seen as representing the land and its health. When the king prospered the land prospered. When the king faltered through sickness or deceit, the land suffered as well.[25] This is why such importance was placed on finding and having the rightful heir to the throne as king. The king had to be of the sacred bloodline, whose roots were long linked through ancient myth and ritual with the land itself.

This concept is a direct link back to the ancient myth of the Tuatha de Danann in which the Lia Fail, *the Stone of Destiny*, which was brought from the realm of Falias, was said to utter a cry when the rightful king touched it.[26] In the Arthurian epic, the sword which imparts kingship, stuck in the stone, takes on new significance when seen in light of these earlier beliefs. Because of this, it now becomes clear that it is the land itself that bestows the power of ruler ship to the king by releasing the sword to him. Yet, it needs to be understood that the land is none other than the Great Earth Mother, the Goddess Herself. It is Her power which manifests in the sword so that the king can rule.

This same theme is repeated later in the myth when, through his own folly, Arthur loses *Excalibur*. In battle with older, powerful forces *Excalibur* is shattered. It is then that the wizard, Merlin, takes Arthur to the Lady of the Lake. She replaces the sword, renewed and potent. Ceremonial magician, Gareth Knight, explains that the lake itself is representative of the astral realm which lies

---

25. Bord, Janet & Colin. *Earth Rites: Fertility Practices in Pre-Industrial Britain*. 1983 p.157-172.

26. Squire, Charles. *Celtic Myth and Legend*. 1975 p.71-72.

behind physical reality. The Lady, he explains, is not only "the mistress of the inner worlds", she also represents the Queen of the faery realm, as well as the Great Goddess of nature Herself. [27]

So we see that in both instances, the power of the sword and, thus, the Athame, ultimately comes from the divine feminine as a gift to the masculine. Perhaps, Dion Fortune described this best in her wonderful paper *The Worship of Isis* when she expressed that the Goddess is the *Awakener* calling to potency that which lays latent -even dormant - until she gives it life through the power of desire. [28]Ms. Fortune explains that it is the male, the God, which lays dormant, until the touch of the Goddess revives the masculine so that He may be effective.[29] The Arthurian myths with the references to the sword of kingship being given not once, but twice, through the power of the Goddess, eloquently portray the esoteric truth which Dion Fortune so beautifully teaches in her writing.

Make no mistake about it, though - the sword and knife are martial tools embodying masculine power. The symbolism and relationship to the phallus are obvious. However, it is only the power of attraction, the desire of the Goddess as the awakener, that gives the blade its potency.

Yet, the sword and knife are so much more. In many respects, they can be seen as the cutting edge and sharp point of the intellect and will of the Witch or magician. Gareth

---

27. Knight, Gareth. *The Secret Tradition in Arthurian Legend.* 1983 p.155.

28. Fortune, Dion. *Aspects of Occultism.* 1983 p.236.

29. For those seeking a deeper understanding of the nature of the relationship between the Goddess as Divine Feminine and the God as Divine Masculine, Dion Fortune's paper 'The Worship of Isis' is an indispensable reference. The concepts which she discusses in this short article form the basis for many of the concepts which Ms. Fortune characterized in her novels *The Sea Priestess* and *Moon Magic*.

Knight even goes so far as to state that the sword (and, thus, the ritual knife by association) represents one's own "inner spiritual dynamic – the spirit striking down through matter, to express the spiritual will".[30]

All of this leads us to the term 'Athame' itself and how this tool came to form such a critical role in the Witch's regalia. A certain amount of controversy surrounds this. The word 'Athame' may very well be a corruption of several different words used in various versions of the medieval grimoire, *The Key of Solomon the King*, also referred to by its Latin name, *Clavicula Salomonis*.[31] These refer to the ritual use of a "knife with a black hilt" used for marking the circle and controlling spirits.[32] One of these gives the name of this knife as an *arclavo* or *arclavum*.[33]

Historian and Professor, Ronald Hutton, suggests that Gerald Gardner, one of the early leaders of the movement which brought Witchcraft as a religion out into the public, was the first to begin using the term 'Athame'. Professor Hutton feels that Gardner arrived at this after reading several different books which reference *The Key of Solomon*. He suggests that one work in particular may have influenced Gardner the most, Grillot de Givry's *Witchcraft, Magic and Alchemy* published in 1931. In this, the black-handled knife from *The Key of Solomon* is referred to as an *Arthame*.[34]

In his book, *The Triumph of the Moon*, Professor Hutton even goes so far as to suggest that the use of the black-handled knife as a primary tool in Witchcraft was essentially an invention of Gerald Gardner with no basis in historical

---

30. Knight, Gareth. *The Secret Tradition in Arthurian Legend*. 1983 p.151.

31. Mathers, S.L. MacGregor. *The Key of Solomon The King (Clavicula Salomonis)*. 1992.

32. *Ibid.*, p.96.

33. British Library, Additional MS 10862, fos. 12v and 13v.

34. Hutton, Ronald. *Triumph of the Moon*. 1999 p.230-232.

fact.[35] Rather, he explains that this was borrowed almost exclusively from *The Key of Solomon*. This is ironic as, in the same dissertation, Professor Hutton goes on to explain that, indeed, the use of a black-handled knife was "a powerful magical weapon in Irish folk tradition, employed to banish malevolent fairies and other unwelcome spirits".[36] This critical, yet often overlooked piece of information is, in my opinion, vital to the discussion of the Athame's relevance for the Witch and one which I will return to shortly.

The actual meaning to the words which may have come to influence the term 'Athame' are obscure. However, Ronald Hutton suggests that the simplest explanation maybe that the word 'Athame' came from the old French verb, *attame*, meaning 'to cut'.[37] Again, I find this ironic as in the same book Professor Hutton had made the statement that the term 'Athame' was an invention of Gardner's drawn from his interest in *The Key of Solomon*. Clearly, the actual origins of this term are nebulous at best.

Still, an important point needs to be discussed here. There is little doubt that Gerald Gardner did draw inspiration from *The Key of Solomon*. Many of the symbols inscribed on the handle of the Gardnerian (the tradition of Wicca developed by Mr. Gardner) Athame are exceptionally close to those found in most versions of *The Key of Solomon* for the markings on the "knife with a black-hilt".[38] Priestess and close associate of Gerald Gardner, Doreen Valiente explains that, in fact, she had firsthand knowledge of Gardner's use of *The Key of Solomon* as a reference, as he sought to piece together the remnants of the Old Religion that had been passed to him by the New Forest coven which had initiated him.[39] Yet, he

---

35. Hutton, Ronald. Triumph of the Moon. 1999 p.230-232.

36. *Ibid.*, p.230.

37. *Ibid.*

38. Farrar, Janet & Stewart. *A Witches Bible Compleat.* 1996 p.253-256.

39. *Ibid.*, p.42.

insisted that the use of a black-handled knife was a part of the original teaching he received when brought into Witchcraft.

Despite Professor Hutton's doubts to this claim, as we saw earlier, his own research found that black-handled knives were an important traditional magical tool in certain folk traditions in the British Isles. Rather, Professor Hutton postulates that Gardner may have known of the traditional Irish use of the "black-handled knife" and that this, too, influenced Gardner to 'invent' his own use of this for contemporary Wicca .[40]

Dr. Hutton's assertions would seem to go almost too far. On the one hand, he claims Gardner drew from medieval grimoires for his source; on the other, the professor claims Gardner had taken this from Irish "folk traditions." One has to ask the Professor, which is it?

As I view it, no matter the term used, it seems entirely plausible that the use of a black-handled ritual knife for magical purposes could have easily survived in the group which Gardner had made contact with in the New Forest. From this, it would have been only natural for Gardner to see the similarity to those listed in the various versions of The Key of Solomon and seek additional information there.

The simple fact is that the use of the black handled knife in Celtic magical practice was widespread. This is evident in the fact that this was referred to in Irish Gaelic as the *Scian Cois Duibhe* 'knife with the black handle'. In song and folktale incidents are told of spirits held at bay through use of this tool. Legend also illustrates the black handled knife as the tool used to draw a protective circle around the wielder of the same, to keep spirits and faeries away. Elisabeth Andrews discusses the Irish legend of Owen Boyle who was pursued by faeries. To protect himself and his new bride, he drew a circle around the two of them using a black-handled

---

40. Hutton, Ronald. *Triumph of the Moon.* 1999 p.230.

knife.[41] Similar magical uses of the black- handled knife can be found in legends from ancient Scotland. There can be little doubt that any surviving circles practicing Celtic Pagan magical folk rites would quite possibly involve the use of this tool.

No matter its origins or the name employed, it is obvious that the function of this implement as a part of the Western Mysteries and Pagan practices remains vital and alive today as the inheritor of the same magical qualities of the swords of legend. Quite clearly the ritual use of knives and swords in Western Paganism is very old, and that their powers were interchangeable between the two. It may be important to note that even *The Key of Solomon* clearly states that the sword and the black-handled knife may be exchanged, both used for the same purpose, and possessing the same attributes.[42]

In our system, the ritual knife employed is almost always black-handled, possessing a double edge. The knife needs to be sharp and functional as a cutting tool. This is opposed to those who may want only a dull edge using this for purely symbolic purposes only. No markings or sigils adorn my own personal knife.

While simple in design, the symbolism embodied in the Athame is rich. The black handle represents the hidden power of life, death and regeneration. In many cultures and magical systems the color black not only represents death, it can also symbolize the fertility of the rich earth which renews and brings forth life.[43] This harkens back to the images of the Arthurian legends with the sword in the stone as well as the sword renewed and given to Arthur by the Lady of the Lake, which were discussed earlier. In both cases, the Goddess provides the raw power through which the blade can become potent and effective.

------

41. Andrews, Elizabeth. *Ulster Folklore*. 1913 p.69.

42. Mathers, S.L. MacGregor. *The Key of Solomon The King* (*Clavicula Salomonis*). 1992 p.x & 96.

43. Wilkinson, Richard H. *Reading Egyptian Art*. 1992.

It is death which gives back to the land, yet it is the land which renews life, giving this to all. So we see the dual yet complementary nature of divinity embodied in this one tool; the blade as the God, the handle as the Goddess.

Looking to the blade itself much can be learned. The dual edge of the blade is a clear reference to the two aspects of the primal God. He is the Lord of Life and the God of Death. This is a reference to the two aspects of the God found in the Oak and Holly kings of Pagan traditions.[44] While being a tool which can kill, the overall form of the blade is very phallic. This shows a deeper meaning of life, regeneration, drive and the ability to make ones will manifest.

In ritual, the black-handled knife has several uses. In many traditions, this is the primary tool used to create the boundary of the sacred space. This is done by focusing the will, envisioning energy flowing through this and forming the boundary itself. So it is with ours in that we use the black-handled knife to demark the first and thus outer circle of the three which we meet in. Keep in mind that this is a martial tool used for defensive purposes. In using this tool for the first of the three circles, this corresponds to the realm of Annwn.

Grandma Julie began all rituals by slapping the flat of the blade against her thigh and then exclaiming:

"Leave thee spirits of evil and darkness for this is place made holy, given over to the Sun, Moon and Stars!"

This harkens back to the consistent use of a black-handled knife in Irish, Welsh and Scottish folklore to banish negativity and evil spirits. This has been an ongoing tradition surviving to this day and undoubtedly lending significant credence to the claim by contemporary Witches that the black-handled knife has been a vital part of the craft for centuries.

---

44. For information on the Oak and Holly Kings please see Farrar, Janet & Stewart. *A Witches Bible Compleat.* 1996.

In our tradition, a simple but effective method for repeatedly energizing the Athame has been handed down. Those who had trained me, I was told, had learned this from their teachers' years before. This technique was called "Sharpening the Blade". On the night of the Full Moon, when the sky is clear, point the tip of the Athame at the Moon. Relax and breathe slowly, deeply and evenly. Then envision the silver-blue energy of the Moon gently flowing down into the tip of the blade. With practice, it is relatively easy to feel the energy flow into the Athame filling this with power.

In this simple, yet vital tool we find such a rich embodiment of the foundations of Western Paganism; the power within the land and gift of the Goddess. This ritual kinfe is the active representation of the masculine force awakened to its true potential by the creative desire of the feminine. This is the God in His ability to both create and destroy. Through death, the land is renewed. The power of the land is returned, fertilized; that life may continue in new and vibrant forms.

The sharp edge and gleaming point is none other than the Witch's own magical desire honed through discipline and creative imagination. This is her will manifesting as the dynamic power of the spirit through which magic is made. This wonderful tool of the Mysteries is one the most potent the Witch can possess.

Chapter Sixteen

✤ DRAIN THE GOBLET DEEP! ✤

The goblet, chalice, grail and ritual cup have long been central to the western mysteries. Their history reaches back to the beginning of written record. Some of the earliest representations of the ritual use of cups and goblets can be found in Ancient Sumerian rites from BCE 4,000. These include rituals of offering to a Goddess and God of vegetation. In these, the participants would hold cups before them in praise of the divine couple.[45]

In Ancient Egypt, cups and chalices held sexual significance as direct references to the intoxicating power of the Goddess Hathor.[46] The pouring of wine and other liquids into the ritual cup, as well as into one's cupped hands were frequently represented in ancient inscriptions. Egyptologists believe that this was symbolic of the sexual act itself. In these depictions wine was seen as the seed of the male as well as the intoxicating state of love and passion that accompanies sexual intercourse.[47] In fact, entire festivals were dedicated to the delirium and ecstasy of intoxication as portrayed in the rites of Hathor. A beautiful inscription from Egypt describes Her festival of inebriation:

45. *Janson's History of Art: The Western Tradition.* 2011 p.21-47.

46. Schumann Antelme, Ruth. *Sacred Sexuality in Ancient Egypt.* 1999 p.122.

47. *Ibid.*, p.125.

"Come, O Golden One, who consumes praise because the food of Her desire is dancing, who shines on the festival at the time of illumination, who is content with the dancing at night. Come! The procession is in the place of inebriation, that hall of traveling through the marshes. The drunken celebrants drum for you during the cool of the night." [48]

In Ancient Egypt, this celebration was a joyous recognition of Hathor as the Goddess of intoxication. While the use of wine was part of the ritual, the sense of drunkenness associated with the festival was also brought on through spiritual devotion, exhilaration, sensuality, joy and dance.[49] It was in this state of ecstasy that the presence of the Goddess was experienced. The cup, goblet and chalice all are symbolic of this receptive and intoxicating state of mind.

Magic cups also form an important part of Celtic practices and myths. This is particularly so in Irish and Scottish traditional lore. Cups thought to bring luck, prosperity, success, as well as "any drink desired" were common in the beliefs of the Celts of the British Isles.[50] The Arthurian quest for the Holy Grail with its mix of pagan Celtic symbolism colored by the overlay of Christian theology is testament to the enduring spiritual nature of the chalice.

In the Art as a whole, the chalice has come to represent the quintessential symbol of the divine feminine. This simple, yet elegant form reveals within its basic shape the transformative and creative powers of the Goddess. In traditional Celtic paganism, the chalice, cup or grail is the very symbol of the Moon and womanhood itself.[51]

In his examination of ancient grail legends, Carl Jones explains that many of the myths which influenced the

---

48. Lesko, Barbara S. *The Great Goddesses of Egypt.* 1999 p.126.

49. *Ibid.*, p.230-231.

50. Spencer, Lewis. *The Magic Arts of Celtic Britain.* 1993 p.37.

51. Carl Jones, 'Legends of the Grail' *Gnostica Magazine* Issue 50, p.21, 1979, Llewellyn Publications, St. Paul, MN.

Arthurian epic repeatedly made reference to the "radiant woman" who resided in the grail castle. In other related legends, a woman *takes the place* of the grail altogether.[52] In these myths, Jones explains, the woman oftentimes appears first as a wise crone who, only after the hero is about to lay with her, does she transform into a beautiful woman. It is through this sexual union that the hero of the legend, representing the God and the Sun, is invigorated and renewed. This is exemplified in the story of Lughaid Laighe. In this Irish legend, the hero prepares to sleep with the wise crone. With this, her transformation into the beautiful Goddess and their subsequent mating brings about his rejuvenation. Through her, he gains the qualities needed to rule as king. After their union she says to the hero:

> "I will tell thee, gentle youth:
> With me sleep the high Kings,
> I, the tall slender maiden
> Am the kingship of Alba and Eriu ."[53]

In his discussion of this legend, Carl Jones equates this encounter with the process that the initiate undergoes in the mysteries. Within many pagan traditions, it is the unveiling of the Goddess, usually in the form of Her priestess or the Mistress, which marks the crucial point in the initiation bringing about the inner transformation intended by the rite itself. As Mr. Jones so beautifully states "she is at once the youthful maiden and the old crone, the land, the earth, and the initiating priestess ."[54]

---

52. Carl Jones, 'Legends of the Grail' *Gnostica Magazine* Issue 50, p.21 1979, Llewellyn Publications, St. Paul, MN.

53. These refer to Scotland and Ireland respectively, but may be seen as representations of the material realm itself.

54. Carl Jones, 'Legends of the Grail' *Gnostica Magazine* Issue 50, p.22 1979, Llewellyn Publications, St. Paul, MN.

This symbolism offers a valuable clue into the meaning of the chalice. For in its simple form, we find a mirror image of itself. The bowl corresponds to the Full Moon and starry heavens above, while the base is the reverse of this resting in the underworld as the Dark Moon. The bowl, with its curved shape and ability to hold the intoxicating and enriching fluids is the womb, beauty, fruition and spiritual awareness. This is the bright Goddess as lover and mother, conceiving and creating.

On the other hand, the base of the chalice is flat on the bottom but curves upward slightly as if emptying its contents. This is the dark moon, the Goddess as the wise and yet sometimes dread death crone of the Celtic underworld and Faery traditions.[55] She is the essence and cause of the transformation that comes through this realm. She is the true power of the grail. For only through the power of the dark Goddess with Her ability to tear down old and outworn modes of thinking and being, can real growth and transformation begin. It is the dark Queen who bears the essence of regeneration within Her, so that life and fulfillment may blossom in time. As such, the root of the power found in the Dark Moon as the base of the chalice, in due course, manifests in the fruitful bowl that is the top of the chalice. It is only because of the transcending power of the underworld that the cycle can continue, emerging as the light of the Full Moon manifesting in Her radiance.

Each is part of the other, yet both aspects represent the Great Sea that is the divine feminine. Dion Fortune expressed this well when she described the Goddess as "the soundless sea" who is at once both "the mother of the gods who made the gods", "the root substance of all existence" and "the giver of form to the formless force whereby it can build." Yet, Ms. Fortune also explained that the Goddess is "the bringer of death" in order that one

---

55. Stewart, R.J. *Earth Light: The Ancient Path to Transformation.* 1992, 1998 p.105-106.

"may be born again to fuller life."[56] In this respect, the Goddess embraces both aspects.

R.J. Stewart elaborates on the dual nature of the Goddess and the connection between both in his writing:

> "In the Underworld tradition there are two aspects of the Goddess that are especially relevant and potent. We might call them She Who Dwells Below, the Goddess of the Underworld, the Dark Mother, and She Who Dwells Above, the universal Goddess of the Stars ."[57]

The mirror image of the divine feminine portrayed so eloquently in the simple form of the chalice expresses both at once the dual nature of the Goddess and yet the enveloping wholeness of her influence. In his important work on Celtic traditional lore, *Earth Light*, R.J. Stewart discusses this connection further:

> "By descending into the Underworld we are paradoxically reaching towards comprehension and experience not only of the Dark Goddess, the Power of Taking and Giving, but also her universal stellar aspect. First the catabolic destroying force that we fear, which is the Dark Goddess, then her universal aspect beyond all concepts of self-hood or false limitation. In this phase we comprehend the Goddess as a conscious power permeating all time, space and energy ."[58]

By reaching toward an experience of the dark Goddess, the Dark Moon that is symbolically tied to the base of the chalice, one opens the door to experience the bright Goddess of the heavens. Only in this way is the chalice filled with the

---

56. Fortune, Dion. *Aspects of Occultism*. 1962 p.34-35.

57. Stewart, R.J. *Earth Light: The Ancient Path to Transformation*. 1992, 1998 p.105-106.

58. *Ibid.*, p.106.

intoxicating wine of ecstasy; only in this way is communion with the divine feminine brought to bear within the spirit of the individual. This is the dual meaning of the chalice. The base of the goblet rests within the underworld as the crone that strips away the ego of materialism, so as to open the individual to the expansive, stellar realm of the bright Goddess symbolized in the bowl at the top of the chalice. In Her bright aspect as the Full Moon, She is Arianrhod, Cerridwen and so many other beautiful representations.

In the Ogdoadic current of the Western Mysteries, the Goddess is likewise seen as dual in nature yet comprising a whole within her. In their treatise on high magic, Melita Denning and Osborne Phillips describe the Great Mother as:

"Beneficent and terrible, she is called 'white rose, with a center of darkness;' neither aspect can be disregarded."

They go on to say:

"In one aspect the Great Mother is giver of mystical enlightenment, divine patroness of many arts, and bestower of all bounties; in the other she presents the allurement of the deeps, she is the fulfiller of the death-wish . . . the bright life giving aspect and the dark binding aspect ."[59]

This dual nature is reflected in Goddess worship the world over; particularly so within the traditions which have come to form the western mysteries. In Egypt, Hathor was seen as the bright Goddess of love, life and intoxicating exuberance. However, Her other aspect was that of Sekhmet, the vicious lioness who protects the Sun God

59. Denning, Melita & Osbourne Phillips. *Mysteria Magica*. 1981, 1986, 2004 p.88.

Ra.[60] We see this, too, in Celtic traditions where there are Goddesses of beauty, love, life and wisdom such as Bridget, Cerridwen, Arianrhod and Danu;[61] and those who preside over war and death as in the three-fold sisterhood of the Badb – Macha, Morrigan and Neman.[62] Some of these Celtic Goddesses embrace both aspects within themselves - particularly Cerridwen and Arianrhod.

For many pagans, the Lady is seen in three phases; maiden, mother and crone. These, too, can be found in this wonderful symbol of the chalice. While the base represents the Dark Moon and the death crone residing deep in the underworld, the stem can easily be seen as the crescent of the waxing Moon on one side. In this form, it corresponds to the maiden. Then, as has been discussed, the bowl relates well to the Full Moon and mother aspect. While on the other side of the chalice the stem once again relates to crescent Moon but, this time, waning.

This latter phase is the crone stage that follows the mother. In this aspect, She is not necessarily the death crone of the Dark Moon, though some traditions do incorporate Her into this phase. Rather, the waning crescent is the experienced woman, past motherhood, but not yet in the transformative stage of the underworld Goddess. Finally, the circle is completed at the base, in the underworld so that transformation and rejuvenation may begin anew.

The opening itself, at the top of the Goblet holds obvious significance - for this is the gate of transition leading from one state of being to another. This is the entrance to the womb, as well as entrance to the tomb because within her, lays transformation. It is precisely because of this that the Goblet filled with a potion of spring water and Vervain acts as a perfect scrying mirror. This is the gateway between Worlds.

---

60. Akhet Hwt-Hrw 'Bezzu Course: Lesson Two' 2005, 2011.

61. Squire, Charles. *Celtic Myth and Legend*. 1975.

62. Fitzpatrick, Jim. *The Book of Conquests*. 1978.

In actual ritual work, most contemporary Wiccan groups will use the chalice almost exclusively for the *Symbolic Great Rite*. This is a beautiful ceremony expressing the union of Goddess and God as emblematic of the dynamic and yet complementary polar forces merging as one. In Traditional Witchcraft, a different set of symbols in relation to the chalice, is used to accomplish the same effect. Near the end of our rituals we pour a combination of red wine and mead into the chalice to draw in and represent the complementary forces that are behind all that is.

As pointed out earlier, wine, particularly red wine, has long been seen as representing the masculine force, the God, his blood and seed. Mead is symbolic of the feminine force and the Goddess. Mead is an alcoholic drink derived from fermented honey. It is essentially a *honey wine*. Traditionally honey has been seen as corresponding to the fluids released by women during sex.[63] This mixture of red and white wines is a wonderful expression of the union of the sexes. The red and white may also be seen as corresponding to the red and white roses of renaissance Alchemical writings which represented the dynamic phase in which transformation begins, the sacred marriage of Sun and Moon.[64]

As alcohol, this mixture relates to the heady ecstasy found in the interplay between the sexes. Together, the wine and mead form the creative substance of the universal and complementary forces within the matrix of the chalice. This is the womb of the Great Mother, and the center from which all originates. In drinking the wine and honey mead potion one partakes of the rich, creative elixir brought to life through the Goddess, both light and dark. This rich intoxication reminds one of the old Italian Strega chant from the *Vangelo: The Gospel of the Witches:*

---

63. Carl Jones, 'Rising Goddess' *Gnostica Magazine* Issue 51, 1979, Llewellyn Publications, St. Paul, MN U.S.A.

64. Hauck, Dennis William. *The Complete Idiot's Guide to Alchemy.* 2008 p.151.

"O Diana! In honor of thee I hold this feast,
Feast and drain the goblet deep!"

Bright Goddess, dark Queen, maiden, mother and crone; the chalice encompasses the extreme poles within the Goddess' nature while expressing the unity and wholeness which is the divine feminine. Both are part of each other. Both express qualities that the other needs. Both represent the transcendent experience the initiate within the western mysteries needs to undergo in order to reach the fullness of her or his potential. Perhaps these few simple lines from the *Consecration of the Grail* ritual found within Ogdoadic ceremonial Orders best describes the essence of the chalice:

"I am a sapphire bowl, dark and immense, that holds in ancient ward the glorious horde of the stars . . . Within me mingle time and eternity . . . I am the Mother of All Living, and I am the Womb of Rebirth."

Chapter Seventeen

❖ THE CAULDRON ❖

Perhaps no other image evokes the immediate sense of magic and Witchcraft in the way that a cloaked figure huddled over a bubbling cauldron does. From the ancient legends of Celtic lore featuring such powerful themes as the cauldrons of Cerridwen, Dagda, the Annwn and more; to the cursing Nganga of African and Santerian tradition; or the Kokumthea of Native American mythology; through thousands of years and across cultures worldwide, the cauldron can easily be seen as a universal symbol representing occult and magical arts.

For early humans, the advent of the cauldron or cooking pot must have had a profound influence on their lives. By placing the raw ingredients of vegetables, roots, herbs, meats and any number of liquids into a pot and setting this over fire, the contents could be transformed into something entirely different, new and unique. Stews, soups, alcohols and medicines all could be made through the careful use of the cauldron. This was a major advancement for tribal communities. Yet the process of exactly how this transformation took place was mysterious, even hidden, while those who tended the cauldron, usually the women of the community, were seen as possessing great knowledge and power. Whereas men usually were the ones hunting or tilling the land, in many cultures the women were the ones caring for the children and tending the cooking fires. So it was that women were frequently the ones who came to learn the secrets of herbs and medicines, and how these could be mixed within the confines of the cauldron.

This association with the feminine is further exemplified by the fact that the cauldron is opaque. Like the womb itself, the transmutation that occurs within the cauldron is hidden, secret and even mysterious. Before long, this simple tool came to be seen as representing the womb itself. Like the cauldron, a woman's womb forms the matrix in which the dynamic elements of nature are transformed into something entirely new and unique. From woman, life is renewed. From the cauldron, nourishment and medicines to sustain life were generated. This correlation between the womb and the cauldron was not lost on our early ancestors. As such, we see that the cauldron has a long association with any number of Goddesses.

In Celtic lore, the primary tool associated with Cerridwen, a legendary Welsh sorceress who over time has been elevated to the status of a Goddess of nature, magic and inspiration is the cauldron. In this, She brewed a potion of wisdom that was distilled down to three precious drops. Legend explains that when the draught was swallowed, one was given universal knowledge. In this myth, the brew is accidentally swallowed by an attendant. Through this, he undergoes a series of transformations into various forms while being pursued by the Goddess. In the end, he is swallowed by Her only to be born as Her son. The legend continues by stating that Cerridwen set the infant a drift in a small boat on the ocean.[65]

This simple legend is filled with rich symbolism indicating the transformative power of the cauldron that ultimately leads to rebirth into new forms of being. At first thought, the idea of the Goddess abandoning her child to the sea would seem inconsistent until one understands that Goddesses worldwide have long been associated with the ocean itself.[66] In giving Her son to the sea, the legend is emphasizing the child's alignment with the divine feminine and the wisdom

65. Spence, Lewis. *The Magic Arts in Celtic Britain*. 1993 p.17.
66. Fortune, Dion. *Aspects of Occultism*. 1962 p.34-35.

that comes through initiation into Her ways. It is interesting that folklorist, Lewis Spence, suggests that a mystery cult may have developed around this Goddess and that the various transformations that Her cauldron legend involves are symbolic of various stages of initiation , concluding that the myth is a metaphor for an actual initiation ritual into the Order of the Goddess.[67]

Other Goddesses, too, were associated with this tool, including Arianrhod, Brigit and more. In Ireland, the cauldron of the Goddess Brigit is said to lay beneath Corghan Hill in Offaly county. Here lays the remains of an extinct volcano that has long been believed to be the entrance to the underworld realm of this Goddess.[68] This is significant for it shows the strong connection to the land, the Goddess and the underworld of transformation, all contained within the symbolism of the cauldron. From this, it isn't hard to see that the cauldron can be viewed as a gateway to the earth mysteries and inner dimensions of reality. This is a theme that reoccurs frequently in myth and one which I will be returning to as we continue this examination of the cauldron.

In Native American lore, the Shawnee speak of a Creator Goddess named Kokumthena, which means *our grandmother.* She is most frequently portrayed as an older woman bent over a cooking pot. Tradition teaches that She can be seen on the night of the Full Moon.[69]

Despite its obvious feminine correspondence, the cauldron has also been long associated with certain male deities as well. One of the most notable of these is the cauldron of Dagda. This was one of the four great treasures brought by the mythical race of the Tuatha de Danann to the shores of Ireland. These people were the Tribes of the Goddess

---

67. Spence, Lewis. *The Magic Arts in Celtic Britain.* 1993 p.158.

68. http://en.wikipedia.org/wiki/Croghan_Hill#cite_note-2   Last accessed 01/25/2012.

69. *Dictionary of Native American Mythology.* 1992 p.160.

Danu. According to legend, the cauldron of Dagda was a kettle from which no one was left wanting.[70] It is significant to note that Dagda is the mate of the great Goddess Danu. As such, it can be argued that the cauldron, while named after Him, was His charge to protect and preserve. He, as the primary mate of Danu, played a vital role as Her partner and defender. So while the cauldron may bear His name in the myths, one could easily see the cauldron itself as a symbol for the regenerative and transformative powers of the Great Goddess of nature.

Another example of a masculine deity's association with the cauldron can be seen in the Gundestrup cauldron discovered in the peat bogs of Denmark in CE 1891. This beautiful Celtic artifact dates back to somewhere between BCE 200 and CE 300. Made of silver, this is richly decorated with scenes depicting a number of human figures, mythological beings as well as animals. One of the scenes shows a clear representation of a Horned God displaying antlers on His head. One can easily surmise that His representation on the inside of the cauldron corresponds to the raw elements of nature itself being placed within, so that the transformative power of the Goddess' womb could revitalize these ingredients bringing forth new life and new forms of being - perhaps not unlike the phallus fertilizing the womb.

The fact that this cauldron is silver links this closely the cauldron of Caer Wydyr, the Full Moon and the bright Goddess of life.

In each of these examples, the cauldron was originally seen as the representation of the creative matrix through which transformation into new and better forms occurs. While its connection with magic and ancient nature centered Pagan religions was always a part of the cauldron's significance, it wasn't until the advent of the dark ages and the onslaught of religious persecution that gripped Europe, that the

---

70. Squire, Charles. *Celtic Myth and Legend.* 1975 p.54.

cauldron became associated almost solely with black magic. With the rise of the Witch hunts, the cauldron soon became a symbol of the dark power of the Witch. From this kettle, the worst fears of a male-dominated Christian religion were thought to brew. Soon, the new religion began to believe that women gathered late at night casting spells, controlling the weather, conjuring demons; blasting crops and more, all while tending the Witch's cauldron.

A woodcut from Olaus Magnus' CE 1555 *Historia de Gentibu Septentrionalibus* depicts the power associated with this tool. In this, a Witch summons a storm that sinks a ship by the emptying of her cauldron into the sea.

Once looked upon as a source of awe, wonder and the very essence of women's ability to create, the cauldron had now become regarded with fear and seen as a quintessential symbol of evil. This same theme appears to be taken up in a German woodcut from CE 1510. We had discussed this engraving earlier in the section discussing the Stang, however, it bears revisiting here as well. In this drawing, a group of witches are casting spells by spooning the contents of their cauldron into the air. Through this, they appear to be evoking a tempest. All around them, a series of Stangs and two pronged pitchforks can be seen. Some of these are lying on the ground while overhead one Witch is shown riding a goat while holding a Stang that has a cauldron resting between its two forks.[71]

Many other engravings from the same period all show similar themes. We find it significant that these two symbols would be repeatedly paired together. As was seen earlier, the Stang is a purely Pagan symbol of great antiquity that corresponds in a large part to the World Tree rising through the various realms recognized in the traditional Celtic magical worldview.[72] These dimensions include the underworld of

---

71. Hans Baldung Grien woodcut from 1510, Germanisches Nationalmuseum, N

 Nuremberg.
72. Gray, William G. *Western Inner Workings*. 1983 p.151-152.

Annwn, the lunar world of the Abred, the sunlit realm of Gwynfyd and the stellar world of Caer Wydyr, the Castle of Glass.[73] This final realm was also known as the Ceugant, a term that is associated with that which is boundless and infinite.[74] The cauldron's long association with the Stang would suggest that this tool also is linked intrinsically with this ancient paradigm of spiritual realms.

A key to understanding the significance of the cauldron and its relationship to the Celtic worlds can be found in the myth, the Spoils of Annwn. We had discussed this legend in relation to the Stang; however, it is important to consider it here in relation to the cauldron. In this legend, a number of knights journey to the underworld to recover the cauldron of regeneration. While residing in the lower realm of Annwn, the cauldron is kept within a series of castles, one of which is the high realm of the Castle of Glass.[75] This would suggest that the journey of regeneration begins in the underworld, yet it is here that access can be granted to all other states of existence.

Like that of Cerridwen, the cauldron of Annwn was known to bestow inspiration and knowledge. Rimmed at the lip with pearls and attended to by nine maidens, the lunar significance is obvious. The venture is met with great hardship and difficulty from which only seven knights return. It may be important to recall that the number seven is frequently equated with the seven celestial bodies that are traditional in the magical arts; Saturn, Jupiter, Mars, Sun, Venus, Mercury and the Moon.[76] It seems likely that these

---

73. The worlds of Annwn, Abred and Gwynfyd are discussed at length by Spenser, Lewis. *The Magic Arts in Celtic Britain.* 1993. Also see our chapter on the Worlds earlier in this text.

74. Spence, Lewis. *The Magic Arts in Celtic Britain.* 1993 p.129.

75. Squire, Charles. *Celtic Myth and Legend.* 1975 p.319-320.

76. An excellent source for understanding traditional correspondences in the magical arts can be found in Skinner, Stephen. *The Complete Magician's Tables.* 2006.

knights are symbolic of the qualities of these orbs. This myth is felt by some scholars to have been a major influence on the later Holy Grail legends.[77]

Beyond its mythological associations, ancient Irish lore uses the symbol of the cauldron to describe different energies within the individual. Known as the Coiri Filiochta, which is Gaelic for *cauldrons of poetry,* this teaching is summarized in the 7th century Irish poem "The Cauldron of Poesy".[78] Said to be located in the body, there are three different cauldrons:

- The cauldron of warming (sometimes known as the cauldron of incubation), located in the groin and abdomen, governing the person's health and basic instincts;
- The cauldron of motion, located in the heart and chest, controlling one's emotional nature;
- The cauldron of knowledge, located in the head, where it collects and engages wisdom for the individual.[79]

The poem itself gives detailed information on the function of these energies within the individual and the ways in which they may be used. The extreme age of the poem (more than 1,400 years old), along with the depth of thought that went into the teaching, shows a rich tradition of esoteric wisdom long overlooked by most scholars today. All too often it is easy for academics to look back at Pagan lore as simply a collection of primitive myths and folk stories with little

---

77. Squire, Charles. *Celtic Myth and Legend.* 1975 p.318-321.

78. Several translations of this poem are available to the reader, some of these include: Henry, P.L., 'The Cauldron of Poesy,' Studia Celtica #14/15, 1979/1980, p.114-128; Breatnach, Liam, 'The Cauldron of Poesy,' Ériu #32, 1981, p.45-93; Matthews, Caitlin and John. *The Encyclopedia of Celtic Wisdom: A Celtic Shaman's Sourcebook.* 1994.

79. Tuathail, Seán Ó. *Foclóir Draíochta – Dictionary of Druidism.* 1993 John Kellnhauser/Cainteanna na Luise.

depth or spiritual insight.[80] However, the few remaining texts from ancient Celtic sources, such as The Cauldron of Poesy, present a different image of a longstanding tradition with deep roots in sacred art and understanding. At the heart of this rests the clear and basic symbol that is the cauldron, the womb of the Great Mother Herself.

In practice, a cauldron that is properly cared for can be invaluable for the brewing of condensers, potions and elixirs. Whether one's cauldron is the traditional iron kettle or a more up to date stainless steel cooking pot, this can and should, be one of the most practical tools available to the magician and Witch.

Beyond its use as a means of brewing, we use the cauldron for the purpose of holding fire when no other means was available. On many occasions, we have used the cauldron or separate *fire pots*, as we have come to call them, to hold cleansing fires set with the sole purpose of burning off negative influences and energies that may be affecting our ritual space, as well as home. As a result, one may wish to have more than one cauldron, each with a different function. One may be used for brewing potions or herbal philters, while another may be used for fire cleansing rites; still another may be used for cooking ritually-charged foods in circle. Witches have always been practical and innovative. The cauldron lends itself to this, particularly well.

Practical magic aside, the cauldron should be a welcome tool in all seasonal rituals, as well. For these, the cauldron can be decorated with the symbols and flora of the festival at hand. If used in outdoor rituals, the cauldron can be

---

80 An example of this can be seen in Charles Squire's description of how the "Gaels and Britons would no doubt accept the purer gospel" of the new religion and abandon the old ways for a "nobler belief and a higher civilization". Such is the common attitude assumed by many regarding the superiority of the religions embodied in the Abrahamic tradition in comparison to the indigenous beliefs of Pagan teaching. Squire, *Charles. Celtic Myth and Legend.* 1975 p.402.

placed directly over a small bonfire and filled with water, liquor and honey; as well as herbs, roots and barks related to the occasion. Each member of the group can then take a portion of the concoction home afterwards, to use for their own purposes.

In her wonderful book "The Complete Art of Witchcraft", Sybil Leek briefly discusses the use of the cauldron in many of the seasonal rites she and her group, observed. Some of these included placing the cauldron in the circle at Spring Equinox as a symbol of regeneration and reincarnation; while at midsummer, she would fill the cauldron with water, adorn this with flowers and plunge the wand into the mixture as a symbolic act of the sexual union. This was done while invoking the Goddess Cerridwen.[81]

At the festival of Imbolc, the group which I first trained with always set a small fire in the cauldron, representing the rebirth of the Sun through the womb of the Goddess. This is a central feature in the ritual, which celebrates the feast of waxing light. If circumstances were such that we couldn't have a large flame in the cauldron, we would set a candle inside as a substitute.

At the Autumnal Equinox, we would set a fire inside the cauldron and burn effigies made of corn and wheat from the previous year, as representations of the sacrifice needed to give thanks for the harvest of the current year. At Beltane and Samhain, one could see the cauldron filled with warmed spiced wines. At Beltane,this can be white wine seasoned with Woodruff. For Samhain, a rich mulled red wine can be warmed in the cauldron as part of the celebration.

It is easy to see that a pattern soon develops over the course of the festival year between the all-consuming desire that cleanses found in fire and the nourishing, even intoxicating, refreshment of liquids prepared in the kettle. Both correspond to vital aspects of the creative matrix of the cauldron as the regenerative womb of the Great

81. Leek, Sybil. *The Complete Art of Witchcraft*. 1971 p.186.

Goddess. Fire and liquid form the interplay of life, death and transformation that this tool so eloquently represents. Sacrifice leads to rebirth. Placing the raw elements of nature into the cauldron (symbolized as the grains, herbs, and liquids gathered in nature) means giving these up to the power of the Goddess. Yet through the mysterious essence of the womb, the heat of the flame without, or within, the cauldron, transforms the ingredients into new and vital forms. Whether these manifest as substances that nourish and delight, or as the raw internal flames that burn away that which is no longer needed in life; the cauldron's power cannot be overstated.

In our own ceremonies, we are careful to always have the cauldron present. Ideally, this would be placed directly over a bonfire; if this isn't available we will set the cauldron either in the center of the circle, to the left side of the altar, or directly in front of the Stang. When near the Stang, this serves as a representation of the Great Goddess's power of regeneration corresponding to the cauldron of inspiration found within the realm of the Annwn. This is largely because the base of the Stang relates closely to the Celtic realm of Annwn. Setting the cauldron here reinforces the ancient connection between our rite and the powerful energies encapsulated in the mythical cauldrons of old.

The tools of traditional Witchcraft are simple items - objects and implements used in life for the natural cultivation of the land, the feeding of the family and defense of the tribe. Whether they be a simple dagger, a two pronged pitchfork, a goblet sitting on the fireplace mantle, or a cauldron hung near the hearth, these and other objects central to the Art, were also a vital part of the everyday living and functioning of the rural family. The simplicity of these tools became all the more imperative once the new religion of the Middle East sought to suppress all indigenous religious practices within Europe and the British Isles. As mentioned before, by necessity the tools of the Witch had to be disguised as household objects hidden in full view.

The tools of Witchcraft are the very tools of life itself. They are tools enabling one to live close to the land, in harmony with the elemental and spiritual forces of nature that form the essence of all that we really are. In an age when the disconnect between much of humanity and the universe around us seems to grow greater day by day, we as the inheritors of the great natural Mystery Traditions, need to embrace the tools of the Old Ways. Simple but elegant in form, each can be a means by which the Mysteries can be reawakened in renewed and vibrant forms, while carrying the spiritual essence offered by the nature religions forward for future generations.

Lastly, we would like to finish this section by quoting from Gemma Gary. She performs a traditional form of Witchcraft which originates in Cornwall, England:

> "A cauldron has its most obvious use as the cooking vessel for magical ointments, or the food for a ritual feast, hung over the 'hood fire' [ritually- charged fire]. In ritual magic, it is a symbolic portal of the Otherworld and a vessel of change; a womb of generation or a tomb of consumption, depending on intent and the phase of the moon. Herbs and magical substances can be cast into a cauldron with smouldering embers, or a small fire kindled within, and the required virtues stirred up with the Pellar's [Witch's] staff, conjuring that which is required into manifestation within the rising smoke issuing forth from the vessel's depths. Visions and spirits can be conjured in this way, to be born forth from the Otherworld during generative workings of the waxing and full moon ."[82]

Indoors, during workings at the hearth, a candle may be burned within the cauldron. Or one may place charcoal

---

82. Gary, Gemma. *Traditional Witchcraft: A Cornish Book of Ways.* 2008 p.62.

smoldering within, burning herbs and resins. Above this, conjurations are made with repetitive stirring gestures. During the waning or dark moon, those things that one wishes removed from one's life can be placed within the cauldron fire, in the form of symbolic items, images, knotted cords or pertinent substances, as the Witch stirs or moves quietly about it in a sinistral, tuathal or widdershins circle, willing the undesired thing to be gone. In seasonal rites, things may be born symbolically forth from the cauldron or sacrificed within; it may also become a vessel for sacred fires of the year.[83]

83. Gary, Gemma. *Traditional Witchcraft: A Cornish Book of Ways.* 2008 p.82-83.

Chapter Eighteen

✤ THE HEARTH ✤
Doorway to the Worlds

Slowly, in voices full and rich, the women in the circle began to chant. At first low, almost in a whisper. Then steadily their voices rose in song, as they wove a pattern of power and tone. *Diana! Diana! Diana!* Over and over they sang the sacred name as we stood before the fireplace in the home of Grandma Julie. I was a young man then, just beginning the journey of a lifetime and was fortunate to have been allowed to train with her. This was despite the fact that hers was a family tradition and I was not a part of the family. It was the late nineteen seventies and membership into a coven was difficult to obtain.

We met through a series of connections brought about by my correspondence with Sybil Leek. Through these connections, I was recommended to her. After much thought on Grandma Julie's part and a series of meetings with her family; she decided to take it upon herself to begin my training. While doing so, she started searching for a suitable group that would best fit my particular needs and skills. I was exceptionally lucky to have had such a wonderful teacher. How accurate her claims of her family's long involvement in Witchcraft were, I really can't say but, that there was power and wisdom in her teachings no one can deny.

Central to this wonderful woman's tradition was the hearth, the meeting place of magic within her family. All of her rituals were performed in a large room before an old fireplace. The hearth was her altar. As she explained, in times of old, it was the hearth that fed the family and kept them warm. It was a symbol of stability and security, as well as the power of the women of the family, for it was they who kept the fire burning. But it was much more. She explained to me that all four elements met in this one place in the home; fire that burned the wood which came from the earth, water which boiled in the cauldron and air that rose as smoke and steam up the chimney. Central to this, was the Witch herself. For she controlled the flame, working in harmony with the four elements, just as spirit acts as the fifth element working in harmony with each of these.

So it was that Julie kept the traditional tools on the hearth; goblet, knife, wand and stone. It was here that she worked candle magic and here that she called on the Gods. Julie was in her fifties at the time and, unknown to me, she was dying of cancer. Yet, she took it upon herself to help me. I was her last student before her passing and I will remember her always for her wisdom, love and kindness. Hers was a hearth tradition, centered in the family with knowledge reaching back generations.

According to Barbara Walker, during the ancient matriarchal periods of humanity "every woman's hearth-fire was her altar." She goes on to state that this was considered the feminine hub of the universe, and the keystone or 'navel' of the temple.[84] She explains that the hearth is strongly tied to such Goddesses as the Roman Goddess, Vesta, as well as with the Saxon Goddess, Ertha or Heartha, the Goddess from whom the name of our planet is derived. This connection to the Mother and center of being is echoed further in the Greek Goddess, Hestia, meaning hearth. She was considered to be one of the oldest matriarchal Goddesses representing the home and center of life. It is no coincidence that the hearth is strongly equated with the nurturing power of the feminine and the Earth itself.[85]

---

84. Walker, Barbara. *The Women's Encyclopedia of Myths and Secrets.* 1983 p.821

85. *Ibid.,* p.400

In traditional Cornish Cunning lore, the hearth is used as the central place of magical practice. Here the Witch's tools are kept. Here, the Cunning Woman works charms and spells. Gemma Gary explains that the hearth is used as a "type of altar" on which magical objects, talismans, etc., are left to "cook". Here, too, food offerings to spirits are made, including the nature elementals of the land and helpful or familiar spirits of the Witch. She states that, frequently, the flames and smoke of the fire are used as an oracle of scrying. Spells will be released through the fire and out through the chimney.[86]

In looking to folklore and ancient traditions, the hearth was always seen as a point of entrance and exit for spirits and other supernatural entities. One is reminded of the accusations from mediaeval records that Witches would anoint themselves with flying ointment and then rise up through the hearth on their brooms and stangs, to attend their meetings. Of course, we need to recall, too, that legend explains that Father Yule or, later, Father Christmas would descend through the chimney to enter the home.

As the meeting place of the four elements, the hearth clearly holds enormous significance for the Art. Beyond being the central altar of the home, the hearth can be a place of entrance to other dimensions. Like the mirror of ceremonial magic, the hearth acts in a similar manner. I would venture to say that the old legends of Witches rising up the chimney are a direct reference to the use of this household center as a type of astral doorway through which one could enter and exit, in trance and ritual. And through this, the use of broom and Stang represent traditional magical images meant to carry one to further levels of awareness.

In the Hermetic order in which I have been trained, we use a series of mental images in much the same way. One in particular that reminds me of this technique, is

86. Gary, Gemma. *Traditional Witchcraft: A Cornish Book of Ways.* 2008 p.62.

the use of an image of an arrow held firmly in the visual imagination to aid in carrying one to the solar realm from the lunar. The broom and Stang were used by Witches, in much the same way.

This was, and is, a classic form of trance work meant to carry one to different realms. It is likely that Family - hearth traditional Witches would gather in the main room of the house. As the ritual would progress, certain members would be anointed with ointment and then enter trance, in order to travel to the various realms to gain knowledge, which would be brought back.

Communion with the Gods would occur on these excursions, as well as, exchanges with other Witches and spirits. There can be little doubt that it was from these astral ventures that the idea that Witches could actually fly, came. Again, one needs to be reminded that actual traditional Witches used those items that were readily available to them and easily disguised, by being placed in open sight. The hearth is one such vital link in the tradition of Witchcraft.

Gemma Gary confirms this practice when she discusses the use of the hearth and chimney. She explains that not only would the spell be sent via the chimney (with a point being to be aware of the direction the wind would carry it), she goes on to discuss the practice of the Witch traveling in spirit, up through the chimney in the form of an animal, to complete the task at hand.[87]

For the contemporary Witch, an actual working hearth may be a luxury. However, if one has access to one, it can be a powerful connection to this ancient tradition. In the absence of an actual hearth, wood stoves can serve in their place. For those who lack both, the cauldron set with fire within can act in ritual in a similar fashion. We are fortunate that, living in New England, both an actual hearth and wood stoves are readily available to us.

---

87. Gary, Gemma. *Traditional Witchcraft: A Cornish Book of Ways.* 2008 p.63.

Chapter Nineteen

✤ THE WITCH'S STEED ✤

For centuries, the broom has been the single item most commonly associated with European and American Colonial Witchcraft. In popular culture, no depiction of a Witch is complete without a besom being present. Yet where does this image originate from and how did it become associated with those of the Art?

In previous chapters, I had alluded to the broom, explaining that it was one of the tools "hidden in plain sight". The magical staff wrapped at the base with twigs, disguised as a household cleaning item is probably the most obvious explanation of the origins for the Witch's broom. Yet, there is much more involved in the inherent symbolism this simple object contains.

For those of the Art, the broom is, primarily, a feminine tool. For while the shaft is phallic in form, it is the bush of straw or twigs at the end into which the shaft is plunged, that gives the broom its purpose. This is clearly an overt reference to sexuality. Grandma Julie explained that, traditionally, the besom *or* a smooth river stone were often a young woman's introduction to sexuality in order, to use Julie's words, that "no man could own her."

Old slang from the 18th and 19th centuries in England refer to a man's penis as a "broom handle" or, conversely a broom handle was thought of as an artificial 'member'. While the same slang referred to a woman's vagina as the "broom". To have a "brush" in this context was to have intercourse. It was common to refer to a woman who was romantically active as a "besom." In some traditional

Witchcraft circles, to "ride the broom" was to have ritual intercourse – perform sex magic.[88]

The meaning, though, is deeper here than just human sexuality. The besom represents fertility, new growth and pleasure. It can sweep clean - clearing the way for new opportunities, as well as sweep in positive energies. Thus, it is a can be used to sweep negative influences away from an area, or conversely, it is used to bring positive influences to an area. A common curse was to use the broom to sweep evil spirits and influences away from oneself and toward the person being hexed.

The old ritual of riding the besom at night in the fields to promote the future prosperity of the crops comes to mind. Passion, desire, lust - all are reflections of the power of nature that now comes to bear on bringing what one desires. Too, this was almost certainly a reference to the ancient custom of making love in the fields to promote fertility of the land.

The custom of couples "Jumping the Broom" to signify marriage is very old. In this, one is reminded of the Celtic legend of the Goddess Arianrhod stepping over Her wand, only to immediately give birth. Again, the theme of sexuality and fertility comes through.

Gemma Gary notes that the broom is emblematic of the horse and used as a vehicle for traversing worlds. It is strongly related to various Goddesses, in part because of this association with horses:

> "The traditional feminine broom becomes the steed and vehicle of fiery sexual force and spirit flight between the worlds, and thus the 'bridge' in and out, of the witch's circle."[89]

---

88. Illes, Judika. Encyclopedia of Witchcraft. 2005 p.686.

89. Gary, Gemma. *Traditional Witchcraft: A Cornish Book of Ways.* 2008 p.56.

Essentially, made of woods corresponding to the feminine force; this acts to draw the vital power, the dragon or serpent power of nature, so that this may be directed by the Witch. Gemma Gary explains that the besom represents the entirety of the Goddess, both bright and dark.

Traditional sources explain that the broom is normally made from three different types of wood, though the types can often vary from group to group.[90] Most sources indicate that the shaft is normally made of Ash. While the brush should be of Birch twigs. These can be lashed to the shaft with Willow. It is important *not* to lash the Birch to the handle with metal.

Ash was selected for its protective powers and for its overall magical influence. Birch relates to the Moon and the Great Goddesses of nature, while Willow is used "in honor of Hecate" a lunar Goddess of magic. Of course, Willow relates directly to the "Willow Path" of Witchcraft.

As a tool that incorporates a shaft, this is strongly related to representations of the tree rising through the worlds. The broom is used to travel between the worlds, representing transition from one phase or plane, to another. The broom is also used in ritual to aid in the *exchange between* worlds.

The broom frequently figures in ritual dances meant to induce heighten states of awareness. In Reginald Scot's "Discoverie of Witchcraft" from CE 1584, he states that the Witches would sing and dance while carrying brooms, often holding them aloft. It has been suggested by many that the image of the Witch riding her broom may stem from such dances.[91] In these, it has been suggested that herbal ointments meant to induce trance states, i.e. flying

---

90 Sybil Leek explains that her group would often tie Heather to the staff to form the brush of the besom (see *The Complete Art of Witchcraft*).

91. See the chapter 'The Tower and the Maze' for more information on the Besom and Stang in ritual use including the rite of 'Riding the Mare' or 'Riding the Hag'.

ointments, were smeared on the Witch and on the shaft of the broom. In this way, the hallucinogenic ingredients of the potion would be introduced into the blood stream when the broom was 'ridden'.

Yet, as insinuated above, the besom can also be used to banish, sweeping negative influences away and out of an area. Perhaps, it was partly for this reason that in ancient Greece the broom was the emblem professional midwives used to advertise their service. For they not only delivered the baby, they also were called on to protect the infant and mother, drive evil spirits away and bring blessings to the new child.

In a similar fashion, many in the Art will begin with the sweeping of the area. This ritualistic action was used in the temples of Ancient Egypt at the start of each ceremony. This is for practical reasons, as well. Sybil explains that for outdoor rituals her meetings always began with this ritual act in part to clear any debris and animal droppings from the site.

The broom's use goes much further in ritual, though. It is frequently laid at the entrance of the circle, after this has been constructed. This represents the point of transition between worlds. This harkens to the ancient custom of laying the broom across the threshold of the home to keep enemies, or unwanted spirits and ghosts, away.

Some forms of the Art will place the besom and the ritual sword cross ways at the entrance of the circle. In doing so, this forms a gate over which the members must step. This act represents the transition from mundane existence to the other, ethereal worlds and states of being.

In ritual, we will frequently place the besom at the edge of the circle in the area corresponding to the season or the Moon, which we are celebrating. In this respect, the purpose is to aid in drawing the forces of the season into the ritual setting. Almost as if one were putting pressure on that point of power in the ritual, drawing attention to the energies of the season. Many of the Art will use the broom's brush to gather and hold in smoke, capturing the essence of the power raised. This is then used to sweep this influence through the circle or the area.

Again, this is one of the most practical tools of the Art holding deep meaning and yet remaining hidden in front of those who can't see.

A Broom Spell to Remove Unwanted People
In a separate room or area point the handle of a broom at the unwanted person and chant:

"Get ye out beyond my door.
For I am weary to the core!"

If the person is just visiting they will leave within the half hour. Having said this, I have used the spell to remove unwanted neighbors, causing them to move within the month.

Chapter Twenty

✤ THE FE OF ARIANRHOD ✤

For the Celts, the Wand was one of the quintessential tools of the magical arts. These were known as a Fe; the same word used to describe states of spiritual ecstasy, trance, prophetic vision and enchantment. It derives from the same source that the words faery or fairy come from. To be 'fairy struck' was a term used to signify becoming enchanted. The Wand was always seen as a primary tool through which this was brought about. But Wands and staves have been part of magical and religious practices, the world over.

Distinctly phallic in form, the Fe or Wand is a tool embodying the creative drive toward life. But it is much more. In our system, the Fe is the manifestation of the art of fascination, desire and compulsion.[92] It is used to stir the forces of the astral, invoking or calling these to the work at hand. As such, it is an excellent tool to be used in all rites designed to manipulate energies within the Annwn and the Abred. As will be seen, when we discuss the working space of the Art, the Fe is used to energize and designate the threshold between the Abred and the Gwynfyd. Thus, as a tool representing transition into the spiritual realm of Gwynfyd, it retains unique powers over the realms leading to this.

We call this tool the 'Fe of Arianrhod', in part, due to the Welsh legend in which the Goddess steps over a Fe,

---

92. The Art of Fascination is an integral practice in Witchcraft. This will be discussed further in our upcoming work 'The Art'.

giving birth to Her two sons immediately, afterward. This is almost certainly a reference to creative masculine force joined with the divine feminine to produce life. This legend is reminiscent of the ancient custom of couples stepping over a broom to ensure fertility. Yet, there is much more involved in this simple legend. This relates directly to the creative and dynamic polar forces which make up all that is. Embodied in male and female symbology, these forces merge as one in the legend. It seems highly likely that the legend, itself, may be a representation of ritual intercourse. These forms of fertility rites have formed an important part of the Shamanic Tradition in cultures across Europe, performed both in actuality and (more frequently), symbolically.

As for the construction of the Fe, this can vary, based on the purpose of the specific Fe. Some in the Arts will have several different Wands for different functions. I've seen healing Wands, Wands of evocation, Wands of necromancy, Wands of prosperity, etc. For our part, while we, too, have different Wands for different purposes, in general, we have one single Fe which is used in most rites.

The Fe we use most is essentially designed to be used in most rites in which the forces are being drawn in and directed into spells. In addition, this Fe is used for the evocation of spirits and otherworld entities residing within the Annwn or Abred, for infusing energy and life into potions; bestowing good fortune on people, homes and animals; as well as the creation of the link with the Gwynfyd. In each case, the Fe acts as a conduit - moving energy from one state of existence to another, just as the phallus moves seed into the womb so that She can create. The phallus itself doesn't create. However, it does carry the essence through which manifestation can come to fruition in the female. Thus, as already noted, the use of the Fe is distinctly sexual in nature, taking the will and desire of the Witch, Shaman or magician and projecting this in a moment of passion, so that the work at hand can occur.

The Fe can be made of any number of woods - each has its own use. The following is a list of some of the more traditional woods used for Wands and their inherent traits:

- Ash wood has strong associations with healing, regeneration, workings with spirits, and the opening of pathways between the realms. It is excellent for dispelling negativity, dispersing curses, driving evil away and setting protective boundaries.
- Generally, Fruit trees and Apple wood, in particular, make for excellent Wands. In Celtic myth, the Apple is emblematic of the paradise realm of Avalon, meaning "Apple Land." Irish legend tells of the "silver bough" which is used to open the doorway between worlds.[93] This "silver bough" is none other than a Fe cut from an Apple Tree. Thus, the Apple wood wand is excellent for invocation, evocation, transition between worlds, spirit communication, and communion with the Gods. Apple wood is very traditional for wands meant to draw on and come closer to, the power of the Goddess. It is useful in bringing love, happiness, prosperity and fertility.
- Birch wood is excellent for Wands tied to lunar workings. Wands of Birch are powerful for the promotion of fertility, new life, and growth. It is also used for wands tied to invocation of lunar influences, including any of the Great Goddesses tied to this orb.
- Beech is associated with knowledge. As such, wands and staffs made from this are useful for divination, increasing wisdom and uncovering secret information.
- Blackthorn Wands are powerful when used in cursing or 'blasting', defensive magic and setting boundaries. Blackthorn also relates strongly to death.

---

93. Spence, Lewis. *The Magic Arts in Celtic Britain*. 1993 p.28-29.

- Box wood is highly toxic and as such should be used with care. Wands made from Box wood traditionally have been used to call on the guides and spirits of those of the Art.
- Elder wood is excellent for spirit evocation, calling on the Sidhe, as well as protective rites and healing. Permission should always be asked of the Sidhe – Faery before cutting this. Elder Wood holds a soft pulp inside that can be removed. Once hallow, we fill this with dried Vervain and seal the ends with wax.
- Hawthorn is strongly related to season of Beltane. It aids in spirit communication, fertility and abundance. While excellent for a Fe, it is not recommended for use as a walking staff. If used as such, problems on journeys can accompany one.
- Hazel wood is excellent for Wands used in divination.
- Hornbeam is known for its ability to bestow strength and fortitude, as well as steadfastness. This tree is strongly related to the Faery traditions. As such, permission should always be asked before taking any of this wood.
- Oak is very traditional for the Fe, carrying with it strength, power, wisdom, virility and abundance. This is an excellent wood for a 'general purpose' Wand.[94]
- Pine wood Wands carry traits aiding in prosperity, healing, wisdom, protection and the increase of power.
- Poplar wands are best used in protection magic as well as in communicating with other world entities.
- Rowan wood makes for Wands that conjure spirits and visions. They are used to lift curses and protect from evil.
- Willow is strongly related to the Moon. Wands

---

94. Tradition teaches that one of the most powerful Fe's come from the wood of a 'blasted Oak', that is an Oak that has been struck by lightning.

made of this wood aid in fertility, healing, love and intuition. Willow is also excellent for wands made to communicate with otherworld entities as well as the dead.

- Yew is another very traditional wood used for the Fe. This is used in rites of evocation of the dead. Rites of transformation, renewal and wisdom.

It is best if the Fe is cut from a live tree during the Waxing Moon, in the spring or summer months, when the energies of the tree are at their peak. The Fe itself should be, approximately, the same circumference as one's middle finger.[95] In addition, this will need to be the length of one's forearm, measuring from the inside of the elbow to the tip of the middle finger. When cutting this, it is wise to speak to the tree, explaining the reason you are asking for this gift, and to *always* leave an offering of some kind to the tree and the spirits of the land that protect the tree. This can be a food offering and some red wine.

Once you have returned to your working space, whether this be a circle, your hearth or a room dedicated to ritual work, you will need to strip the bark, and then carve the tip into the general rounded form of a phallus head. This does not need to be excessively graphic. Rather, it should have the general suggestion of the form without necessarily being too overt. Once dry and sanded, one may inscribe or paint the sigils related to the function of the Fe.[96] The inclusion of these characters

---

95. Some authorities state that the Wand should be no more than 'one years growth' and 'cut with a single stroke of a knife'. We have found that in practice this is impractical. A Wand that is of one year's growth is very small indeed. Further, many of the woods used simply are too durable to be cut with a single stroke.

96. Frequently we will add a small amount of powdered Vervain to paint that we use on ritual equipment. This adds a tremendous amount of inherent power to the operation

are meant to draw on the energies of the realms desired, enabling them to manifest in our dimension. As such, a properly prepared Fe is capable of channeling these energies as needed.

The tip of the rounded end of the Fe will then need to be hollowed out with a small hole. In this, one places a small piece of white linen or cotton that has received a few drops of one's blood. To this, one may also add a drop or two of their own sexual essence (whether male or female depending on the gender of the practitioner).[97] While this isn't essential, it does provide an additional dimension of power and personal will to the Fe. Once filled, the hole is then sealed with wax.[98]

In some forms of traditional Witchcraft, a lodestone is inserted into the hollowed Fe before it is sealed. This, of course, is then used to draw forces to one.

Despite its obvious phallic representation, the Fe is used by both men and women members of the Art, just as the Goblet and Cauldron are used by both. In the case of the Fe, this represents the magician's or Witch's will. It is her power to arouse, fascinate (in the traditional Witch's sense of the word) and direct energy. It is the desire and passion of the Witch magnified and pointed singly toward a specific goal, that is being used here. As such, to use the Fe successfully requires both intense drive and the discipline to focus this. The use of the Fe is at once an act of sheer joy and pleasure and yet the single focus of energy, culminating

---

97. Despite the obvious masculine character of the Wand, a female Witch, magician or Shaman can include her own fluids for these will embody her will and form that connection between her and the Fe.

98. As a final touch to the Fe one may stain this with one's own Fluid Condenser described further in this series. While this, too, isn't essential it will add a tremendous amount of power to the Fe. Because the Condenser is made individual to the Witch, its inclusion as a coating and dye will serve to solidify the Fe's link to the Witch. Thus, it becomes theirs only, serving that person alone.

in the powerful release of energy in one moment of intense passion, so that the work at hand can come into manifestation. So, while to the onlooker the use of the Fe may appear as one is simply 'waving a magic Wand', the reality is that a tremendous amount of inner drive, desire and focus is occurring in order to manifest the goal.

Julie, as well as other teachers of the Art whom I have studied with, frequently pointed out to me repeatedly, the practice of magic is best understood through sexuality.[99] That is the intense interplay of dynamic, complementary opposites merging in passion.

Thus, the use of the Fe is best understood in these terms. In the sexual act, all of one's desire, passion and will is focused in the moment on that one single function. During sex, there is no past or future, there is only the present. Seldom is this seen as work. Rather, it is a joyous act of pleasure that reaches a climax of ecstatic release. This, then, is a magical act. In the same vein, a ritual act of magic should hold this same focus, desire, joy and release. There really is no difference.

---

99. Sybil Leek, writing in the late 1960s and early 1970s, was always careful to distance her teaching on the Art from the tendency to think of Witchcraft as an excuse for 'free love' which was a common theme in the media, then. Nevertheless, she consistently reaffirmed that Witchcraft is a philosophy based on nature, fertility and sexuality.

Chapter Twenty One

❖ BONE, STONE, WIND & FIRE ❖

The tools we have examined so far form the foundation of the Art as we practice it. Yet, there are other items we use, many of which come directly from nature, itself. These are just as vital to practical magic. As has been stated repeatedly in this work, there is power in the land, in all of nature; the timeless essence that is the Geassa itself. It is this energy, this all pervasive consciousness resting just below the surface of most people's awareness, which comprises the forces which we work with. This is the Willow Path: the path of the Art. Traditional Shamanic practice has the ability to tap into, understand and channel these energies to achieve one's goal. As a part of nature we, too, become aware of items of power around us.

Bone

In the Art, natural bone forms a link between worlds perhaps better than almost any other material. Whether it be antler, tooth, or actual bone, this is the remains of the living transitioning from one stage of existence to another. As such, bone can be used to represent death, regeneration, and rejuvenation; the wisdom of nature and of the ancients. Links to the ancestors through which the tradition flows, can be formed through the use of bone. It is used in the calling of spirits and assisting with sending the fetch. Except on rare occasions, bone is present on the Hearthstone during all rituals as it helps make the connection between worlds.

Finding the right bone for ritual use can be a challenge. This should be something that comes to one, as opposed to taking this from cooked food. In our experience, the most powerful items are those found in nature. In our rituals, we currently use a stag's antler, as well as an old bear bone found near our stone circle atop the mountain in New Hampshire, where we practice. The bear bone had been gnawed on by scavengers, its marrow gone. Yet, there is a strength to this piece and with its center hollowed by time, it makes a perfect vehicle to call other world beings in our rites.

Stone

In the Art, the use of stone holds enormous power. Stone represents the manifestation and culmination of the forces of nature coalescing into a single mass. A number of stones, gems and minerals hold specific qualities that are of value to those of the Art. We will be discussing the specifics of these further in this series. For our purposes here, there are four different 'types' of stones that hold power for the Witch and have direct links to the tradition.

The first of these to consider is the 'holy stone' or, as some call them, 'hag stones'. In our experience, unless one lives near the ocean, these are exceptionally rare. The holy stone is any stone in which a natural hole is formed through it. To find one has always been considered extremely lucky and it is believed that the Goddess favors those who do. The obvious symbolism is that of the vagina, as passage from one state of being to another. As such, it is one of the quintessential representations of the divine feminine found in nature.[100]

An old Strega invocation documented in Charles Leland's "Aradia, the Gospel of the Witches" was said,when finding a holy stone:

---

100. Another item found in nature that is strongly associated with the divine feminine are cowrie shells. With their clear resemblance to the vagina this simple shell has been used for thousands of years around the world to represent Her.

"I have found a holy-stone upon the ground.
O Fate! I thank thee for the happy find,
Also the spirit upon this road
Hath given it to me;
And may it prove to be for my true good
And my good fortune!"

In practice, the invocation may, or may not, be used. Rather, the reality is that this is a tremendous gift which has several uses.

In ritual, one will pass small items or pour fluids through this to 'give them life' - thus energizing them. Potions, oils, philters and tinctures - all can be 'charged' in this manner. Too, incantations and spells spoken through the opening will have power, causing one's will to be 'born' and begin to come to fruition. Naturally, this technique will be used for positive acts of magic meant to promote health, life, love, prosperity, as well as spiritual fulfillment. During the Full Moon, it is common to gaze at the silver orb through the opening while meditating on Her beauty and invoking Her to the rite. For me, this is one of my most prized possessions, keeping it close at all times.

Traditional cord magic will frequently involve passing the cord through the hole in the stone, giving birth to the energies being bound with the cord. Knots are then tied in the cord representing the intent of the Witch for what she is bringing into the world.

As amulets, they can be worn with cord strung through the hole. Many people will string them on knotted cord, often times with keys (particularly old skeleton keys) and hang these near doorways for protection and to attract luck.

An old custom holds that one can take a holed stone into the forest. Holding this out in front of one and looking through the hole, walk in a circle three times tuathal (widdershins). While doing this, relax your mind and open yourself to the energies and forces in nature. Tradition states that doing this simple ritual will help draw nature spirits and otherworld beings to one. In many cases, these may make their presence known, by appearing to the Witch.

As with shamanic traditions the world over, quartz crystals also are important to our system of magic. These minerals are alive with power, gathering in the energy of nature, concentrating this and allowing it to transition from one state to another at the will of the Witch or magician. It is for this reason that 'seeing' stones were often made from quartz.[101] Many will place a quartz crystal on or near the Hearthstone to concentrate the power of ritual, directing this toward the work at hand.[102] We regard this mineral as being linked directly to lunar forces, whether clear, white or colored. As such, it is excellent for use at the Full Moon.

A third stone that has held tremendous importance in this system is Granite. This igneous rock is at once dense, solid and heavy and yet holds an inner fire and energy that the Witch uses with care. It holds high quantities of Quartz, thus, not only possessing its own force of inherent passion but also drawing on the power of the Moon. It is for this reason that many Witches prefer to use this stone as the material to set up their Hearth or altar.

In addition to these, the lodestone – natural magnetite – has a long history of involvement in the Art. This is used in spells meant to attract what one desires. In practice these have proven to be highly effective. We have used

---

101. However, because of the enormous cost involved in purchasing an actual crystal ball, these were very rare items for common village Witches. However, a quartz crystal not formed into a ball will work well. In addition, other items were and are available to the Witch for the purpose of scrying, which will be discussed in our up-coming work 'The Art'.

102. Quartz has long been a part of native shamanic traditions of both North and South America in a similar manner as described above. In Central America the symbolism of the human skull was combined with the power of this mineral. In fact, several examples of 'crystal skulls' from this culture exist. One can see the uses of such a tool as an oracle.

these in prosperity spells, wrapping a lodestone in green cloth with a High John root and placing this in the highest portion of the home. The lodestone could be similarly employed with other types of enchantments.

Stone of Destiny
In addition to the 'holy stone' or 'hag stone', many in the practice will have a representation of the Stone of Fal on the hearth. This may take the form of the pentacle engraved into metal or wood. Others may prefer to choose an actual stone in nature which holds power and meaning. In such cases, one will want this to be relatively flat. On this one may paint or carve the Witch's Foot, or as we prefer, mark the triple Celtic spiral on this. In any case, this serves to represent the divine manifest, and the ability of the magician or Witch to bring her will to bear fruit in the mundane world.

Wind
One of the oldest, most universally used tools in the Art is the Wind Roar. While it is nothing more than a flat, smooth, oblong piece of wood tied to the end of string or twine, the effect when used can be powerful. This is used by twirling it overhead while it cuts through the air emitting a fluttering roar. It can be quite eerie in its tone as the Witch or magician uses this to call spirits and otherworld beings to the working space.

Fire
Closely allied with the Roarer, is the Bramble Switch. For this, one gathers thirteen branches from a blackberry or raspberry bush. These are cut and left to dry completely. Then they are tied together at the base to form a handle. The other end of the switch is ignited, allowing the ends to smoke. This is then waved around the area, the smoke warding off evil while drawing in positive spirits, forces and otherworld beings. This can be very effective, although one should be careful as the embers on the ends of the stalks tend to drop off easily.

Fire is also used extensively in the Art to cleanse objects, areas and people. For this, one can build a small bonfire if working outdoors. The fire should be made of natural woods gathered from the local area. Pine is particularly good as it burns easily and is used extensively for purification.

Indoors, we will fill a layer of sand in the bottom of our cauldron. We then set a smaller cast iron cauldron inside the larger one, atop the sand. In this smaller cauldron, we will pour a layer of salt. We then cover this with just enough rubbing alcohol to moisten the salt. To this, we will often times add herbs such as silver sage and vervain. We then set this alight. In practice, be very careful as it takes very little alcohol to create a nice flame. Too much and you can have a dangerous situation. To help avoid any mishaps, we keep the cauldron's lid nearby to cover the cauldron should the fire become too large.

We call this the "Fire Pot". It is used frequently in cleansing rites. For this, we will let it burn out, to clear the space of negative forces. We will also use this to cleanse objects by passing these through the flames. During many of the 'Fire Festivals' as discussed in the chapter on Sun Tides, we will set up a fire pot in the center of the working space. It is common for the more agile members of the group to jump over this during the celebrations.

The Spirit Gad

In traditional forms of the Art, we find the use of the Gad or whip. This is usually made from the branch of a Rowan tree or from Blackthorn. In many cases, to the end of this, horse hair, sisal, or leather thongs will be attached, although this is not always the case. There are some traditions which will make this by tying twigs and brambles together. Forms of the Gad have been used throughout folk traditions in Great Britain for centuries, primarily to gently whip a person, animal or object in order to drive out any evil spirit or curse that may be present.[103] [104] In some forms of the Art, it is part of the initiation rites where in the candidate is lightly struck with it to help purify them as they enter their new life as a Witch.[105] Beyond these uses it can function as a means to bring lesser spirits and elementals under one's control.

When the Gad is made from Blackthorn this is also frequently used as a "Blasting Rod" gathering the energy that it has banished, storing this within itself. The Witch is then able to direct this through the handle to curse "blast" those whom she may feel deserve this.

The Spirit Hook
This is a wooden branch that has been carved with a hook on the end. It is important that where the shaft and hook meet a point is formed. The Spirit Hook is used to literally pull or "hook" the energies, spirits or forces to one. In this way the Witch may use the hook to pull elemental energies from the appropriate direction. It can be used to pull the attention of one desired by directing this toward the place the person lives. Once the energies have been gathered they can then be directed by willing these through the shaft of the Hook through the point at the end.

These are both very old tools of traditional European folk magic. I find this interesting as they seem to be vaguely reminiscent of the crook and flail that forms such an important part of the Egyptian Osirian Mysteries. This is yet another example of the Geassa finding expression in different cultures and across vast regions both in time and locale. The similarities are too striking to be ignored.

103. Hartley, Marie and Joan Ingilby. *Life and Tradition in The Moorlands of North-East Yorkshire*. 1990.123

104. Gary, Gemma. *Traditional Witchcraft: A Cornish Book of Ways*. 2008 p.80 and photo insert. Also, Howard, Michael. *Liber Nox*. 2014 p.36.

105. Leek, Sybil. *The Complete Art of Witchcraft*. 1971.

Chapter Twenty Two

✤ THE APPAREL OF THE ART ✤

The horizon dwellers see me as the sole one with the
secret seal.
I don the raiment,
I wear the robe,
I receive the wand,
I exalt the Great Lady in Her dignity."

So reads part of a ritual invocation of the Goddess
Hathor drawn directly from Ancient Egyptian coffin
texts. The attire one wears when practicing magic can
have a tremendous effect on the success of the operation,
but it need not be so. Further, what one wears in ritual can
and does vary from tradition to tradition, coven to coven,
order to order, or even as a solitary worker.

In high ceremonial magic it is very common for the
magician to have a variety of robes, many which will
correspond in color and with specific sigils related to
planetary forces, or other esoteric influences. Generally,
when a robe is employed this is a one piece, loose fitting
garment covering one from the shoulders to the floor. Some
groups will include hooded robes or cloaks.

The advantage of the use of robes is that in putting this
on, this sends a signal to the deep mind that one is about
to perform magic, as such it can be an excellent method of
helping to alter consciousness in preparation for the work at
hand. In group workings, the robe also helps to put everyone
on an equal standing; that is assuming that the robes are all
the same.

In rural expressions of the Geassa – Traditional Witchcraft – basic one piece robes or shifts have been frequently employed. However, this is not always the case. There are some rites in which the participants perform naked. In contemporary circles, this is sometimes referred to as 'skyclad'. The thinking behind this is that nudity is natural, and thus the state of being that a fertility-based system should adopt. Within Gardnerian Wicca this is a requirement, following a ritual statement from the "Charge of the Goddess" which reads "ye shall be naked in your rites."[106] Yet in many rural traditions of Witchcraft, especially family traditions such as that of Grandma Julie it is common to wear street clothes in ritual.

Looking to the historical record we find all three methods used; robed, naked, and mundane clothes. Numerous woodcuts exist which depict Witches performing the Art while nude. Yet many others have been found showing both robed figures as well as those in everyday attire.

It would seem logical that during the height of the persecutions it would be an almost certain death sentence to be caught owning an elaborate ritual robe. Rather, this would almost certainly be disguised as a simple night shirt, shift, cloak or some other common form of clothing minus any symbols that would identify it as anything more. Yet there is no doubt that for magicians living in urban centers, with the wealth to afford these, robes were a part of their regalia.

Today, we live in a time when we have choices in how we approach the Art. For our part, we have and do practice

---

106. 'The Charge of the Goddess' is a beautiful recitation used primarily in Gardnerian Wicca, having been written by Doreen Valiente. She, in turn, drew portions of this from Leland's *Aradia, The Gospel of the Witches* and elements of the rituals Gerald Gardner received from the New Forest Witches. Sybil Leek quotes this moving ritual script in her book *The Complete Art of Witchcraft* acknowledging this as an important contribution to the growth and evolution of the Art.

at different times in all three of these modes. The choice largely depends on the circumstances as well as the rite being performed. Like Sybil Leek, generally we prefer to don simple robes for ritual. Ideally, we prefer rich, green-colored robes corresponding to the natural Willow Path of magic, which we follow. However, we have also practiced in black robes and white robes. The main point is that one should keep the solar plexus area loose while being as comfortable as possible.

Often times, when circumstances require a more spontaneous use of magic, street clothes have remained. Also, for outdoor rituals in areas when we seek not to draw too much attention to ourselves, these have necessitated keeping street clothes as the garb of choice.

For us, nude rituals are rare. Yet, they have their place in our system. As with others in the Art, for us the naked body is nothing to be ashamed of. Nor is there any sense of depravity or sin attached to the sight of one's own or another person's body. This is the way the Gods made us.

Beyond the robe (or lack thereof), there are a number of items traditionally worn in the practice of the Art. Some of these include; the Cord, the Silver Bracelet, the Necklace and the Ring.

The Cord of Art

Perhaps no other item represents one's commitment to the Geassa more compellingly than this. In almost all forms of the Art that we are aware of, some form of cord, griddle, or belt is kept by the initiate. Generally, this is composed of rope or cording (frequently braided from three strands by the Witch).

While many groups have tassels on each end of the cord, we prefer to tie one end off in a loop and give the other end a tassel. The looped end is representative of the female while the tasseled end corresponds to the male. When wearing this, the male tassel is pushed through the loop of the female end of the cord.

This is highly reminiscent of the Tyet, or "buckle of Isis", depicted from very ancient times in Egypt. The Tyet was worn on the waist by both women and men. In Egypt this was seen as a protective amulet drawing upon the creative power of the divine with an emphasis on the Goddess forces of nature.

The color of the cord varies from tradition to tradition. In many systems, the color will denote the level one has attained in the Order. This is, particularly, so of Hermetic circles where degrees of initiation occur. In Traditional forms of Witchcraft, generally, one cord is kept by the individual for the entirety of their life. In traditional forms of the Art, the color depends on the path or type of magic and spiritual aspirations that the individual follows. Having said this, some groups will use a plain cord without coloring.

The cord is one's link to the tradition, the Gods generally and to the Great Queen Herself. In this sense, it acts as a sacred umbilical cord to Her. The cord also represents the Geassa itself; that is, the Bond. With it, the cord is our commitment to the Old Ways. Through this we are bound to the ancient path. As such, the cord is our word spoken in the form of an oath taken when we step into the Cauldron of Annwn - the Roth Fail, at initiation.

The cord will frequently have a series of knots tied into it - the number of which depends on the tradition or path which the Witch follows. In some systems, four knots are tied into the cord at one's initiation, corresponding to the four elements. Once one becomes a Mistress, Master or elder, a fifth is tied signifying spirit. In other traditions, nine knots are tied corresponding to the center of one's power, the Full and Dark Moon, the light and dark forces of power and the four elements. Yet, other systems tie thirteen knots corresponding to the thirteen lunar months of the year.

The Silver Bracelet & Necklace

In the Art, a silver bracelet is traditionally worn by the Mistress, Master and elders designating their position as leaders in the group. It represents the Lady and Her lunar essence as a link guiding and protecting the Witch. In general, the silver bracelet is a powerful, protective amulet.

With the bracelet, we often find the necklace as a traditional amulet of those of the Art. Like it, the necklace forms a link to the Lady and acts to draw Her power to the Witch, while repelling negativity. That both have a long history in the Art is attested to in Sybil Leek's work. In describing the traditional ritual attire of members of the Art across England, Germany and France she states, "the traditional necklace and silver bracelet are always worn".[107]

Sometimes, those of the Art will wear necklaces made of beads. One of the most frequent that I have seen are some made with Amber. This is popular as Amber holds magical energy easily. Other stones are used as well. I am also aware that some traditions will use snake vertebrae, stringing the necklace with red beads between the bones. These necklaces are meant to draw in the serpent energy of the land, making this more accessible to the Witch. The hagstone is also frequently worn as a necklace, representing the Witch Goddess, bringing protection and luck to one.

The Ring

Rings have a long history in occult lore as bestowing power upon the magician. Their effectiveness corresponds, in part, to the metal the ring is made of, the type of stone (if any) set in it, any markings or inscriptions placed in the metal and any ritual consecration that may have been conducted over this.

Yet, there is much more involved in the choosing and wearing of a ring of power. As it has been taught to me, the ring is highly personal and should represent the magician's highest spiritual aspirations. In donning the ring, one is sending a powerful signal to the mind that, for this moment, the mundane tasks of the day are set aside and in their place

---

107. Leek, Sybil. *The Complete Art of Witchcraft*. 1971 p.19.

a channel is now open, allowing one's true or spiritual self to come through. As such, the ring is primarily worn for magical ceremonies and those times when one may feel the need to forge that link between the layers of the self during difficult and challenging times.

Enough can't be said in regards to this. In many Hermetic circles, the training of a member's use of the ring involves deep ritual techniques and meditation. This is directly related to a process frequently thought of as preparing the "magical personality". This, in turn, acts as a vehicle for the true self or as some more Abrahamic leaning Orders often refer to this - "The Holy Guardian Angel".[108] To be certain, this is not a term used in more traditional forms of the Art, yet, the principle remains, essentially, the same despite the titles involved.

The core of these exercises is meant to steadily build on the Abred (astral) - a suitable body that the true self can use, embodying its consciousness within this. In wearing the ring, this vehicle then is accessed giving the magician a conduit to the deeper immortal aspects of the self. In those moments there is, in theory, a relatively free flow of energy and wisdom coming from the deepest parts of the self, reflecting all the way into the personality of the magician. This power is then used in ritual for the task at hand.

Having gone through this training, I can say that this can be a very effective tool of those of the Art. Crowley explains that the ring is a symbol of the Goddess in Her form of Nut (he spelled Her name after the French spelling for night "Nuit"). He explained that the ring represents the "totality of the possible ways in which he [the magician] may represent himself and fulfil himself".[109]

---

108. This term is not used in our tradition. The various 'spiritual' aspects of the self as understood and taught in our system will be discussed at length in the upcoming work 'Horns of the Moon.'

109. Crowley, Aleister. *Magick in Theory and Practice.* 1929.61, footnote 3.

In practice, the ring is a powerful tool representing one's spiritual aspirations and identity. The actual practice for 'building' the form on the Abred and forming the link with this through the ring will be described elsewhere in the Geassa series. Over time, this simple tool will prove a valuable asset, drawing much power to the one who wields this.

Even without the formal ritual of linking these together, we strongly recommend that one choose a ring that represents one's deepest spiritual feelings, with links to the Old Ones and the Geassa. Use the basic cleansing ritual from the next chapter to consecrate this. Then wear this in your rites.

Beyond these few items, there are a number of other ritual objects that can be worn depending on the ritual involved. These can include various amulets and talismans, stoles, crowns and masks. All of these have their place in ritual, the design of which depends on the tradition or Order involved.

Chapter Twenty Three

❖ PREPARING THE TOOLS OF THE TRADE ❖

Having considered many of the tools normally used in the Art, I would like to present a simple but effective ritual which the student can use to cleanse and then endow the items with power as needed. For obvious reasons, some tools may require additional steps depending on their function. For example, the consecration of the goblet draws on different energies than that of the black hilt knife. Nevertheless, the ritual which is given here is an excellent start, clearing the item and infusing this with a measure of energy which will build over time.

In our system for all items, this rite should be done either during the Waxing Moon, on the Full Moon, or during one of the Fire Festivals noted earlier. You will need to have gathered a black candle, a small bowl filled with salt, a similar bowl filled with fresh water, some dried Silver or White Sage, Wormwood, Vervain or Rosemary (any of these alone will do, or a combination of these). If none of these are available, fresh Pine needles can be very affective as well.

In addition to this, you will need an oil to anoint the object. We use an infusion of Vervain in Olive oil. However, you may use an infusion from any of the herbs noted above. An infusion of any of these can be made by placing the dried herb in a clear bottle and covering the herb with Olive oil. Seal this and let this stand at room temperature in a window that gets direct sunlight for two weeks. At the end of that time, strain the oil and seal this, storing it in a dark cupboard for use, later. If this is not an option, essential oils are very good. Rosemary essential oil is easily accessible and can be diluted by cutting this with Olive oil or Mineral oil.

Following the instructions given earlier in this book, choose a day and hour that embodies the planetary energy that best corresponds to the tool being cleansed. Prior to the rite, you want to have abstained from eating for a minimum of three hours. You will also need to have avoided any physical sexual stimulation for a minimum of twelve hours, preferably twenty four hours, prior to the ritual.

Place all of the items gathered on a working table, Hearthstone, or as many contemporary groups call it the 'altar'. For extra light, you may want to place two candle sticks at the two back corners of the Hearthstone. These can be white, or of a color corresponding to the energy being called on to charge the item. Do not use black candles for these. You should only have the one black candle which will be placed at the back center of the Hearthstone.

In the center of the Hearthstone itself, mark out an equal-sided triangle. This can be done with chalk, flour, or the leaves and herbs related to the nature of the force being called on. The apex of the triangle should be facing the black candle. In front of the triangle the bowl of water should be placed at the outside left point of the triangle, the bowl of salt needs to be set at the outside right point. The dried herbs, with a fireproof container that can be used to hold these, should be placed to the right of the triangle. The oil which will be used to anoint the object should be placed to the left of the triangle. Clear your mind, as you stand before the Hearthstone. If you are using candles at the back corners of the Hearthstone light the right candle as you say:

Between the Horns,

As you light the left candle state:

Lays the path we keep.

This phrase, "Between the horns, lays the path we keep", is a direct reference to the deep spiritual realms embodied in the Stang and the silver cauldron of the Moon that sits in Caer Wydyr. This simple invocation should not be changed in any way as it is a key to opening the paths within this tradition.

Next, light the herbs so that they smoke. It may be helpful to have tied these together in a type of stick or roll. In this form, it is easy to light one end and let this burn. Once this is smoking suitably, pick up the item to be cleansed, and pass it through the smoke of the herbs, several times. Take your time as you do this, purposely.

When finished, light the black candle. Then pass the item through or over the flame. Be careful not to set fire to the item or to injure yourself. As you do this, envision any negative energy, thoughts, spirits, emotions, etc. being pulled out of the object and being absorbed by the candle. As before, take as much time as needed. There is no need to rush through this process.

Following the candle, sprinkle three pinches of salt into the bowl of water. Then dip your fingers into this and anoint the item with the water. Again, see any negative energy being washed away. Do the same with a few pinches of salt. When finished with the four elements, replace the item back in the center of the triangle.

Again, calmly clear your mind with some relaxed even breathing. Then, when ready, think of the energies you are calling on as your recite:

Three worlds encircle the one,
Annwn, Abred, Fair Gwynfyd.
The Lady calls from Caer Wydyr,
Her Cauldron deep and pool clear.
I call to the forces of this hour,
Gathering in this place of power.

With the middle finger of the right hand, trace the invoking pentagram of spirit as described in the "Witches'

Foot". Then, if the item being charged is related directly to an element, trace the invoking pentagram of that element using the appropriate finger corresponding to that element.

If the item being consecrated is more aligned to a specific planet, trace the invoking heptagram, starting with the point corresponding to the planet related to the item and proceeding deosil/clockwise. For this, it would be best to use the middle finger of the right hand.

In addition, should you desire to call on a specific other world being, such as a God or Goddess, you would intone their name while tracing their sigil (identifying symbol), above the item in the triangle. Finish by reciting:

> Come with your power,
> Charge this [name the object] here!
> For between the Horns,
> Lays the path we keep.
> Come Ancient Ones
> Your company I seek!

In drawing these pentagrams and sigils, use your creative imagination to visualize the forms burning with an electric blue flame in the air, over the triangle. Remember, force follows will and imagination is the vehicle through which that force is directed. The greater you can envision the form, the more power that is directed to its actual existence on the astral. It is this force which will draw in the energies you seek for the rite.

Once finished, hold your hands over the object being charged. Allow yourself to envision a brilliant gold energy in your chest. Take a few moments to picture this. Let this energy grow in brilliance. Then, let this gold light rush through both arms and out through the palms, down into the object. See this in your mind as the energy fills the object. Take as long as you need to let this image build. It is very common to feel a warm sensation in the hands and palms. Some people feel a pulling or tugging of energy come out of the palms. Whether you feel anything or not, let this image flow and build, for several moments.

Then, pick the object up and gentle exhale onto this. As you do, imagine the same type of energy flowing through the breath into the object. Do this with at least three exhales - more if you feel it is needed. In essence, you are breathing energy and life into the item. As you do this, anoint the item with the oil. This acts as a condenser, holding the energy raised, while at the same time distributing this into the object that it is applied to.

Finish by replacing the item in the triangle, leaving this overnight to let this absorb the energies you had brought to bear on it. In rural traditions, this is known as letting the item "cook". The triangle of Art acts as a means of focusing and containing the energy drawn to the object. Put out all of the candles and leave the item until the next day. The object is now ready to be used in ritual.

Chapter Twenty Four

✤ COMPANIONS OF THE ART ✤
'Familiar Spirits'

One of the most potent allies one of the Art
can have is a 'familiar'. Unfortunately, much
misunderstanding and fear has grown up around
this subject, fueled primarily by the Christian hysteria
during the middle ages. To this day, black cats, crows, snakes
and other animals are tinged with the stigma of evil and
loathing in western society, because of their association
with Witchcraft in mediaeval Europe.

In reality, the familiar can take any number of forms. For
our purposes, we will talk of four different, distinct 'types'
of familiar available to those of the Arts. Which type, or
how many different ones the Witch uses, is largely a matter
of choice.

While the mediaeval 'traditional' view of the familiar
is that of a 'servant' spirit that the Witch uses to assist
with delivering spells, the truth is that these are more of a
companion and assistant to the magus or Witch.

The first type of familiar had been alluded to early in this
series, when we spoke of the overarching group mind or
spirit that a tradition or occult group taps into and draws
on. In traditional Witchcraft, this can and frequently does,
come through in an animal form. Crows, snakes, toads,
hares, wolves, horses, dragons and other creatures often
manifest as the form which this spirit will choose to take in
order to relate to the group in question. Initiation into the
group gives one access to this spirit. As such, the spirit will
begin to manifest in the new member's magical and spiritual

life, acting as a channel of information and wisdom to the member. In addition, it is common for members of the group to use this manifestation when sending forth their energy to accomplish their goals. This includes 'sending forth the fetch' - an astral form.[110]

This type of familiar is strengthened by the rituals of the group and is meant to open the lines of communication with it. In addition, it is strengthened by the controlled regular visualization of the form it normally takes. The stronger, clearer and more frequent the visualizations are, the more likely that the form will take on an objective life of its own, being visible to others who are sensitive enough to perceive it.

There are several advantages to accessing these types of familiar. The most obvious is that it is the repository of the wisdom of the group tradition. Thus, access to this being brings with it an older, shared knowledge. Too, the familiar acts as a guardian helping to protect the group and providing psychic and spiritual strength to those within the group.

It is important to understand that this type of familiar is more than an astral manifestation of the group's structured visualization come to life. Rather, the group had attracted this spirit force to it through the rituals and traditions they had embraced. Conversely, it can be argued that the spirit attracted these people to it, as their Mistress or Master. The familiar acts as the otherworld contact and messenger, linking the members of the group to the tradition, the group is part of. Further, the familiar works as a liaison between the group and those beings within the realms which the group seeks to call on.

---

110. It is important to know that the concept of 'the fetch' is very complex and involves a number of practices; from relations to specific spirits some of whom will come as otherworld teachers, guides and lovers, to the practice of sending etheric energy sometimes referred as the 'second skin'. This topic is best left for a more advanced volume on the Art.

While this first type of familiar pertains mostly to those working within a living group tradition, the lone Witch or magician have other options available. The most common form of familiar thought of by people today, is that of the pet. As noted above, black cats, crows and other animals closely associated with Witchcraft, come to mind. In reality, the living animal familiar can take any form the individual forms a bond with. The important point to understand here is that turning an animal into familiar is a huge responsibility. Having said this, for those of the Art, often times animals may be drawn to one solely for this purpose. Aleister Crowley explains the responsibility well:

"You can always use the body inhabited by an elemental, such as an eagle, hare, wolf, or any convenient animal, by making a very simple compact. You take over the responsibility for the animal, thus building it up into your own magical hierarchy. This represents a tremendous gain to the animal."

He continues:

"The magician must realize that in undertaking the Karma of any elemental , he is assuming a very serious responsibility.[111] The bond which unites him with that elemental is love; and, though it is only a small part of the outfit of the magician, it is the whole of the outfit of the elemental ."[112]

---

111. Crowley doesn't use the term 'familiar', rather substituting this with 'elemental'. Nevertheless it is clear that he is referring to the same procedure used in traditional Witchcraft. This is significant as most ceremonial magicians are quite adverse to the use of 'familars'. It is interesting to learn that Crowley uses many techniques found in traditional Witchcraft. This may well be due to his friendly and frequent acquaintance with a certain family that followed the Old Ways.

112. Crowley, Aleister. Magick in the Theory and Practice. 1929 p.90.

It is important to understand that for us, animals are seen as equal to humans, possessing emotion and a certain level of intelligence which varies from species to species. We see them as sisters and brothers. For sacred myth confirms that spirit embodies animal and human form, alike.

For those so inclined to have an animal familiar, it is best to choose an animal that one has an affinity with. Cat, dog, crow, whatever the animal, be sure it is one you relate to easily. The stronger the inherent link to the species itself, the more successful you will be in creating this partnership.

It is best to work with an animal that is very young. You will want to 'imprint' yourself into this animal's mind and emotions early on, as its primary, if not sole, companion. This includes spending as much time as possible with the animal. To strengthen the bond, it is traditional to mix a few drops of your blood into the animal's food when they are young. As they grow older this is not needed and, in fact, not advised.

You will want to spend time getting to know the animal's personality, mannerisms, likes and dislikes. It is important to set aside specific times every day to work with the animal. Make this part of their and your daily routine. During these periods, mentally allow yourself to open to their mind. Envision yourself as them. Try to see what they see, hear what they hear; experience what they experience. In turn, allow them to reach into your soul, allowing them to experience a measure of who you are.

Some sources recommend sitting facing the Moon with your familiar each evening. Looking to the Moon, begin stroking the animal, allowing your breathing to match the rhythm of theirs. Through this nightly ritual, according to older sources, you will begin to merge in will, "your eyes will see as its eyes see and your thoughts will travel together." The teaching goes on to state that once this has been accomplished "the time has come to work spells and cast enchantments for power is doubled through the agency of your familiar."[113]

Once the animal is able to remain calm for periods at a time, introduce them to ritual. Let them be present when performing spells and ceremonies. This isn't always easy. The last thing one needs is a cat knocking over candles at the peak of spell casting. However, given time and practice the animal will become used to the setting. This can be invaluable as animals tend to be more sensitive to occult influences than humans. As such, their presence in ritual can aid the Witch in knowing when entities are present, or when energies are truly raised.

After some time, the animal familiar can be an effective vehicle to deliver the energies of spells. To do this, an object can be ritually 'charged' with one's intention. This is then attached to the animal's collar. The animal is then set loose in the vicinity of the person intended for the spell, with the talisman attached. When the person touches the animal, the intention is released into the person's consciousness. This is a very common means by which love and seduction spells are introduced to the person desired.[114]

As can be seen, an animal familiar is a big commitment, requiring work, patience and steady practice. Nevertheless, it can be very rewarding for those who have the time and means to work with them.

---

113. Quoted from the article 'The Cat as Familiar' from the 1972 *Witches Almanac*, by Amanda Martin, who in turn, states that the material quoted stems from magical instructions written in the eighteenth century.

114. While some do, I would not recommend this type of action in the case of 'blasting' or otherwise introducing negative influences to the intended target. To do so may backfire causing the familiar to suffer the effects of the curse. This is particularly true if the intended target person is protected through magical means. In the case of a love spell though, if this were to rebound, the worst that would happen is that the familiar would become more affectionate.

A third form of familiar is more akin to the 'spirit guide', thought to exist for some with mediumistic ability. There is some controversy over this. On the one hand the concept has been a part of the Arts for thousands of years. Simply put, this teaching states that we all have a spirit or spirits which take an active interest in our life. Learning who this spirit is and opening one to communication with it, can be a source of knowledge for the individual. The controversy comes from the ability to recognize when a spirit's influence is in one's best interest. This is not unlike deciding who in one's life is a valued friend whom you would not only allow into your home but whom you would take real, life-changing advice from. This can be difficult to determine.[115]

Having said this, should one be so inclined to work with this type of familiar the best advice is be certain of their identity. Any advice or communication received should be scrutinized carefully. This, of course holds true with any relationship in life, whether corporeal or spiritual. Should you find that the relationship is mutually good and that the spirit has your best interest at heart then this may be a familiar worth forging a lasting relationship with. Still, this form of familiar was very common among medieval Witches and can be very effective, today. Once a relationship has been formed that is mutually beneficial and in which trust and respect for each other has been formed, this can be a very potent ally in the practice of the Art.

In the magical system which we follow, our relationship to nature, the land and spiritual forces inherent within the land,

---

115. It is important to note that not all 'mediums' have 'spirit guides' or advocate the use of such entities. Sybil Leek was a noted medium who worked with parapsychologists on a number of cases, yet she was one who to my knowledge did not use 'spirit guides'. Having said that, I have had moments in my life when otherworld beings have communicated with me clearly with solid and useable information that later proved accurate and important at the time. And, for whatever reason, these beings had an active interest in my wellbeing.

is paramount. As such, the type of familiar which we prefer to work with is that of the Alraun. As explained earlier in this work, the word itself has ancient Germanic roots referring to female "long-haired, bare-legged" Witches and sorceresses first encountered by the Romans when they entered northern Europe. In time, the word Alraun came to represent a Spirit Root and totem, or as anthropologists might term it, a fetish.

This is identical to the Mandrake root of the Mediterranean region. However, in the case of the Alraun, this familiar is drawn from the root of an Ash tree.

The preparation of the Alraun is essentially like that of the Mandrake. In doing so, one is giving form and a vehicle to a spirit on an elemental level. In essence, the spirit is one invited from nature, the local land and forces of the region. Yet, while she may have physical form, the Alraun retains her link to the world of spirit.[116]

To prepare an Alraun locate an Ash tree in a quiet place far from the activities of most humans. The more sacred and powerful the land feels to one, the better. The best time of year for this is during the Beltane May festival period, especially so if this falls during the Waxing to Full Moon .[117] For at that time the tides have turned and the impulse of life and rejuvenation have begun. Once located, bring the Black Hilt Knife, a shovel and small tools to carefully cut and remove the section of the root desired. You will also want to bring an offering for the tree and the spirits of the land. This can be wine and sweet bread, or cakes.

---

116. I use the word 'she' here only for the sake of this writing. The gender of the spirit depends primarily on that drawn to the ritual during preparation. Almost always female nature spirits are drawn to male Witches, and male spirits to female Witches.

117. Under no circumstances should you perform this rite during the Waning or Dark Moon. If needed wait until the Waxing Moon following Beltane.

At the location, begin by drawing three circles around the tree with the knife. Then, facing the tree, state your intention, thanking the tree for the gift you are about to receive. You will then call on the spirits of the land, welcoming that which is compatible and wants to be your assistant to manifest in the root you are about to dig up.

Now, carefully dig around the root desired. My own Alraun was cut from a larger root that had branched forming two 'legs'. The beauty of Ash trees is that often times the roots are visible, at least in part, above ground. As such, it can be easier to locate a 'human' looking form before digging.

Once the desired root is exposed, carefully and respectfully cut this away from the tree. You want to do as little harm as possible. Once free of the ground, brush any soil away and wrap the root in a white cloth. Now, present the offerings to the tree, putting the food in the hole where the root had been and pouring the wine into it. Then bury the offering with the soil that had been covering the root.

Returning to your ritual space clean the root completely and then begin to carve this into the appearance of a human. If you are a woman, you will want this to appear male, if you are a man, the root will need to be female in form. Don't be put off if this ends up being somewhat crude in form. You want this to appear as a root that had grown naturally into a human form of sorts. The important points to consider are that the familiar will need a face, and the gender of the familiar will need to be easily identifiable. Naturally the more artistic the better but by no means is this essential.

All the while that you are preparing the root, invite the elemental spirit most compatible to you, to enter the Alraun. While carving the root, ask that the spirit reveal itself to you, guiding your hand. Again, don't worry if this comes out somewhat basic in form. Rather, the intent is to form a link between yourself and the spirit. The root is the channel and vehicle through which the nature spirit can come.

Once carved, allow the root to dry. It is customary to cense the Alraun in the smoke of Vervain. The drying process can take days, even weeks. Unlike the Mandrake, we do not advocate re-burying the Alraun for a lunar cycle. Rather, we bath this in red wine, wrap it in white linen and place it in a wooden box. The box is then set on, or near, the hearth.

From this point on the Alraun is seen as the embodiment, or living vehicle through which a specific natural spirit comes through for the Witch. It needs to be treated as a partner, companion and assistant in each sense of the word. Daily one should address it, talk with it and ask for advice or assistance. Each week the root should be bathed in red wine.

In ritual, the Alraun should be present each time. She will act as an aid adding power to each rite. The Alraun is particularly useful for astral workings, rites involving moving between worlds, as well as prosperity, good fortune and protection. I have found the Alraun acts as an excellent ambassador between myself and the spirits of the land.

Like the other types of familiars, the Alraun comes with tremendous responsibility. In working with a familiar, one is entering into a relationship that goes beyond the bonds formed by even most earthly friendships. In each case, the Witch or magician is sharing very intimate details about their inner life with the spirit itself. This is a long term commitment with all the implications that this entails. If you decide to pursue this, be aware of the responsibilities. However, having said this, this commitment may lead to great reward. In our experience, the results of working with a familiar may not be instantaneous; however, they do produce real, objective and long lasting results beyond that which can be ascribed to other methods.

In the practical application of the Art, it is very common for the Witch to appeal to their familiar for assistance in all magical practice. In the case of an actual living animal, this can be as simple as having them present in ritual and consciously drawing their power into the enchantment itself. In the case of a group familiar, a spirit and an Alraun, the preferred method of practice is to clear the mind and then allow this being to merge with oneself, so that your energies are combined.[118] This can be accompanied by a simple incantation inviting them into oneself. In such cases, at the peak of power, frequently, the Witch will experience the energy then flow from her chest, mouth, as well as palms in an ecstatic rush. The feeling is unmistakable.

Before leaving this chapter, it needs to be stressed that the familiar is not 'something' that is 'made'. Rather, in each case, this is a covenant, a relationship formed between oneself and an otherworld being. Once forged, they become your companion in the Arts. It is only through reaching out to them through trance and ritual, that this link is forged. Keep in mind as well, that this is a mutual arrangement with expectations for both parties involved. Respect, communication, companionship and a certain amount of affection are involved. Like any relationship, how this develops is up to both beings involved.

---

118. It is common among some Traditional Witches to allow the spirit to 'reside' in the Witch themselves. In such cases, this has been described as having the spirit in their chest. During ritual, its power is then projected through the chest and mouth. In the case of the Alraun, I prefer to have her reside in the root; however, in ritual, I will invite her to merge with me as we combine our power.

Chapter Twenty Five

✤ THE FOUR FAMILIARS ✤

Within European Witchcraft, four distinct energies characterized in the form of animals are traditional emblematic images. Each is very powerful and needs to be understood. Some see these as guardians of the tradition. However, we feel that these are the equivalent of Familiar spirits representing distinct strands within the tradition. These four are the Crow, the Hare, the Serpent or Dragon and the Toad.

The Crow is known for its keen intelligence, its ability to understand and communicate. In the Art, the Crow is the messenger of the spirit world traversing between realms. It is the embodiment of the haunted realm; spirits who seek to communicate, or otherwise wish to influence, the living. This is the energy of the Black Spirits but as was shown earlier, black has many occult attributes ranging from death to fertility.

The Morrigu, the three War Goddesses of Celtic Mythology, take the form of ravens. As such, they are at once revered and feared. The Crow also accompanies Herne, the Horned One, as he rides with the spectral Wild Wind Riders during storms. Yet, the Crow is intensely clever. In the wild, they have been proven to be able to recognize specific people by face. In the Art, the essence of the Crow is called on for spirit communication and magic, divination and communication with the Gods. On a negative note, works of cursing and blasting also draw on its energies.

In Sybil Leek's "The Complete Art of Witchcraft" a rare photograph from an initiation ceremony shows the Mistress of the group wearing a Crow mask as she approaches the candidate. Clearly, she represents the powerful dark and wise aspect of the Lady in the ceremony.

Serpents and Dragons have a long history in the Art. Until the eventual demonization of these by the Abrahamic traditions, both images were venerated and revered as emblems of the great Goddesses throughout many parts of the world. The red serpent represents the raw sexual power of creative energy inherent in nature. This is the power which awakens in spring. This is the power residing at the base of the spine within each of us. This is will and desire, passion and flame waiting to rise, bringing life and power to those who can understand and channel Her energies. This was particularly true in Ancient Egyptian magical practices. We see this in the serpent form of the Goddess of magic, Heka. She was almost certainly the inspiration, if not the actual Egyptian being, who was also the Greek Goddess of Witches - Hecate. The Great Goddess Hwt-Hrw often appears in this form, as does the winged guardian Goddess Wadjet.

In Celtic myth, we find the twin red and white serpents coiled together. This is analogist of the masculine and feminine energies embraced in passion. Here, they create the dynamic interplay of creative energies that lay at the heart of the mysteries.

The Dragon is essentially this same energy. The Dragon is the power of the land awakening in the spring, bringing life to all that is. In geomancy, lines of power in the Earth are known as 'Dragon Currents'. Dragon energy, too, has long been linked to many sacred sites, hills, wells and stone circles.

It is through the power of the Serpent, the Dragon, that sexuality, passion and desire can manifest. Theirs is the power of the Besom. Theirs is the entrance of light. In Egypt, we find numerous representations of the Winged Serpent. This was particularly so in the very late period, with the mysteries surrounding the Agathodaimon or 'the good spirit'. This god-form, figures highly in some of the older traditions within the Hermetic Arts, specifically those related to the Ogdoadic stream. The Serpent totem is the energy of the Red Spirits.

The Hare, too, has a long history in Witchcraft. It is renowned for its ability to reproduce. It represents fertility, life and abundance. This totem is sacred to the Goddesses of spring and summer because of the Hare's sheer ability to propagate. Folklore tells us that this is one of the forms that Witches have traditionally sent their 'fetch' or double, as. It is interesting that in medieval Europe and early colonial America, the Hare was feared precisely because of its association with Witchcraft.

In Ancient Egypt, the Hare was seen as an embodiment of sexual endurance, passion and ability. As an amulet, representations of the Hare were worn to extend a measure of the hare's sexual powers and ability to procreate. As such, this represents abundance, prosperity and an increase in one's love life.[119] They are the embodiment of the energies that bring fruitfulness, success; the drive to survive and grow. In ritual, the energy of the Hare is used in healing, luck, prosperity and good fortune. This is the power of the White Spirits.

The Toad has long been associated with Witchcraft. This highly misunderstood creature is very intelligent. Further, many produce toxic chemicals which have long been used to induce visions and altered states. This is the power of the well, of seas, rivers and lakes. The depths of other realms are reached through the West Road of the Toad.

In Ancient Egypt, frogs, and presumably toads, were seen as symbolic of the energies within the creative force that made all. Amulets in the shape of frogs related to this ancient force and to the fertility Goddess Heket, a

---

119. Andrews, Carol. *Amulets of Ancient Egypt.* 1994 p.64.
Lurker, Manfred. *An Illustrated Dictionary of the Gods and Symbols of Ancient Egypt.* 1980 p.57.

Goddess of Birth. They were used to promote fertility, prosperity and abundance.[120]

Theirs is the realm of the Grey Spirits. Works of transformation, those evoking deep emotion, cleansings, memory and reaching into the creative depths of the past are all part of the West Road.

Each one of these animals embodies energies traditionally sought and used in Witchcraft. Further in this series, we will be referring to these energies, giving rites, incenses, oils and sigils, all corresponding to these powerful totems of the Art. Again, it is important to understand that some in the Art equate these four animals and the directions to the elements in a different pattern than normally used in the Western Mysteries. For our part, we continue to use the normal pattern but in doing so we also recognize that within each direction, underlying energies related to these totem animals are present, powerful and easily accessible. We see no conflict or confusion between the two systems. Rather we feel that these complement each other.

---

120. Lurker, Manfred. *An Illustrated Dictionary of the Gods and Symbols of Ancient Egypt.* 1980 p.52-53.
Andrews, Carol. Amulets of Ancient Egypt. 1994 p.62-63.

Chapter Twenty Six

✦ THE WHEEL OF TLACHTGA ✦

For those of the Art, the place in which one practices is always carefully prepared. Whether this be an elaborate chamber designed for ritual magic, the circle set before the hearth, or a clearing under moonlit sky - the goal is the same. That is the creating of a separate, sacred space, which is meant to be, at once, a microcosm of all that is and yet removed from the mundane. When properly prepared, the place in which one performs magic exists between Worlds, acting as a vehicle that carries those present to realms of consciousness and being not normally experienced in this world.

In varying factions of the Art, this can be called the Maze, the Mill, the Compass, the Wheel, the Circle, the Ring, the Castle, the Crossroads, the Blood acre, the Lodge, the Chamber, the Temenos. In our system, we prefer to use the Gaelic term 'Roth Fail', meaning 'Circle of Light' or 'Wheel of Light'.

This is a direct reference to the Celtic legend of Tlachtga. She was a great Druidess taught by her father. Her name means 'earth geassa'. She was also known as 'thunderbolt-wisdom-woman'. Depicted as a maiden, she frequently could be seen as the young Goddess.

In the legend Tlachtga created and governed over a 'swift and mobile' wheel which carried her wherever she wished .[121] So marvelous was this, it could carry one to

---

121. Spence, Lewis. *The Magic Arts in Celtic Britain*. 1993 p.36 & 71.

other worlds and heavenly realms.[122] She named this the Roth Fail - the Wheel of Light. In time, the Roth Fail came to be strongly associated with the fires set on the hearth at the festival of Samhain.

For us, the Circle, or Roth Fail, is a living vehicle that *engages* the Worlds as we have discussed them, thus far. It also draws upon the tides of power mirroring these. Thus, the proper setting of the Roth Fail opens time, space and dimensional realities, making these available to those of the Art.

In our system, the Roth Fail consists of three concentric circles. Traditionally, the inner circle should be nine feet in diameter. In practice though, this can be larger or smaller, as space dictates. For our outdoor working, we meet in a stone circle deep within the forest that is approximately twenty-two feet across on the inside.

The first, outer circle is traced with the Black Hilt Knife, beginning in the north and proceeding Sunwise, while reciting the appropriate enchantment. This circle draws upon the realm of Annwn and the cauldron of inspiration resting in the heart of the castle. When tracing this, all of the Witch's attention needs to be in the visualization of a great wall of electric blue flame rising up surrounding her space. With this, there is the realization that the vast and wondrous realm of Annwn *is* this first, outer circle.

As noted above, this magical process *engages* the Worlds. The circle doesn't 'represent' the Worlds. Each circle draws upon and becomes an extension of the realm involved. It is imperative that the student understand this. When setting the Roth Fail, one is working with very real forces in this operation. Thus, the Roth Fail is a miniature version of the realms involved.

A somewhat primitive example that may help the reader to understand this concept can be found in a comparison

---

122. In this respect She was seen as a form of Arianrhod who bears the title of "Silver Circle".

between a nuclear reactor and the Sun. The Sun is a natural product of nuclear fusion on a massive scale. A nuclear reactor isn't 'symbolic' of the Sun, nor does it 'represent' the Sun. Rather, it is a devise meant to create and harness the power of nuclear fusion on a much smaller scale than the Sun. Nevertheless, it is using the same principles and forces as the Sun. As such, both the Sun and the reactor are vehicles for and extension of, the force of nuclear fusion.

In a similar manner, the Roth Fail is engaging the same Worlds, the same dimensions as those discussed thus far but on a microcosmic level. Make no mistake about it; these are real forces being brought to bear on the ritual work at hand.

It is important for the reader to know also that each of the three circles relate directly to certain Hermetic and Alchemical principles. The circle of Annwn corresponds to the black step of the Ogdoadic 'House of Sacrfice' as salt, body and the outward manifestation of the Art. It is for this reason that the outer circle of Annwn *can be* marked with a barrier of sea salt. In fact this can be a very effective mineral for keeping unwanted influences out and holding energies raised within.

Beginning in the north (the realm of the Gods), one traces the second circle Moonwise / tuathal or widdershins with the Stang, again, while using the enchantment for this realm.[123] In doing so, one envisions a curtain of silver mist being stretched all the way around the circle. With this operation, the forces of Abred are called to the Roth Fail at once lending power to the rite, opening the consciousness of the participants to the forces contained in this realm, protecting the place and containing the energies raised within, until the forces are released through spell and incantation.

---

123. The North has long been seen as the 'realm of the Gods' largely because the stars in the North never rise or set. Thus the Ancient Egyptians saw them as 'the imperishable ones'. It is in the north that the 'pole' or 'nail of heaven' exists. It is here that the Witch derives knowledge and power.

Alchemically, this second circle corresponds to the second step of the Ogdoadic House of Sacrfice, which is red in color. This, too, relates to Sulphur and the soul or 'astral' forces.

Returning to the north once more, the third circle is traced with the Fe of Arianrhod - the wand. While each action in this process is important, it is with the drawing of this final circle that the Witch will perceive significant changes in the atmosphere of the room. It is common to feel the outer world fall away.

In drawing this third circle, point the Fe out and, walking Sunwise once again, visualize a gold light emanating from its tip, projecting out. Doing this, envision a beautiful field of sunlit golden grains, wild flowers and the abundance of nature, all around. This is the realm of Gwynfyd, evoked through action and word. This is the Field of Reeds of the Egyptians, and the Eleusinian Fields of the Greeks.

This third circle is tied to the Alchemical element of Mercury, spirit and the third white step of the Ogdoadic House of Sacrifice.

Once the three circles are formed with the appropriate tools and invocations, the Witch takes up the Stang, once more. Walking to each quadrant she faces the direction and evokes the elemental guardian for each. This is done while raising the Stang toward the guardian. For the Stang, as the World Tree, reaches across all realms and realities acting as a conduit bringing the entities called to the circle.

In the Hermetic system of the Ogdoadic tradition, this evocation of the four quarters relates to some extent to the four pillars of the sacred 'House of Sacrifice'. In the Celtic paradigm, this act corresponds to erecting the four walls of the tower or castle. For with the three circles laid and the guardians in place, the Castle of Glass is formed. This is Caer Wydyr, the Tower of Arianrhod.

The Witch now stands in the center of the Roth Fail, before the cauldron, as she utters the final enchantment. With this last act in the ritual, she is forging a link between the cauldron present in the circle to the sacred cauldron of inspiration resting at the heart of the Castle of Glass. This is the same cauldron that is the rim invoked with the casting of the circle of Annwn. They are one in the same. For the essence of all is the Great Goddess. She is the Mystery at the heart of existence. She is, at once, the spiritual cause and the manifestation of spirit in everything we see. She is the Great Mystery and the Roth Fail embodies all of these energies as one living vehicle through which those of the Art transcend time, space and multiple realities.

Because of the nature of the powers involved, the Roth Fail must always be constructed with care. Yet, when set properly, it is one of the most powerful tools available to the Witch.

At this point, it may be important to discuss the function of imagination in the Arts. Frequently, we will instruct students - the reader - to 'envision' a specific scene, image, set of symbols or a series of events as with the forming of the Roth Fail. In doing so, one is actively engaging the imagination. This will often lead those new to the Art to wonder if "it's all in my head". The fact is that every ritual act that is successful begins with intention and a disciplined desire to bring a goal into reality.

It is important to understand that in the Art, *force follows will*. One must first imagine and visualize a goal before the energy raised can be directed toward making this a reality. This is similar to the task of the architect who first imagines the building to be constructed. She then will draw this out (the 'magic symbol') which will be used to bring this into manifestation. From this, energy is applied to make this a reality.

The Art is the same. We visualize the goal, creating the sigil through which the force is directed, to attain the desired effect.

Chapter Twenty Seven

❧ THE ROTH FAIL - CIRCLE OF LIGHT ❧

The following ritual is the actual one we use to create the platform in which we perform the majority of our rites related to the Art. As such, this is at once a protective barrier keeping unwanted influence out of the area, while also functioning as a vehicle between worlds, enabling us to become aware of realms and dimensions beyond those normally perceived in mundane life. In preparing the Roth Fail, nothing should be done heedlessly or without intention. Rather, the best approach is to relax and gently move through each ritual action. Beyond the physical words and actions involved, you will want to carefully envision the images and energies involved. Again, force follows will and to imagine a thing through the careful functions of a disciplined mind is to give the energies form and direction. For this ritual, you will need the following items:

- Cauldron
- Goblet
- Fe (Wand)
- Black Hilt Knife
- Stang
- Wind Roarer

Each of these items should be on the Hearthstone with the feminine tools on the left, masculine on the right. The Cauldron should be placed in the center of the Roth Fail.

Ideally, you will place a candle at each of the four quadrant directions. Normally, these are white in color though you can use colored candles depending in the work being done.

On the Hearthstone have a representation of the four elements - salt, water, incense and flame. The incense will vary depending on the work being done. For us, we will frequently use a mixture of dried herbs grown on our property. Oftentimes, this will take the form of traditional 'smudge' sticks with the herbs rolled and tied together. Having said this, we have had wonderful success collecting the hardened resins of local trees. In particular, pine and cherry resign (sap that has hardened and dried) is very fragrant and providing no bark is present in these, it can be very pleasant. For us too, we like to use local plants and resins primarily because this is all that a country Witch or Shaman would have had available. In colonial times only the wealthy could have been able to obtain many of the more exotic ingredients described in mediaeval magical texts. Having said this, we are so fortunate to live in an era when we can purchase these non-native ingredients. As such, we can and do use these. Nevertheless, in our tradition with its rich emphasis on forming and maintaining links to the land, the use of incenses and oils which come from the land on which we live, is an important part of our system.

On the Hearthstone, place two candles; one on the left back corner and one on the right back corner. For general purposes, a green candle can be on the left and red candle on the right, though the color can and will, vary based on the work at hand. On Full Moon, we will use white candles at both positions. These two candles correspond to the feminine and masculine forces of nature; female on the left, male on the right. Ideally, we will lay three concentric circles:

The outer circle can be marked with salt;

The middle circle can be marked with dried Birch bark;

The inner circle can be marked with dried herbs.

Oftentimes, space or circumstances can't accommodate this. For example, if the coven is meeting in a member's home where it would be impractical to use these substances, we simply place the four quadrant candles at the directions and draw the three circles with the appropriate tools, as described in the following ritual.

It needs to be noted as well that in our outdoor ritual setting, we have a permanent stone Roth Fail set atop a high point on the mountain. In this case, we frequently don't feel the need to use the materials above as the boundary is clearly set in stone. Having said this, we can use the stone circle as the boundary of salt, then mark out the Birch and herbs circles within this. On other occasions, we draw the three circles with the tools within the stone boundary.

The Ritual

Light the right candle while reciting:

> Between the Horns,

Light the left candle while reciting:

> Lays the path we keep![124]

Facing the Hearthstone slap the flat of the blade of the Black Hilt Knife against your thigh, then lift the knife skyward as you recite:

> Be gone spirits of evil for this place is sacred, given over to the Sun, Moon and Stars!

Taking up the *Wind Roarer*, spin this allowing the Roth Fail to fill with the sound, calling attention to the space from the forces desired. Replace the Wind Roarer.
With the knife place three tips of salt into the bowl of water. With the knife face north and trace a circle, deosil (clockwise

---

124. This is not to be altered in any way.

or Sun-wise), envisioning this as a brilliant wall of blue flame. Doing this, recite:

> By the blade of the black hilt knife the cauldron of Annwn encircles us/me, rimmed in pearl and fire blue. Its beauty and power protect us/me now!

Replace the knife on the Hearthstone. With the Stang, face north and trace a circle tuathal (counterclockwise or Moon-wise) while envisioning a silver mist current. Doing this recite:

> By Stang and horn the silver mists of Abred surround us/me, as the maze is laid here.

Replace the Stang. With the Fe face north and trace a circle, deosil, while envisioning the golden sunlit field of Gwynfyd opening up all around the Roth Fail (or barring this, envision a screen of gold light encircling the Roth Fail). Doing this, recite:

> By the Fe of Arianrhod the golden lands of Gwynfyd open to us/me now, that the Gods shall know us/me in this place of power!

Return the Fe to the Hearthstone. With the Stang, face east holding this high. Recite the following while envisioning the Guardian of that quarter:

> Hear me O Mighty One,
> Ruler of the Whirlwinds,
> Guardian of the East Gate!
> We welcome you to this place of power,
> To aid us in this rite,
> And to protect this circle!

With the Stang, face south holding this high. Recite the following, while envisioning the Guardian of that quarter:

Hear me O Mighty One,
Ruler of the Sacred Flame,
Guardian of the South Gate!
We welcome you to this place of power,
To aid us in this rite,
And to protect this circle!

With the Stang, face west holding this high. Recite the following while envisioning the Guardian of that quarter:

Hear me O Mighty One,
Ruler of the Mysterious Depths,
Guardian of the West Gate!
We welcome you to this place of power,
To aid us in this rite,
And to protect this circle!

With the Stang, face north holding this high. Recite the following, while envisioning the Guardian of that quarter:

Hear me O Mighty One,
Ruler of Land, Forest and Field,
Guardian of the North Gate!
We welcome you to this place of power,
To aid us in this rite,
And to protect this circle!

At each of the directions, take the time to build up the mental image of the scene and guardian associated with the quadrant. It may be helpful to read through the descriptions given earlier in this book, holding these in the mind while calling out to the guardians. Remember, force follows form; will creates the matrix through which the energies flow. With this, the mental forms build on the Abred, becoming vehicles for the energies and beings involved to come through and work with the Witch in ways that can be understood and related to.

Returning to the center, stand before the Cauldron. If no Cauldron is to be used, lift the Goblet and say:

> From the starry heavens,
> Our circle is formed;
> The center from which,
> All is born.
> Silver Cauldron of Caer Wydyr,
> Radiant star,
> Jewel of light,
> Our magic begins,
> With this rite!

Once the Roth Fail is laid, any acts of the Art can now be safely conducted. Sybil Leek gives some excellent advice on this matter:

> "After this, the circle is safe for ritual magic to be performed within it; the student should know exactly the right invocation for whatever she is requesting. Be word perfect at this point if you are an initiate, and put your reason for the invocation into clear language, without any attempt to barter. A straightforward request for help is rarely left in limbo, as the vibrations go out soundly on the ether waves and are caught up in the universal mind. If the student mumbles, or becomes verbose, the quality of the vibrations is distorted and perhaps destroyed ."[125]

Closing the Roth Fail
With the Stang, face north holding this high. Recite the following, while envisioning the Guardian of that quarter:

---

125. Leek, Sybil. The Complete Art of Witchcraft. 1971 p.184.

Hear me O Mighty One,
Ruler of Land, Forest and Field,
Guardian of the North Gate!
I thank you for your presence and protection,
As you return to you beautiful realm,
I bid you farewell!

With the Stang face west, holding this high. ecite the following, while envisioning the Guardian of that quarter:

Hear me O Mighty One,
Ruler of the Mysterious Depths,
Guardian of the West Gate!
I thank you for your presence and protection,
As you return to you beautiful realm,
I bid you farewell!

With the Stang face south holding this high. Recite the following while envisioning the Guardian of that quarter:

Hear me O Mighty One,
Ruler of Sacred Flame,
Guardian of the South Gate!
I thank you for your presence and protection,
As you return to you beautiful realm,
I bid you farewell!

With the Stang face east holding this high. Recite the following, while envisioning the Guardian of that quarter:

Hear me O Mighty One,
Ruler of the Whirlwinds,
Guardian of the East Gate!
I thank you for your presence and protection,
As you return to you beautiful realm,
I bid you farewell!

In reciting these enchantments, it is very common to get the sense of these great beings are withdrawing from the space. The reality is that they don't leave at all. Rather, our perception and awareness changes and the Witch begins to shift to mundane levels of consciousness. The guardians are sentient beings inherent in nature. As such, they exist as part of the elements and yet on dimensions within and beyond, our own. In thanking these high beings and bidding them farewell, we are acknowledging their aid and allowing our awareness to return to mundane tasks.

The circles can then either be taken up completely by retracing in the opposite direction using the appropriate tool or doorways through the three can be made, by using the tools.

To take up the Roth Fail, begin with the inner circle, using the Fe, start in the north and trace your steps this time moving tuathal (counterclockwise or Moon-wise), while envisioning the gold energy of Gwynfyd being pulled into the Fe. Then, with the Stang, return to the north, move deosil or Sun-wise, as the silver mists of Abred are absorbed back into this tool. Lastly, return to the north with the Black Hilt Knife and, walking tuathal, envision the electric blue energy of Annwn returning to the blade.

To Move between Worlds

An alternative to taking up the Roth Fail is to simply cut a doorway in the circles. There are several reasons why one would do this. For example, should one have a room or an outdoor space that is dedicated solely to the Art, it is often desirable to begin to build up an astral presence of energy in the space by leaving the Roth Fail psychically intact. In this way, each time the Roth Fail is recreated, this energy builds up, in essence becoming stronger with each rite performed.

There are other occasions when a doorway is not only desirable; it is essential. This is the case in many traditions in which the Roth Fail is created by set members while the remainder of the group wait outside. In such cases, some groups will lay the besom and sword across the doorway and each person steps over this as they enter. Initiation, too, is a case in which this is a vital part of the rite. In such cases, the candidate is made to wait outside the area, only to be invited or led into the Roth Fail via the door.

To cut the doorway, the Witch will use the three tools involved; Fe, Stang and Knife. In each case, the tool will be drawn across the edge of the circle in the opposite direction to that taken when creating the boundary. In doing so, the energy in that one spot is seen as being absorbed into the ritual item and a gateway is envisioned opening out to the mundane world.

Once the participants have traveled through the door, these are once again sealed using the appropriate tools to project the energies back into the boundary, while imagining the doorways closing and being sealed.

Chapter Twenty Eight

✤ THE TOWER AND THE MAZE ✤

In all forms of the Art that I am aware of, the simple act of circumambulating the ritual space has been used since ancient times. In Witchcraft, this is referred to as "walking the maze", "dancing the maze", "treading the mill", "walking the compass" and by many other titles. It is the act of circling the ritual space and is done for a variety of purposes. The first among these is to alter consciousness. When combined with chant, it can induce light trance states. Even without chanting, it can have profound effects on the participants. This is done at key moments in the rite and is combined with deep mental imagery in order to bring the ritualist into an awareness of other worlds and energies.

This act, too, is used to 'stir the astral light'. In other words, when introduced into key moments of ritual, circumambulation draws in the energies of other realms making these accessible to the Witch or magician. In this way, one is quite literally creating "a vortex of energy" which then is used for the rite at hand. The important element to remember when performing this is to relax and let the movement flow on its own. Circling the space should not be a forced effort. Rather, it is an opportunity to take the ritual, and one's awareness, to richer levels of experience.

Generally, circling to the right, clockwise or deosil, is used for rites of a positive and celebratory nature. It is used to invoke or create. It, specifically, relates to the apparent circle the Sun makes daily in the sky.

Walking to the left, counterclockwise, widdershins or Tuathal, is considered by many to be of a negative nature.

As such, it can be used in acts of blasting or cursing, as well as banishing. However, this movement also relates to the cycle of the Moon as She changes phases through the month. Too, it is used in rites meant to draw on the powers of the deeper worlds of Annwn and Abred.[126]

In Traditional Witchcraft, often times the participants will face their bodies at a right angle to the center of the circle. They then turn their heads focusing on a center point in the circle while making the circumabulations. This is done to help avoid dizziness and to keep one centered on the task at hand. In all cases, the act of circumabulation is used to envision the 'journey' from one state of being or awareness to another. As such, it is common to experience a sense of climbing the stairs of a tower, or conversely, to feel one descending deep within a cavern or vault. When working with specific planetary energies, or specific realms other than the planets, the colors, images and symbols related to those realms will be foremost in the mind of the ritualist.

Remember, in magic, force follows will. As such, the active employment of images related to a realm, coupled with ritual actions, will draw those forces and energies to the site.

Riding the Mare

In circumambulation, it is often common to carry magically-charged tools and items related to the energies involved, to act as further aids in drawing the forces, or to help the Witch transcend this realm as she journeys to the next. It is an ancient Witchcraft technique to ride the Besom or Stang

---

126. When Sybil Leek published her book *The Complete Art of Witchcraft* she received considerable criticism from contemporary Wiccans (Alexandrain and Gardnerian Witches) because she described cutting the circle in a Tuathal manner. Now, more than forty years after its publication, Traditional Witches are publishing their methods, many of which readily cut the circle in the direction as Sybil's group had.

during circumabulations. Both are tools which, among other things, are used to assist with moving between worlds. This technique has been traditionally termed "riding the mare" or "riding the hag". This can be difficult to do in a small circle, yet when performed in an effortless almost spontaneous manner, it can be very effective. Almost undoubtedly, this practice resulted in the later folkloric ideas that Witches fly on brooms.

A chant derived from mediaeval Witchcraft sources calls for the following to be enchanted during this:

> "Round and Round,
> Throughout and About,
> I traverse the hedge,
> Astride the mount!
> Round and Round,
> Throughout and About,
> Across the bridge,
> Into the night,
> Over the hedge,
> I take flight ."[127]

A vital form of circumambulation is the Aral or "closed" circling. By linking hands and chanting while circling, the group creates a closed circuit of energy. The force travels from person to person through the centers in the palms, building momentum until the energy can be released and directed toward the goal at hand. In the Hermetic Order to which I was trained, this was always performed deosil, never tuathal, as it was used solely of positive purposes. Having said this, I have personally known of times when this has been performed tuathal (not within the Order) to banish negative situations, spirits, forces and people.

---

127. This is a modern interpretation of an old chant. Several versions exist which the reader may find useful. See Nigel Pearson's *Treading the Mill: Workings in Traditional Witchcraft*. 2016. Troy Books.

The number of revolutions that the maze is walked depends on the circumstances. If specific realms or forces are being sought, then the number must relate directly to those forces or realms. However, if this is being done simply to slip into trance, then the number of revolutions will depend solely on when the Witch finds herself in that state. In "riding the mare", I have maintained this act for a considerable time until I felt the entire area outside of the Roth Fail fade away. In that state, time changed and there was no sense of the material world. As for the number of times I traversed the circle, I have no idea.

Circumambulation can easily evolve into dance in some groups. This was and is, extremely popular in rural expressions of the Art as opposed to more ritualistic, ceremonial and Hermetic Orders. In these dances, it is common to form a Maze pattern, linking hands or arms and forming a processional dance that often times circles back on itself. Some refer to this as the "Spiral Dance." Another form of dance used, is for all to place an arm around the shoulder of the person next to them, while staring in at a fixed point of the circle. This is usually the fire or the cauldron. Then a kicking or skipping motion is begun, in the direction desired. In each of these, the members alternate the sexes as much as possible.

Another method I've used involves facing the center of the circle. The arms are raised with the palms of the hands facing upward. Then one steps in a crisscross pattern, being careful to pivot on the bottom of the 'big' toe. This is done because of the ancient teaching that stimulating the 'big' toe helps to open the centers located in forehead, thereby increasing one's psychic perception. This has proved to be an excellent way to enter into meditative or trance states; especially so when chant are used with this.

Lastly, it can be very useful to incorporate ritual gestures into the act of circumambulation. For example, in the Ogdoadic tradition, it is common to circle three times deosil with arms raised, in order to form the Greek letter psi, when drawing in higher spiritual forces. In Ancient Egyptian magic, it was very common to incorporate specific ritual hand gestures into ceremonial processions and dances.

Chapter Twenty Nine

✤ IN PRAISE OF THE ANCIENT ONES ✤

[Much of this chapter first appeared as an article in "Circle" magazine in 2012 reprinted here with permission by Ruty Aisling.]

On a warm night, a small group of women and men gather deep in a New Hampshire forest. A full moon shines brightly illuminating the clearing where three distinct, concentric circles have been laid. The outer circle is marked in salt; the middle circle is made from dried birch bark, while the third inner circle is set with a rich mix of fresh herbs. In the center a small fire has been lit. A cauldron filled with spring water, herbs and honey is suspended above the flames.
The group begins to chant:

> Three worlds encircle the one,
> Plough, Tree, and Golden Sun,
> The Lady calls from Caer Wydyr,
> Cauldron deep and pool clear . . .

Ritual is the outward expression of the tradition it embodies. There are many today involved in the reawakening and transformation of the ancient traditions of our ancestors. Those who practice will recognize that the opening of ritual, with its invocations and calls of power to the circle are vital. Yet, one area of ritual that is often underestimated and frequently overlooked is the closing. So much work with beautiful invitations to the Gods and Goddesses are brought to bear at the opening of many rites, only to have the ceremony end on an abrupt note. Often times, this may seem as if any wording at the close of the ritual was added almost as an afterthought.

One can imagine that magical rituals of this sort would be similar to holding an important meeting in which guests of honor were to be present. Care is taking to send invitations and make the follow-up calls to be sure that all will go as planned. The guest is encouraged that the meeting will be special, something that they really will want to attend. However, once they have arrived and their favors are asked, the party abruptly ends. The guest is barely acknowledged and then asked to leave. At such rituals, one is often left with the feeling of, *well, that was a good start, but now what?*

In practice, we find that the closing to any ritual needs to be as distinctive and powerful as the opening. It is for this reason that we consistently close our rites with a rich incantation that captures the essence of ancient teachings and ancestral myth. At the end of each ritual, the Mistress holds the goblet out. Her partner, the Master, then takes up two containers - one has red wine, the other holds mead or honey wine. He pours these into the goblet, mixing these together while everyone in the circle chants:

> Three worlds encircle the one,
> Plough, Tree and Golden Sun.
> The Lady calls from Caer Wydyr,
> Cauldron deep and pool clear.
> Four treasures hide in the keep.
> Four realms the wise do seek.
> We call the Ancient Ones.
> We honor them still.
> In grove, in glen, on sacred hill.
> So sing the songs and walk the Maze.
> The great stag bounds through moonlit haze.
> Cer and Cerri are in us found.
> In the three worlds we are bound.

Then, the *Maiden* of the circle takes the goblet carrying this to each member. As she approaches, she addresses the women as *Cerri* and the men as *Cer*.[128] These are some of the names used in our circle to represent the Goddess and God, respectively. Each member takes a sip and then, in their words, briefly gives thanks to the Gods and forces which they feel moved to.

When performing rites and rituals with members, it is important that *all* feel involved. The closing allows each member an opportunity to participate in the ceremony. Everyone actively shares in the ritual, even if only at the end, with their personal communication directly to the God and Goddess. For those few brief moments of oral thanks, they have contributed and participated in the works.

Ours is a path that draws heavily from Celtic tradition. The closing rite, with its chant, encompasses so much of the essence of our practices. Rather than a *Symbolic Great Rite* that is used in so many Wiccan circles, we use the pouring of the red wine and mead into the goblet to draw in and represent the complementary forces that are behind all that is.

The red wine is seen as the masculine force; the God, his blood and seed. Mead is symbolic of the feminine force and the Goddess. Traditionally, honey has been seen as corresponding to the female sexual fluids.[129] As alcohol, this mixture relates to the heady ecstasy found in the interplay between the sexes. Together, the wine and mead form the creative substance of the universal and complementary forces within the matrix of the bowl of the goblet. This is the womb of the Great Mother and the center from which all originates.

---

128. These are drawn from the Celtic names of Cerridwen as Cerri, and Cernunos/Cernowain as Cer. In doing this we feel we create simple yet clear links with these deities.

129. Carl Jones, 'Rising Goddess' *Gnostica Magazine* Issue 51, 1979, Llewellyn Publications, St. Paul, MN.

It is the chant, though, that carries this dynamic energy forward. Through imagery and word, this creative force becomes manifest within each member of the circle.

> Three worlds encircle the one,
> Plough, Tree and Golden Sun.

These first lines are a reference to the three circles within which the group meets. They also correspond to the three spiritual realms of the Celtic people - *Annwn*, *Abred* and *Gwynfyd*.

These three realms are further emphasized by the three symbols of the wisdom of the Gods of the Celts, the Tuatha de Danann. These were the silver plough, representing the crescent moon. The plough was the tool by which the earth could be turned, releasing its transformative, creative powers. Thus, it relates to the fertile essence of the earth and the underworld.

Next the tree, with its roots reaching deep below, draws on the essence of the underworld, as it rises high into the heavens. This is the Abred, the gate and realm that links the lower to the higher. Then, finally, we have the Sun itself; the perfect symbol of the Gwynfyd with its brilliant fields and light.

> The Lady calls from Caer Wydyr,
> Cauldron deep and pool clear.

Beyond the summer fields of the Sun and spirit lays the Castle of Glass, Caer Wydyr.[130] This is the divine realm of the celestial forces. This is the home of the Goddess. In Welsh pagan practices, She is Arianrhod. Her castle is in the northern stars; the stars that, in the northern hemisphere, never set.[131] The ancient Egyptians referred to these as the

---

130. Spencer, Lewis. *The Magic Arts of Celtic Britain*. 1993 p.129-130.
131. Gray, William G. *Western Inner Workings*. 1983 p.144-147.

imperishable ones. The altar in our circle is in the north for these reasons.

The Goddess is the owner of the cauldron, the great kettle that transforms all, bringing life in renewed forms. Yet, it is the cauldron that reflects the beauty of the heavens in the waters which warm in this crucible. Bringing us full circle the cauldron's qualities relate so closely to those encountered in the underworld - transformation and rejuvenation. We find the message here is that the divine is manifest in all of nature. The creative essence of the Mother is in everything.

Four treasures hide in the keep.
Four realms the wise do seek.

This is a clear reference to the four treasures of the Tuatha de Danann; the mythic race of Gods that form such an integral part of Celtic tradition. These four treasures were:

Cliamh Solais, the Sword of Light;
Slea Bua, the Spear of Victory;
Coire Dagda, Dagda's Cauldron of Plenty;
Lia Fail, the Stone of Destiny.[132]

These correspond closely with the tools of contemporary magical systems which use a knife or ritual sword; a wand or staff; the bowl, chalice, or drinking horn; and the pentacle. They also relate to the four elements of air, fire, water and earth.

The next three lines of the incantation are intended to capture the feeling of praise felt for the Gods, as well as the fact that they are found in all of nature.

We call the Ancient Ones.
We honor them still.
In grove, in glen, on sacred hill.

---

132. Fitzpatrick, Jim. *The Book of Conquests*. 1978.

In the last four lines, the dynamic forces that were initially combined in the bowl as the wine and mead mix now manifest within the members themselves. This is the creative essence of Goddess and God realized through joy and passion.

> So sing the songs and walk the Maze.
> The great stag bounds through moonlit haze.
> Cer and Cerri are in us found.
> In the three worlds we are bound.

These last four lines also carry powerful esoteric imagery. The maze has long been a symbol in the west for the spiritual path. To *walk the maze* is an ancient term describing certain rituals which induce altered states of consciousness, allowing one to become aware of worlds not normally perceived with the five physical senses.[133] The stag is a powerful symbol of the lunar forces, frequently represented as a guide to the initiate on their journey of spiritual discovery.

Throughout it all we find that the very force which was invoked in the first place, the dynamic power of Goddess and God, are within us. This is reflected in the final two lines. With it, in the circle of the three worlds, comes the bond to the ancient ways and the wisdom that they contain – the Geassa.

The ritual then ends with the normal process of either taking up the circle or cutting a doorway through which to leave. This, of course varies from tradition to tradition. Frequently, we prefer to keep the three circles intact, creating a doorway so that we can pass. If outdoors, we leave this for the elements of nature to disperse. In this way, the site begins to retain the residue energy from our meetings, becoming a place that draws the forces to it easily.

Afterwards, we follow the ceremony with eating, drinking and a certain amount of celebration and, if

---

133. Gray, William G. *Western Inner Workings.* 1983 p.151-152.

appropriate, we leave a small amount of food and drink as an acknowledgment to the forces invoked.

For us, the closing of the ritual is as important as the opening. This should be worthy of all your guests. All members of the group should feel as if they are active participants in each working. Ensure that the endings are as dynamic and rich as the beginnings. Make it something that everyone, including the forces invoked, enjoys, so that they will look forward to the next gathering.

Conclusion

✤ WALKER ON THE LAND ✤

This book began with a simple thesis; the premise that within nature there is a flow of energy, a deep consciousness, lying just beyond the perception of most people today. This living consciousness, the Geassa, has manifested in Shamanic practices across the world. The west is no exception. In this volume, I have attempted to present the rich tradition and practical application of western Shamanism as it has been taught to me. From Egyptian teachings to Celtic beliefs, the practices of Wise Ones and Witches to the Hermetic teachings of magicians, Alchemists and Astrologers; all have come to form the wonderful tapestry that is The Art.

Throughout this book, it was important to show the deep roots of the Art, with its reverence for nature, its knowledge of multiple universes and realms that are inhabited by countless otherworld beings. We have seen, too, that in essence all is consciousness and, as such, we can access and move within these various worlds through the techniques of ritual magic. Beyond this, though, lays the hidden reality that all of nature is governed by basic universal principles; that there are spiritual forces at work in nature. Further, the divine feminine is central to western forms of the Art.

As we saw earlier, the recognition and honoring of the Lady has remained vital and alive across vast expanses of time and through multiple regions and cultures. Today, this practice continues; revitalized and renewed, yet retaining the older teachings that have sustained this through the terrible persecution of the last sixteen hundred years.

Through that time, countless women and men risked their survival to keep the mysteries alive.

In looking at society today, I am of the opinion that we are still in the grips of a terrible dark age; one which descended on humanity an eon ago. With it came a patriarchal paradigm centered on the lesser cult of a warrior god within the Hyksos and Canaan pantheon. Driven by greed, cruelty and power many within that cult rose in authority, seeking to destroy any who were not a part of their world view. The matriarchal religions of the Pagan world were seen as a direct threat to this new cult. The terrible persecution of any and all whose spiritual practices differed from theirs, has led to the near genocide of countless cultures and belief systems, including the destruction of much that was the basis of western Shamanic practice.

Today, that cult has grown to such proportions that its members have turned on themselves, savagely attacking each other. Such is the result when a warrior god, from a people who sought to steal - by force - the lineage of ancient wisdom, rises in power. And yet, through it all, the Geassa, the Bond, the ancient well spring of knowledge, has remained. It continues on in the Art, given expression in part through this work here.

Today, we stand on the threshold between two great Astrological epochs. The choices made will affect humanity and the world for thousands of years to come. With this comes great opportunity and hope, for many who served the mysteries in the past have returned. The great wheel spins as the thread of truth weaves through the ages. The Willow Path of the Bond remains for those who seek it.

Bibliography

Andrews, Carol. Amulets of Ancient Egypt. Copyright 1994. University of Texas Press,
Austin TX, U.S.A.

Andrews, Elizabeth. Ulster Folklore. Copyright 1913.

Assmann, Jan. "Death and Initiation in the Funerary Religion of Ancient Egypt." Yale Egyptological Studies. 1989. Yale University, New Haven, Connecticut, U.S.A.

----------, The Search for God in Ancient Egypt. Copyright 2001. Cornell University Press. Ithaca, New York, U.S.A.-

----------, The Mind of Egypt. Copyright 2002. Metropolitan Books. New York, N.Y., U.S.A.

Barry, Kieren. The Greek Qabalah: Alphabetic Mysticism and Numerology in the Ancient World. Copyright 1999. Samuel Weiser, Inc. York Beach, Maine, USA.

Bias, Clifford. Ritual Book of Magic. Copyright 1981. Samuel Weiser, Inc. York Beach, Maine, USA.

Bills, Rex. The Rulership Book. Copyright 1971, 1976. Macoy publishing.

Bord, Janet & Colin. Earth Rites: Fertility Practices in Pre-Industrial Britain. Copyright 1982. Paladin Books/Granada Publishing Limited. London, Great Britain.

Breatnach, Liam, "The Cauldron of Poesy," Ériu #32, 1981

Burton, Robert. Anatomy of Melancholy. 1621

Cauville, Sylvie. Dendera: Les Chapelles Osiriennes. Volumes I & II. Copyright 1997. Institut Francais D'Archeologie Orientale.

----------. Dendera I - Traduction. Copyright 1998. Orientaliste, Leuven. Belgium. (Translation into English by Kerry Wisner 2000-2001)

Christian, Paul. The History and Practice of Magic. 1969 printing. The Citadel Press, New York, USA.

Crowley, Aleister. Magick in Theory and Practice. Copyright 1929. Castle Books. New York, USA.

"Cunning Folk and Wizards in Early Modern England" Copyright 2010. Warwick, RI. ID Number: 0614383.

Denning, Melita & Osborne Phillips. The Magical Philosophy, Book I: Robe and Ring. Copyright 1974. Llewellyn Publications, St. Paul, Minnesota, U.S.A.

----------, Mysteria Magica: Fundamental Techniques of High Magick. Copyright 1981, 1986, 2004. Llewellyn Publications, St. Paul, Minnesota, U.S.A.

----------, Magical States of Consciousness. Copyright 1987. Llewellyn Publications, St. Paul, Minnesota, U.S.A.

----------, Entrance to the Magical Qabalah. Copyright 1997. Thoth Publications, Loughborough, Leicestershire, Great Britain.

"Dictionary of Native American Mythology" Copyright 1992. Oxford University Press

Farrar, Janet & Stewart. A Witches Bible Compleat. Copyright 1996. Magickal Childe printing. USA.

Feder, Walter. "The "Transformations" in the Coffin Texts: A New Approach." Journal of Near Eastern Studies. October 1960.

Fitzpatrick, Jim. The Book of Conquests. Copyright 1978. E.P. Dutton, New York, NY, U.S.A.

Fletcher, Anthony. A County Community in Peace and War: Sussex 1600-1660. Copyright 1975.

Fortune, Dion. Moon Magic. Copyright 1956, 1978, 1979. Samuel Weiser, Inc. New York, New York, U.S.A.

----------, Aspects of Occultism. Copyright 1983. Aquarian Press, London, England

Fortune, Dion & Gareth Knight. An Introduction to Ritual Magic. Copyright 1997. Thoth Publications. Loughboough, England.

----------, Principles of Hermetic Philosophy. Copyright 1999. Thoth Publications, Loughborough, Leicestershire, England.

Gary, Gemma. Traditional Witchcraft: A Cornish Book of Ways. Copyright 2008. Troy Books. London, England.

Glass, Justine. Witchcraft, the Sixth Sense. Copyright 1965. Melvin Powers. Hollywood, California, USA.

Gray, William G. Western Inner Workings. Copyright 1983.

Samuel Weiser, Inc. York Beach, Maine, USA.

Gonzalez-Wippler, Migene. The Complete Book of Spells, Ceremonies, and Magic. Copyright 1978. Crown Publishers, Inc. New York, New York, U.S.A.

Greenacre, David. Numerology and you. Copyright 1971. Lancer Books, Inc. New York, New York, USA.

Grimassi, Raven "The Ancient Roots of Italian Witchcraft" (on-line article – no copyright date noted).

Harner, Michael. The Way of the Shaman. Copyright 1980. Harper & Row. New York, New York, USA.

Hart, George. A Dictionary of Egyptian Gods and Goddesses. Copyright 1986. Routledge & Kegan Paul. London, England.

---------- Egyptian Myths. Copyright 1990. University of Texas. Austin, Texas, U.S.A.

Hartley, Marie and Joan Ingilby. Life and Tradition in the Moorlands of North-East Yorkshire. Copyright 1972, 1990. Smith Settle Ltd. West Yorkshire, England.

Hatsis, Thomas. The Witches' Ointment. Copyright 2015. Park Street Press. Toronto, Canada.

Hauck, Dennis William. The Complete Idiot's Guide to Alchemy. Copyright 2008. Alpha Books, New York, NY, USA.

Hedva, Beth, Ph.D. Betrayal, Trust, and Forgiveness; A Guide to Emotional Healing and Self-Renewal. Copyright 1992, 2001. Celestial Arts. Berkeley, California, U.S.A.

Henry, P.L., "The Cauldron of Poesy," Studia Celtica #14/15, 1979/1980

Hornung, Erik. Conceptions of God in Ancient Egypt: The One and the Many. Copyright 1982. Cornell University Press. Ithaca, New York, U.S.A.

Howard, Michael. Liber Nox: A Traditional Witch's Gramarye. Copyright 2014. Skylight Press. United Kingdom.

Huson, Paul. Mastering Witchcraft. Copyright 1970. G.P. Putnam's Sons. New York, New York. USA.

Hutton, Ronald. Triumph of the Moon. Copyright 1999. Oxford University Press, England

Illes, Judika. Encyclopedia of Witchcraft. Copyright 2005. HarperCollins. New York, New York, USA.

Janson's History of Art: The Western Tradition. Copyright 2011. Pearson Publishing.

Jones, Carl. "Legends of the Grail" Gnostica Magazine Issue 50, pg 21 1979, Llewellyn Publications, St. Paul, MN, USA.

Jones, Prudence and Nigel Pennick. A History of Pagan Europe. Copyright 1995. Barnes & Noble Books. USA.

Knight, Gareth. The Secret Tradition in Arthurian Legend. Copyright 1983. Aquarian Press, London, England.

Leek, Sybil. Diary of a Witch. Copyright 1968. Prentice-Hall, Inc. Englewood Cliffs, New Jersey, USA.

----------, Numerology: The Magic of Numbers. Copyright 1969. Collier Books. New York, New York, USA.

----------, Cast your own spell. Copyright 1970. Pinnacle Books, New York, NY. USA.

----------, The Complete Art of Witchcraft. Copyright 1971. World Publishing Company. Canada.

----------, My Life in Astrology. Copyright 1972. Prentice-Hall, Inc. Englewood Cliffs, New Jersey, USA.

Leland, Charles. Aradia, the Gospel of the Witches. This edition published by Buckland Museum, New York, USA. 1968

Lesko, Barbara S. The Great Goddesses of Egypt. Copyright 1999. University of Oklahoma Press. U.S.A.

Lurker, Manfred. An Illustrated Dictionary of The Gods and Symbols of Ancient Egypt. Copyright 1980. Thames & Hudson Ltd. London, England.

Manniche, Lise. Sexual Life in Ancient Egypt. Copyright 1987. Kegan Paul International. London, England.

Markale, Jean. The Pagan Mysteries of Halloween. Copyright 2000. Inner Traditions. Rochester, Vermont, USA.

Martin, Amanda. "The Cat as Familiar" 1972 Witches Almanac.

Mathers, S.L. MacGregor. The Key of Solomon The King (Clavicula Salomonis). Copyright 1992. Samuel Weiser, Inc. York Beach, Maine, U.S.A.

Matthews, Caitlin and John. The Encyclopedia of Celtic Wisdom: A Celtic Shaman's Sourcebook. Copyright 1994. Element Books, Rockport, MA, USA.

Moser, Robert E. (Bob), Mental and Astral Projection. Copyright 1974. Esoteric Publications. Sedona, Arizona.

Parker, Richard A. The Calendars of Ancient Egypt. Copyright 1950. Oriental Institute of the University of Chicago. Chicago, Illinois, U.S.A.

----------, "Egyptian Astronomy, Astrology and Calendarical Reckoning. Dictionary of Scientific Biography, vol. XV, Suppl. I New York: Charles Scribner's Sons, 1978, pp.706 - 727.

Paulsen, Kathryn. The Complete Book of Magic and Witchcraft. Copyright 1970, 1980. New American Library. New York, New York, USA.

Pearson, Nigel. Treading the Mill: Workings in Traditional Witchcraft. Copyright 2016. Limited Edition. Troy Books. London, England.

Phillips, Osborne. Aurum Solis: Initiation Ceremonies and Inner Magical Techniques. Copyright 2001. Thoth Publications, Leicestershire, England.

Progoff, Ira. Jung's Psychology and Its Social Meaning. Copyright 1973. New York, New York, USA.

Regardie, Israel. The Tree of Life: A Study in Magic. Copyright 1969. Samuel Wiser, Inc. York Beach, Maine, USA.

Richardson, Alan. Priestess: The Life and Magic of Dion Fortune. Copyright 1987. Aquarian Press, Great Britain.

Roberts, Alison. Hathor Rising: The Power of the Goddess in Ancient Egypt. Copyright 1997. Inner Traditions. Rochester, Vermont, U.S.A.

----------. My Mother, My Heart: Death and Rebirth in Ancient Egypt. Copyright 2000. Northgate Press, Rottingdean, East Sussex, England

Rudhyar, Dane. The Astrology of Personality. Copyright 1970. Doubleday. Garden City, New York, USA.

Schumann Antelme, Ruth and Stephane Rossini. Sacred

Sexuality in Ancient Egypt: The Erotic Secrets of the Forbidden Papyrus, A Look at the Unique Role of Hathor, the Goddess of Love. Copyright 1999, 2001. Inner Traditions. Rochester, Vermont, U.S.A.

Scot, Reginald. Discoverie of Witchcraft. 1584. London, England.

Seán Ó Tuathail, "Foclóir Draíochta - Dictionary of Druidism" 1993 John Kellnhauser/Cainteanna na Luise

Sharpe, Elizabeth & J.K. (Editors). Splendor Solis: Alchemical Treaties of Solomon Trismosin. Written 1582. Copyright 1920. Reprinted by Kessinger Publishing U.S.A.

Spence, Lewis. The Magical Arts in Celtic Britain. Copyright 1945, 1993. Barnes & Nobel reprint.

Squire, Charles. Celtic Myth and Legend. Copyright 1975. Newcastle Publishing Co. Van Nuys, California, USA.

Stewart, R.J. The Underworld Initiation: A Journey Towards Psychic Transformation. Copyright 1985. Aquarian Press. Wellingborough, Northamptonshire, England.

----------, Living Magical Arts: Imagination and Magic for the 21st Century. Copyright 1987. Blandford Press. England.

----------, Advanced Magical Arts. Copyright 1988. Element Books. England.

----------, Earth Light: The Ancient Path to Transformation Rediscovering the Wisdom of Celtic & Faery Lore. Copyright 1992, 1998. Mercury Publishing. Lake Toxaway, NC, U.S.A.

----------, Living the World of Faery. Copyright 1999. Mercury Publishing, Lake Toxaway, NC, U.S.A.

----------, Robert Kirk: Walker Between the Worlds. Copyright 1990, 2007. R.J. Stewart Books.

Thiselton-Dyer, T.F. The Folk-Lore of Plants. Copyright 1889, 2003 release as E-Book through Project Gutenberg.

Thomas, Keith. Religion and the Decline of Magic, Studies in Popular Beliefs in the Sixteenth-and-Seventeenth-century England. Copyright 1991

Valiente, Doreen. An ABC of Witchcraft. Copyright 1973. St. Martin's Press. New York, New York, USA.

Wang, Robert. The Qabalistic Tarot. Copyright 1983. Samuel

Wiser, Inc., York Beach, Maine, U.S.A.
Walker, The Witches. Copyright 1970
Walker, Barbara. The Women's Encyclopedia of Myths and Secrets. Copyright 1983. HarperOne, New York, New York, U.S.A.
Wente, Edward F. "Mysticism in Pharaonic Egypt?" Journal of Near Eastern Studies, 1982. University of Chicago, U.S.A.
Wilby, Emma, Cunning Folk and Familiar Spirits, Shamanistic Visionary Traditions in Early Modern British Witchcraft and Magic. Copyright 2005. Brighton, England.
Wilkinson, Richard H. Reading Egyptian Art. Copyright 1992. Thames and Hudson Ltd. New York, New York, U.S.A.
----------, Symbol & Magic in Egyptian Art. Copyright 1994. Thames and Hudson Ltd. New York, New York, U.S.A.
----------, The Complete Temples of Ancient Egypt. Copyright 2000. Thames and Hudson Inc. New York, New York, U.S.A.
Wind, Edgar. Pagan Mysteries in the Renaissance. Copyright 1980. Oxford University Press. London, England.
Wisner, Kerry. Eye of the Sun: The Sacred Legacy of Ancient Egypt. Copyright 2000. Hwt-Hrw Publications. Nashua, New Hampshire, U.S.A.
----------, Mdw Hwt-Hrw: Reconstructions of Religious Rituals from Ancient Egypt, Vol I. Copyright 2001. Hwt-Hrw Publications. Nashua, New Hampshire, U.S.A.
"Witches All" Copyright 1977. Grosset & Dunlap. New York, New York, USA.

Index

Abrahamic, 15, 26, 36-39, 46-47, 49, 62, 71-72, 102, 133, 154, 210, 243, 260

Abred, 64-68, 72-74, 77-81, 86, 88, 98, 107, 112, 114, 119, 134, 156, 208, 224-225, 243-244, 247, 266, 272-273, 276, 279, 286

Air, 96, 111, 122-124, 128-129, 150-151, 159, 164, 207, 216, 235, 248, 287

Alchemical, 23, 133, 152, 201, 266, 267

Alchemy, 18, 153, 188, 201

Alraun, 112, 256-258

Annwn, 62-68, 72-74, 77-83, 85-86, 93, 98, 100, 102-103, 106-107, 114, 119, 135, 149, 192, 203, 208, 212, 224-225, 241, 247, 265-268, 272, 276, 279, 286

Aradia, 40, 232, 239

Arianrhod, 40, 66-68, 77, 82-83, 124, 168, 199-200, 205, 220, 224-230, 265, 267, 272, 286

Assmann, Jan, 23, 175

Astral, 30, 65-66, 72, 74, 80, 86-88, 108, 113, 118-119, 134-135, 142, 146, 156, 158, 161, 186, 217, 218, 224, 243, 248, 251, 258, 267, 276, 278

Astrology, 12, 18, 95-96, 103, 124, 157

Athame, 185, 187-193

Atum, 26, 139

Atziluth, 74

Beltane, 44, 90, 94, 96, 109-113, 211, 227, 256

Bible, 36-38, 41

Bless, 57

Bridget, 42, 104, 106, 111, 200

Caer Wydyr, 66-68, 72, 74, 77-78, 82, 86, 88, 101-102, 124, 144, 175, 206, 208, 247, 267, 274, 283, 284, 286

Castle of Glass, 66-68, 82, 93, 102, 124, 208, 267, 286

Cernowain, 101, 285

Cernunnos, 90, 101, 127

Cerridwen, 114, 168, 199-200, 203-204, 208, 211, 285

Christian, 26, 39-41, 43, 49-50, 71, 104, 107, 112, 144, 195, 207, 250

Circle, 40, 66-68, 78, 106, 109, 114, 124, 127, 188, 190, 192, 200, 210-214, 215, 220, 222-223, 228, 232-233, 264-277, 278-281, 283-288

Cliamh Solais, 123, 125, 287

Coire Dagda, 124, 126, 287

Corn Dolly, 117, 120

Crowley, Aleister, 70, 86, 243, 252

Cunning, 20, 35, 44, 50, 123, 149, 217

Curse, 57, 20, 236, 237, 254

Diana, 39-41, 46, 202, 215

Druid, 185

Earth, 62, 68, 78, 82, 87, 89, 91, 96, 103, 105, 107, 109, 115-116, 122-123, 127-129, 132, 152, 161, 164, 186, 191, 196, 216, 261, 286, 287

Egypt, 12, 23, 26, 64, 73, 80, 93, 98, 118, 121, 136, 139, 142-144, 148-154, 168-170, 194-195, 199, 222, 241, 261- 262

Equinox, 78, 90, 96-97, 104, 107-109, 119, 164, 211

Faery, 63-64, 77, 80-81, 99, 114, 187, 197, 224, 227

Fal, Stone of, 123, 127, 235

Falias, 123, 184, 186

Familiar, 250-259, 260

Faunus, 101

Fe, 106, 224-230, 267, 269, 272, 276-277

Fetch, 30, 231, 251, 262

Findias, 123, 184

Fire, 101, 104-111, 113-117, 120, 122-124, 128-129, 144, 152, 158-160, 164, 203, 210-214, 215-218, 231-237, 245- 247, 272, 281, 283, 287

Fire Festivals, 98, 109, 111, 115

Fludd, Robert, 69

Fortune, Dion, 82-83, 106, 187, 197, 204

Gardner, Gerald, 188-190, 239, 279

Gary, Gemma, 129, 213-214, 217-218, 220-221, 237

Geassa, 11, 13, 15, 16-24, 25, 28-29, 47-51, 55-60, 66, 71, 74-75, 79, 92, 109, 112, 116-117, 121, 127, 139, 148, 154, 166, 171, 174-176, 179, 181-182, 231, 237, 239-241, 244, 264, 288, 290-291

God, 21, 25, 29-31, 50, 62, 66, 76, 78-83, 87, 90-91, 93, 99-106, 111, 115-119, 123, 135, 139-144, 148-150, 152, 154, 157, 168-170, 184, 192-193, 194, 196, 199, 201, 206, 218, 226, 240- 241, 248, 260, 272, 283, 285-288, 291

Goddess, 21-22, 25-27, 31-32, 35-51, 66-68, 72-73, 80-83, 84-86, 88-90, 93, 98-99, 101-108, 110-11, 116-119, 124, 135, 140, 142, 149-151, 153-154, 168-169, 185-187, 191-202, 204-206, 211-212, 216-217, 220-221, 224-226, 232, 238-239, 241-244, 260-264, 268, 283, 285-288

Gonzalez-Wippler, Migene, 177
Gorias, 123, 184
Grandma Julie, 18, 20, 43, 50, 52, 56, 85, 96, 105, 122, 127, 183, 192, 215, 219, 239
Gray, William, 76-77, 82, 207, 286, 288
Green Man, 21, 113-4
Gwelen, 75
Gwynfyd, 65-68, 72, 77-81, 86, 88, 102-103, 113-115, 118, 208, 224-225, 247, 267, 272, 276, 286
Habondia, 39
Hathor, 26, 64, 104, 118, 150, 168-169, 194-195, 199, 238
Hearth, 31-32, 100-101, 106, 113, 152, 212-214, 215-218, 231, 234-2235, 246-247, 258, 264-265, 269-272
Hebrew, 71, 73, 136, 145
Hedva, Beth, 177
Hermetic, 11-14, 18, 22-23, 34, 45, 56, 69-74, 77, 85-86, 88, 123, 132-137, 142, 144, 146, 154-162, 182-183, 217, 241, 243, 262, 266-267, 280-281, 290
Herne, 99, 101, 260
Hieros gamos, 111
Holda, 39
Honey, 91, 115, 126, 161, 201, 211, 283-285
Hornung, Erik, 169
Horus, 140, 142, 151
Huson, Paul, 50
Hutton, Ronald, 188-190
Imbolc, 94, 96, 104-109, 111, 211
Isis, 72, 98, 102, 118, 140, 142, 151, 187, 241
John Barley Corn, 115-116
Jung, Carl, 27
Jupiter, 130, 132-138, 146-147, 155, 160, 208
Kern Baby, 117
Khnum, 26
King James, 36, 38, 41
Knight, Gareth, 178-179, 182, 186-188
Llawforwyn, 33
Leek, Sybil, 12-13, 20, 35-36, 43, 50, 52, 55-60, 84, 87, 96, 105, 109, 116, 119, 128-130, 140-141, 143, 145, 147, 153, 162-163, 176, 180, 183, 185, 211, 215, 221, 230, 237, 239, 242, 255, 260, 274, 279
Leland, Charles, 40-41, 232, 239
Litha, 113-115

Loki, 50

Lugh, 115-117, 123, 126

Lughnasadh, 94, 96, 115-118

Mabon, 119-120

Mandrake, 160, 256, 258

Mars, 130, 132-138, 146-147, 158, 208

Master, 21, 35, 76, 115, 117, 149, 241, 251, 284

Maze, 264, 272, 278-282, 284, 288

Mead, 91, 115, 126-127, 201, 284-285, 288

Medium, 255

Mercury, 130, 132-138, 141, 147, 159-160, 208, 267

Mistress, 21, 32-33, 39, 51, 85-86, 118, 126, 152, 187, 196, 241, 251, 260, 284

Moon, 16, 25, 30, 40, 43, 46, 66-67, 78-79, 84-94, 101, 104, 106-107, 109, 112, 115, 117, 132-135, 137-138, 147, 149, 151-154, 156, 158, 162, 164, 192-193, 195, 197-201, 205-206, 208, 213-214, 221-222, 227-228, 233-234, 241, 245, 247, 253, 256, 264, 266, 270, 271-272, 276, 279, 283, 286

Morgana, 32, 99

Morrigu, 140, 149, 260

Murias, 124,184

Music, 18, 110, 117, 131

Nephthys, 98, 102

Nuada, 32, 123, 184-185

Ogdoadic, 12, 122, 154, 199, 202,262, 266-267, 281

Osiris, 98, 102, 116, 140, 142-144, 148-149, 151

Ostera, 107

Pagan, 18, 22, 30, 35, 39, 45-47, 49-50, 55-56, 71-73, 75-78, 82-83, 85, 101, 107, 136, 152, 166, 186, 191-193, 195-196, 200, 206-207, 209, 286, 291

Pan, 101

Parker, Richard, 103, 137

polarity, 25, 27-28, 60, 82, 108

Ptolemaic, 132

Pythagoras/Pythagorean, 71, 133, 135-137, 139, 141-142, 147, 156, 158-161

Qabalah, 56, 69, 70-73, 77, 132-133, 136-137, 142

Quartz, 87, 234

Ra, 26, 93, 118, 142-143, 151, 200

Ring, 63, 129, 240, 242-244, 264

Roberts, Alison, 23, 144

Roth Fail, 241, 264-269, 271-272, 274, 276-277, 281

Rudhyar, Dane, 95

Samhain, 76, 89, 94, 96-100, 104-105, 110-113, 211, 265

Saturn, 130, 132-134, 137-138, 146-147, 161, 208

scrying, 200, 217

Sekhmet, 140, 151, 199

Shaman/Shamanic, 19, 20, 22, 28, 30, 35, 50, 66, 71, 73, 81, 83, 112, 166-167, 181, 225, 231, 234, 270, 290-291

Slea Bua, 123, 126, 287

Solstice, 78, 96-97, 100-104, 109, 113-115, 164

Spell, 46, 50, 85, 87, 129, 162-163, 218, 223, 254, 266

Spence, Lewis, 42, 44, 205

Spirit, 28, 52, 59-60, 87, 90, 112, 116-117, 122-124, 128-129, 141-142, 149, 158, 161, 176, 188, 193, 199, 216, 218, 220, 226-227, 233, 237, 241, 241, 250-251, 253, 255-258, 260-261, 267-268, 286

Spirit Gad, 236-237

Stang, 67, 68, 73, 75-83, 85, 98, 101, 105, 107, 109, 112, 114, 118-119, 150, 207-208, 212, 217-218, 221, 247, 266-267, 269, 272-277, 279

Strega, 201, 232

Sun, 16, 25, 30, 43, 78, 80, 89-91, 93-94, 97-110, 113-119, 123, 125-127, 132-135, 137-138, 142, 146-147, 151-154, 156-157, 162, 164, 184-185, 192, 196, 199, 201, 208, 211, 236, 266, 271-272, 276, 278, 283-284, 286

Thoth, 104, 143, 150, 153

Tlachtga, 264

Trance, 14, 30, 217-218, 221, 224, 259, 278, 281

Trulliad, 33

Tuatha De Danann, 141, 149, 184-186, 205, 286-287

Venus, 42, 130, 132-135, 137-138, 142, 147, 151, 160, 208

Wand, 67, 106, 109, 182, 184, 211, 216, 220, 224, 226-228, 230, 238, 267, 269, 287

Wang, Robert, 69, 171

Water, 17, 41, 44, 93, 96, 109, 114, 117, 122, 124, 126-127, 129, 132, 150, 152, 155, 157-158, 161, 163-164, 200, 211, 216, 245-247, 270-271, 283, 287

Wep-Renpet, 117-118

Wine, 90, 115, 117, 195-195, 199, 201, 211, 228, 235, 256-258, 284-285, 288

Woden, 50, 135

Yule, 100-101, 152, 217

Printed in the USA
CPSIA information can be obtained
at www.ICGtesting.com
JSHW022027250224
57999JS00002B/91

9 781909 602403